CATALOGUE OF COINS
IN THE
PANJAB MUSEUM, LAHORE

CATALOGUE OF COINS
IN THE
PANJAB MUSEUM, LAHORE

BY

R. B. WHITEHEAD

INDIAN CIVIL SERVICE (RETIRED), FELLOW OF THE ASIATIC SOCIETY OF BENGAL CORRESPONDING MEMBER OF THE AMERICAN NUMISMATIC SOCIETY

Vol. III

COINS OF NADIR SHAH AND THE DURRANI DYNASTY

'Men read coins in the name of each one who smites with the sword.'

GYAN

Published by

GYAN

Gyan Publishing House
5, Ansari Road
Daryaganj, New Delhi-110002
Phone: 011-47034999, 9811692060
E-mail: books@gyanbooks.com

Distribution Network
gyanbooks.com
India, USA, Canada, UK, Australia, France

ISBN : 978-81-212-2100-9 (Set)
ISBN : 978-81-212-2097-2 (PB)
First Published, 1934

2nd Impression 2021

Printed at: Gyan Press, Delhi.

Catalogue of Coins in the Panjab Museum, Lahore, Vol. III
Author: R. B. Whitehead

CATALOGUE OF COINS
IN THE
PANJAB MUSEUM, LAHORE

BY

R. B. WHITEHEAD

INDIAN CIVIL SERVICE (RETIRED), FELLOW OF THE ASIATIC SOCIETY OF BENGAL
CORRESPONDING MEMBER OF THE AMERICAN NUMISMATIC SOCIETY

VOL. III
COINS OF NĀDIR SH̲ĀH AND THE DURRĀNĪ DYNASTY

هر که شمشیر زند سکه بنامش خوانند

'Men read coins in the name of each one who smites with the sword.'

PUBLISHED FOR THE PANJAB GOVERNMENT

OXFORD
AT THE CLARENDON PRESS
1934

Brit. Mus. Add. 25 609 Fol. 10.

NADIR SHAH

PREFACE

THE third volume of the Panjab Museum Coin Catalogue describes the money of Nādir S͟hāh and of the Durrānī dynasty struck at mints in Afghanistan and India. The general plan is that of the preceding volumes.[1] The coins now described include those from the two separate Cabinets at Lahore, the Government Collection proper and that of Mr. C. J. Rodgers which was purchased by the Panjab Government.[2] The series is by no means common and few pieces were added in subsequent years till the great Bahāwalpūr treasure became available. Through this unique opportunity our Durrānī Cabinets have been much extended and improved. The Panjab Government has generously authorized and financed the production of the present work. Coins from all available sources have been incorporated in the Catalogue which is in fact a Corpus.

This work is the outcome of a happy opportunity. In December, 1908, by the direction of the Panjab Government, Mr. E. D. (now Sir Edward) Maclagan being Chief Secretary, and with the consent of the Council of Regency on behalf of the infant Nawab, I was allowed to inspect the old coins in the Bahāwalpūr State Tos͟hak͟hāna at Bahāwalpūr in the south-west Panjab.[3] The treasure, probably only a part of what formerly existed, had been conveyed to the present capital some time previously from the desert stronghold of Derāwar on the bank of the extinct river Hakra. There were fifty thousand gold and more than four hundred thousand silver pieces; most of the coins were issues of the Durrānī

[1] Vol. I, *Coins of the Indo-Greeks.* Vol. II, *Coins of the Mug͟hal Emperors of India.* Oxford, 1914.

[2] *Catalogue of the Coins in the Government Museum*, Lahore. C. J. Rodgers. Calcutta, 1891. *Catalogue of the Coins collected by Chas. J. Rodgers and purchased by the Government of the Panjab.* C. J. Rodgers. Part II. Calcutta, 1894.

[3] Tos͟hak͟hāna literally means storeroom, wardrobe.

dynasty of Afghanistan and India. In the two weeks at my disposal I could only touch the fringe of so vast a mass of material but I did everything possible; the results were communicated in a Report to the Panjab Government, the substance of which was published in the *Journal of the Asiatic Society of Bengal*, August, 1909. The Bahāwalpūr State generously accepted proposals that moderate prices should be fixed for the selected specimens which in this way could be acquired by museums and private collectors. During the course of the next twelve years I was able to pay five more visits to Bahāwalpūr and I am much indebted to the State authorities for their kindness and hospitality.

A rupee of Nādir S͟hāh was published during his lifetime (J. D. Koehler, *Historische Münz-Belustigung*, Nürnberg, 1746, vol. 18, p. 105). O. G. Tychsen mentions one or two specimens in his work *In Rem Numariam Muhammedanorum. Additamentum* I, Rostock, 1796. There are a few Durrānī coins in the second volume of Marsden's *Numismata Orientalia*, London, 1825. These issues did not escape the researches of C. M. Fraehn; a number are described in *Pars Prima Opusculorum Postumorum*, Petropoli, 1855. Mr. C. J. Rodgers took a considerable interest in the money of the eighteenth-century invaders of India. His paper 'On Some Coins of Nādir S͟hāh struck in India' (*Num. Chron.*, 1882) was followed by a substantial contribution on 'The Coins of Aḥmad S͟hāh Durrānī' (*J.A.S.B.*, 1885). The latter was supplemented three years later by Mr. M. Longworth Dames's excellent monograph entitled 'The Coins of the Durrānīs' (*Num. Chron.*, 1888). The work of Mr. W. H. Valentine, abundantly illustrated, is valuable for the copper coins.[1] The Lahore Catalogues already mentioned, together with Mr. C. J. Rodgers's Indian Museum Catalogue, about complete the scattered literature on the

[1] *Modern Copper Coins of the Muhammadan States.* Spink. London, 1911. *The Copper Coins of India.* Part II. *The Panjab.* Spink. London. I have seen the coins of Mr. R. Sutcliffe and cannot always accept Mr. Valentine's hand-drawn versions of the legends and dates.

subject.[1] In 1885 Mr. Rodgers had observed that 'the coins of Aḥmad S͟hāh Durrānī are becoming rarer every day, indeed it is seldom they are now met with'. Twenty-three years later the enlightened action of the State gave access to the great Bahāwalpūr hoard of nearly half a million coins. Fortunately I found that the issues had been roughly classified; many of the bags contained old money of the Bahāwalpūr State, gold and silver double and single pieces of the Durrānī kings Maḥmūd and S͟hāh S͟hujā' minted at Bahāwalpūr and debased Hirāt silver of Maḥmūd. Next in number came mixed coins of the Durrānī dynasty, many thousands altogether. Imperial Mug͟hal coins were only a residue of the whole, but even so were of great numismatic importance because there were quite six thousand Mug͟hal gold mohurs in mint condition. The Mug͟hal rupees, as a rule much worn, were scattered at random throughout the bags of mixed silver and often only a score would turn up out of a bag of a thousand, but the results justified the labour expended. At first I confined my attention to a search for new or rare Mug͟hal coins; my later visits were devoted to completing the Durrānī lists. The oldest coins in the hoard were a few gold pieces of the Great Mug͟hals, Akbar and S͟hāh Jahān. There were hundreds of Aurangzeb's gold coins, mostly of Akbarābād (Agra) mint. The Mug͟hal silver may be said to start from Aurangzeb and to end with 'Ālamgīr II (1759 A.D.); it yielded several novelties from the Sind mint towns. The great mass of material consisted of Durrānī money and must have contained almost every type, year, and mint (except Kas͟hmīr) of Aḥmad, Taimūr, and Zamān. Coins of the later Durrānīs, except of Bahāwalpūr and Hirāt mints, were scarce; fractional pieces and money of Kas͟hmīr mint were entirely lacking. Coins of the rebel princes Sulaimān and Humāyūn came to light for the first time; I do not know of them from any other

[1] *I.M. Coin Cat.*, Part IV, Calcutta, 1896. As regards private Cabinets there is amongst others the *Catalogue of the Eugene Leggett Collection*; the Collection of the late Dr. White King sold at Amsterdam in 1904–05 by J. Schulman is outstanding.

source.[1] The hoard was rich in money of Kābul and Qandahār (Aḥmad Shāhī) and naturally of such mints as Multān, Bhakhar, Dera, and Derajāt. All known specimens of the rare Camp (Rikāb) mint, except the gold coin of Taimūr, came from Bahāwalpūr as did the rupees of Prince Qaiṣar struck at Kābul and Aḥmad Shāhī mints.[2] I added two or three new mints and types to the scarce series of Nādir Shāh struck in India.

The character of the State treasure reflects the circumstances of the ruling family, the Dāūdpotra chiefs of Bahāwalpūr, old allies of the British. The territory, lying along the edge of the Great Indian Desert, between the Panjab and Sind, came into notice with the disintegration of the Mughal empire. The first Nawab of Bahāwalpūr was Amīr Ṣādiq Muḥammad Khān I who captured Derāwar fort in A.H. 1146, A.D. 1733. When Nādir invaded the Derajāt six years later, the Dāūdpotra went to meet him at Dera Ghāzī Khān and was granted the title of Nawab; this was when Nādir partitioned Sind among certain chiefs in the month of Zilḥijj, 1152. During the reign of the fourth Nawab, Muḥammad Bahāwal Khān II, A.H. 1186–1224, A.D. 1772–1809, the State was virtually a part of the Durrānī empire. Mountstuart Elphinstone visited Bahāwalpūr in November, 1808, at the head of a Political Mission, and was cordially received by 'Bahawul Khaun, the chief of one of the king of Caubul's eastern provinces' (Elphinstone's *Account of the Kingdom of Caubul*, London, 1839, vol. I, p. 20). In February, 1833, a treaty was negotiated with the British Government by the sixth Nawab, Bahāwal Khān III; this was supplemented by further agreements in succeeding years culminating in an alliance for the restoration of Shāh Shujā'. The royal exile,

[1] Except the Kashmīr rupee of Sulaimān which I found in Srīnagar. The coins of Sulaimān and Humāyūn in the Michael Cabinet—Ithiel J. Michael Sale Catalogue, J. Schulman, Amsterdam, March, 1914—came from the specimens selected by me at Bahāwalpūr.

[2] The beautiful Rikāb mohur of Taimūr Shāh was purchased for the British Museum at the Da Cunha Sale, Messrs. Sotheby, 1889.

accompanied by the Bengal contingent, passed through Bahāwalpūr at the end of December, 1838. Sufficient has been said to explain the connexion of Bahāwalpūr with Nādir Shāh and the Durrānī kings. I have little doubt that the Mughal gold came from Nādir's loot of Delhi. The State still possesses superb stones which were once crown jewels of the Great Mughals.

Afghanistan and the Afghans played a great part in India and Iran during the eighteenth century. There were repercussions on the one side with the Mughal, Mahratta, and Sikh powers and on the other with the Persian empire. Nādir Shāh, the Persian, and Aḥmad Shāh, the Afghan, are best known in connexion with the tremendous misfortunes they brought upon the decaying Mughal empire of India. The fate of Delhi at the hands of the rapacious Nādir Shāh is one of the object lessons of history. His invasion reduced Northern India to anarchy and he took away jewels and specie to the estimated value of eighty-seven million pounds sterling; this immense treasure included the historic peacock throne and the Koh i Nūr, preëminently the great diamond of legend and romance.[1] Nādir annexed Sind and all Mughal territory west of the Indus. This catastrophe occurred only thirty-two years after the death of Aurangzeb.

An outstanding triumph of Indian art was the peacock throne; the body was of enamelled gold, the eyes diamonds, and the outstretched tail shimmered with sapphires and emeralds. The jewels of the Mughal Court were unrivalled. With that prodigy of diamonds, the Great Mughal, were the Daryā i Nūr, Sea of Light, the Koh i Ṭūr, Mountain of Sinai, the Tāj i Māh, Crown of the Moon, and the Koh i Nūr, Mountain of Light. The great gems were still more widely scattered upon the assassination of Nādir Shāh, and it is possible that some of the finest crown jewels of Europe come

[1] *The History of Nādir Shāh.* James Fraser. London, 1742. *The History of Nādir Shāh,* being Vol. IV of Jonas Hanway's *Historical Account of the British Trade over the Caspian Sea.* London, 1753.

from the hoards of Delhi. In the battle of Pānīpat, A.D. 1526, the Rajah of Gwalior was slain and his most precious jewel, the Koh i Nūr, valued 'at half the daily expense of the whole world', came to Humāyūn, son of Bābur. Two centuries later the wonderful store of gems belonging to Humāyūn's descendants was carried off to Afghanistan. The treasures of Nādir were looted by the Durrānīs. The Koh i Nūr was taken from S̲h̲āh Zamān when he was dethroned and blinded by his half brother Maḥmūd but was later recovered by Zamān's full brother S̲h̲ujā', together with a famous ruby called Fak̲h̲rāj. S̲h̲ujā' in his turn was driven out of Kābul; he fell into the hands of the Sikhs and was constrained to deliver up the Koh i Nūr diamond to Ranjit Singh. After the Sikh Wars the priceless stone came to the British Crown.[1]

The invasion of Nādir S̲h̲āh was terrible enough in itself; it also showed the way to others. The tyrant was assassinated in June, 1747 (A.H. 1160) and was succeeded in Persia by his nephew 'Adil S̲h̲āh. The rest of the empire fell to Aḥmad K̲h̲ān the Afghan, of the Sadozai section of the Abdālī tribe, the first ruler of an independent Afghanistan. The Sadozai assumed the titles Aḥmad S̲h̲āh, Durr i Durrān (Pearl of Pearls), and made Qandahār his capital; the Abdālīs were henceforth known as the Durrānīs.[2] Aḥmad, like his master Nādir, was a great leader of men and his thoughts at once turned towards India. He invaded the Panjab several times during his reign, penetrating as far as Delhi on two occasions;

[1] Tavernier visited Delhi in the reign of Aurangzeb and described the peacock throne (*Tavernier's Travels in India.* Edited by W. Crooke, Oxford, 1925, vol. I, p. 303). See also Jadunath Sarkar, *Studies in Mughal India*, London, 1920, p. 18. For the Koh i Nūr see E. W. Streeter, *The Great Diamonds of the World*, London, 1882. *The Koh i Nūr Diamond*, London, 1895. W. Crooke has an appendix on this famous gem, *op. cit.*, vol. II, p. 343. He refuses to believe that the Koh i Nūr was Bābur's diamond.

[2] See p. xxiii; also Elphinstone's *Caubul*, London, 1839, vol. II, p. 95; and W. Irvine, *Indian Antiquary*, 1907, p. 63. The Durrānīs were the populous tribe settled in and around Qandahār whose best-known clans were the Popalzai and the Bārakzai. The Sadozai section of the Popalzais gave Afghanistan its first dynasty and the second royal line was to come from the Muḥammadzai sub-division of the Bārakzais. According to Edward Thomas the term Durrānī may go back to the ninth century (*J.R.A.S.*, 1888, p. 85).

the Mughal capital was devastated.[1] Lahore, the north-west Panjab, and Kashmīr were added to the Durrānī empire, the rising Sikh power was repeatedly chastised and a large Mahratta army was destroyed at Pānīpat, one of the decisive battles of India. Aḥmad Shāh Durrānī, the virtual emperor of Hindustan, could have established a new dynasty at Delhi. His power extended from Lahore to Meshed and from the Oxus down to Qandahār. Yet Aḥmad Shāh, 'the very ideal of the Afghan genius, fitted for conquest yet incapable of empire', never attempted to improve a victory or to organize the government of a conquered country.

Aḥmad's successor was the indolent Taimūr Shāh who moved the capital from Qandahār to Kābul. His father's prestige barely kept the ramshackle empire together. East of the Indus the Durrānīs still held Kashmīr, Sind and Multān, though Lahore was already lost to the Sikhs. West of the Indus were Pashāwar and the Derajāt, together with the country of Hirāt, Kābul, Ghazni, and Qandahār, or modern Afghanistan south of the Hindu Kush. Money struck at Meshed and Balkh testifies to precarious authority in Khurāsān and Turkistān.

The Durrānī empire was founded by violence and built upon the blood and treasure of Hindustan; its history has been called an almost unparalleled series of treasons, rebellions, plots, and murders. Only the distractions of war against a common enemy and the personality of the ruler kept the structure together. By the time of Shāh Zamān foreign war had ceased to be easy and profitable. Delhi was gutted and nothing but hard knocks could be got from the Sikhs of the Panjab; on the other side were the Qājārs of Persia. The Afghans turned upon one another and the struggle began between the twenty-three sons of Taimūr Shāh, the Sadozai, and the twenty-two sons of Pāyanda (Sarafrāz) Khān, the

[1] Thirty years later the palace fort itself was sacked by the infamous Rohilla chief Ghulām Qādir Khān who left the emperor Shāh 'Ālam not even his eyes to weep with.

Bārakzai, which ended in the transfer of power from the Durrānī Shāhs to the Bārakzai Amīrs.[1] The first decade of the nineteenth century witnessed the capture of Delhi by Lord Lake (September, 1803) and the consolidation of the Sikh commonwealth under Ranjit Singh, the Lion of the Panjab. By the treaty of 1809 the River Sutlej was declared the boundary of the Sikh power towards Hindustan, and Ludhiāna became the British frontier station. Ranjit Singh captured Multān and Pashāwar, occupied Kashmīr and annexed the Derajāt. All the foreign possessions of the Durrānīs were lost and the future of Afghanistan lay within her own boundaries. The Bārakzai brethren were masters of the country but at first made use of Sadozai princes as puppet kings. Dost Muḥammad waited a number of years before striking coin in his own name.[2] Anonymous silver pieces and autonomous copper coins are known of this intervening period; they were struck by the Bārakzais.

The coins of Nādir Shāh struck in India are interesting relics of the invasion. There is no issue of a special character to commemorate his seizure of the Mughal capital. On the other hand, a few rare pieces bear witness to the fear inspired by the ferocious tyrant in the remote capitals of Gujarāt and Bengal. The mintmaster of Murshidābād invented a new couplet for the occasion; his colleague at Patna was equally obsequious but less ingenious. The initial coinage in gold and silver of independent Afghanistan is of full weight

[1] The history of the Sadozais and Bārakzais illustrates the drawbacks of polygamy. Twenty-three sons of Taimūr Shāh are enumerated on p. 106 of J. P. Ferrier's *History of the Afghans*, London, 1858. The names of the twenty-two Bārakzai brethren are given on p. 36 of vol. III of Charles Masson's *Narrative of Various Journeys in Balochistan, Afghanistan*, &c., London, 1844. Both Sadozais and Bārakzais are Durrānīs. Mr. G. P. Tate has noted that the title Shāh, like Sultān, signifies a despotic ruler. It was established by the great Aḥmad Shāh at the risk of offending his turbulent nobility and implies a power over the person and property of the subject repugnant to the character of the Afghan race. The Bārakzais had filled the office of Amīr ul Umarā under the Sadozais and were content with the lesser title Amīr, which denotes the possessor of delegated authority. G. P. Tate, *The Kingdom of Afghanistan*, Bombay, 1911, p. 152.

[2] The earliest piece noted by L. White King is dated A.H. 1250, A.D. 1834-5, 'Coinage of the Bārakzai Dynasty', *Num. Chron.*, 1896, p. 333.

and good quality; consisting of Indian metal, it appropriately follows the Indian and not the Persian model. It is Mughal money with a difference; a true Durrānī style is soon evolved. The Durrānī money is the equal of the contemporary Mughal coinage in conception, execution, and metal quality. Shāh Zamān was a great moneyer. His short reign of eight years saw the issue of an artistic coinage in good metal, broad, well struck, of full weight, in considerable variety; the Qandahār (Aḥmad Shāhī) issues are about the finest of the dynasty. It is surprising to find such lavish strikings and so much care devoted to the coinage in a poor and barbarous country; the prevailing insecurity is only betrayed by the frequent aberrations of regnal date. The explanation must lie in the almost superstitious regard paid in the Muḥammadan world to the *khuṭba* and the *sikka*; the bullion was the loot of unhappy Hindustan.[1]

The copper pieces struck in India and old Mughal territory outside Afghanistan are as a rule on the Indian model; they display the royal name, Hijri and regnal dates, and the mint. Copper coins struck in Afghanistan are autonomous pieces of Persian design and weight. It was the custom in Persia for towns to issue their own copper money. On one side is a heraldic or geometrical device, a sword, the figure of an animal, bird or flower; on the other appear just the word فلوس 'copper money', the mint, and Hijri date. There is neither the word *sikka* nor a regnal date. The pieces are local money in the nature of tokens; Dr. R. Stuart Poole correctly classified them by towns and not by reigns.[2] It was my intention to exclude autonomous money from this work but on second thoughts I have added to the Catalogue specimens selected from those described by Mr. Rodgers and Mr. Valentine.

The Catalogue is based upon the Collection in the Panjab Museum, Lahore. I have added issues, unrepresented at

[1] خطبة Friday sermon with a kind of bidding prayer. سكّه The mint stamp, the royal prerogative of coining.

[2] *British Museum Catalogue of the Coins of the Shāhs of Persia*, London, 1887, pp. 212 f.

Lahore, from other Museums and from various papers and catalogues; the sources of these coins are given. The coins of Nādir Shāh and of the Durrānīs in the British Museum are very fine; they include those of my own Cabinet which was acquired in April, 1922. These issues are now well represented in the Indian Museum, Calcutta. The number of coins catalogued from all sources is 1,327—167 gold, 1,007 silver, and 153 copper—from 27 mints; the Panjab Museum contingent numbers 673—55 gold, 559 silver, and 59 copper. The Lahore Cabinet is thoroughly representative and contains some fine series in silver.

The Catalogue is concerned largely with place names in India and Afghanistan; I have adhered to a modified Hunterian system of transliteration. A separate Table of this is not given because the Catalogue exhibits the Persian and English forms of the mint names together. I write Hirāt and Pashāwar; the names appear in this way on the coins. There is no Glossary because words and phrases are explained in the Introduction.

The Introduction contains enough historical matter to elucidate the mintages; the money in mint and date faithfully reflects the vicissitudes of empire. The historical part is followed by Sections on inscriptions and weights; then come the Mint Notes and the Catalogue proper. The Durrānīs, following both Mughal and Persian practice, inscribed Persian couplets on their gold and silver coins. I have incorporated in the Catalogue a metrical version of each Persian couplet as it occurs, and have added English translations.

The coins of each king are classified according to their mints, the mints come in the Persian alphabetical order and the issues of each mint are arranged chronologically. In the mint and date columns a line means that the coin is defective in consequence of the fact that the die was too large for the flan, or is illegible in these particulars. If a coin is mintless or dateless, or both, the appropriate spaces are left blank.

The weight is given in grains and the size in inches; if these particulars are omitted, the coin is the usual gold mohur or silver rupee. The marks on Durrānī coins much resemble those on the Mughal series.

A short list of works is given by Mr. Longworth Dames on p. 327 of *The Coins of the Durrānīs.* I would add H. W. Bellew's *Afghanistan and the Afghans*, London, 1879, and G. P. Tate's *The Kingdom of Afghanistan*, *The Times of India* Office, Bombay, 1911; I commend the latter as an introduction concise yet full of detail. The inset of the Map is taken from Mr. Tate's book and the Genealogical Table is a modified copy of that prepared by Mr. Dames. I repeat the motto which is on the Title Page of my *Catalogue of the Coins of the Mughal Emperors.* It aptly describes the coins of those men of the sword Nādir Shāh and Aḥmad Shāh Durrānī.

The greater part of this work has been done in the Coin Room of the British Museum and I am most grateful to Mr. J. Allan, Keeper of the Coins, for all the help he has given me. I record my acknowledgments to the Directors of other Museums who have kindly permitted me to mention their coins. The casts for the Plates were made by the late Mr. A. P. Ready, electrotypist to the British Museum, while the Plates themselves have been produced by the firm of Messrs. McLagan & Cumming, Warriston Road, Edinburgh, to whom I am also indebted for the Frontispiece. The original of the Frontispiece is in the Museum Print Room and is reproduced by kind permission of the Trustees of the British Museum. The Map is from the Geographical Establishment of Messrs. Edward Stanford, Longacre, London. Finally, I wish to thank the Staff of the Clarendon Press for the great care and ability devoted to the production of this work.

R. B. WHITEHEAD

CAMBRIDGE,
January, 1933.

CONTENTS

CATALOGUE

[1] Shāh Nūru-d-dīn is a local saint, see p. xxix.

LIST OF ABBREVIATIONS

A.D. . . .	Anno Domini.
Æ . . .	copper.
A.H. . . .	year of the Hijri Era.
AR . . .	silver.
AV . . .	gold.
Bah. . . .	Bahāwalpūr Toshakhāna.
B.M. . . .	British Museum Collection.
C. J. R., 1891 .	C. J. Rodgers, *Catalogue of the Coins in the Government Museum, Lahore*, Calcutta, 1891.
C. J. R., 1894 .	C. J. Rodgers, *Catalogue of the Coins collected by Chas. J. Rodgers and purchased by the Government of the Panjab*, Part II, Calcutta, 1894.
Cunn. . .	J. D. Cunningham, *History of the Sikhs*, London, 1849.
I. M. . .	Collection of Indian Museum, Calcutta.
I. M. Cat. .	Vol. III of the *Catalogue of the Coins in the Indian Museum, Calcutta* (Mughal Emperors).
J.A.S.B. . .	*Journal of the Asiatic Society of Bengal.*
J.R.A.S. . .	*Journal of the Royal Asiatic Society.*
L. D. . .	M. Longworth Dames, 'The Coins of the Durrānīs', *Numismatic Chronicle*, 1888.
M. . . .	mint mark or ornament.
N. S. . .	Numismatic Supplement to the *Journal of the Asiatic Society of Bengal.*
Num. Chron. .	*Numismatic Chronicle and Journal of the Royal Numismatic Society.*
Pl. . . .	Plate.
P. M. Cat. .	Vol. II of the *Catalogue of Coins in the Panjab Museum, Lahore* (Mughal Emperors).
R. S. P. . .	R. Stuart Poole, *Catalogue of Coins of the Shāhs of Persia in the British Museum* (London, 1887).
S. . . .	size (in decimals of an inch).
W. . . .	weight (in grains).
W. K. . .	*White King Sale Catalogue*, Part III, J. Schulman, Amsterdam, June, 1905.

LIST OF THE DURRĀNĪ SHĀHS

		A.H.	A.D.
I.	Aḥmad Shāh	1160	1747
	Taimūr Shāh as Niẓām	1170–86	1757–72
	Sulaimān	1186	1772
II.	Taimūr Shāh	1186	1772
	Humāyūn. At Qandahār	1207	1793
III.	Shāh Zamān	1207	1793
IV.	Shāh Shujā'. First reign	1216	1801
V.	Maḥmūd Shāh. At Hirāt	1216–45	1801–29
	Maḥmūd Shāh. First reign	1216–18	1801–3
	Shāh Shujā'. Second reign	1218–24	1803–9
	Shāh Shujā'. At Pashāwar and Kashmīr	1227–8	1812–13
	Shāh Shujā'. At Pashāwar[1]	1233	1818
	Qaiṣar Shāh. At Qandahār	1218	1803
	Qaiṣar Shāh. At Kābul and Kashmīr	1222–3	1807–8
	Maḥmūd Shāh. Second reign	1224–33	1809–18
	Shāh Nūru-d-dīn.[2] In Kashmīr	1223–8	1808–13
	Sulṭān 'Alī. At Kābul	1233	1818
	Aiyūb Shāh. At Pashāwar and Kābul	1233–45	1818–29
	Kāmrān. At Hirāt	1245–58	1829–42
	Shāh Shujā'. Third reign	1255–8	1839–42
	Fatḥ Jang	1258	1842
	Shahpūr Shāh	1258	1842

[1] See p. xxviii.

[2] Shāh Nūru-d-dīn is a local saint, see p. xxix.

GENEALOGICAL TABLE

- I. Aḥmad Shāh
  - II. Taimūr Shāh
    - (1) By Sadozai mother
      - Humāyūn
    - (2) By Popalzai mother
      - V. Maḥmūd Shāh
        - Kāmrān
    - (3) By Yūsafzai mother
      - III. Shāh Zamān
        - Qaiṣar Shāh
      - IV. Shāh Shujā'
        - Fatḥ Jang
    - (4) By daughter of Shāh Rukh Shāh
      - Sulṭān 'Alī
    - (5) By Popalzai mother No. 2
      - Aiyūb Shāh
  - Sulaimān

LIST OF PLATES

NUMERICAL SUMMARY OF COINS CATALOGUED[1]

	Panjab Museum			Total		
	Gold	Silver	Copper	Gold	Silver	Copper
Nādir Shāh	2	19	—	10	52	4
Aḥmad Shāh	15	137	6	51	214	18
Taimūr Shāh Niẓām . .	4	48	1	9	55	1
Sulaimān	—	2	—	1	7	—
Taimūr Shāh	17	190	17	43	281	43
Humāyūn	—	1	—	1	1	—
Shāh Zamān	10	69	13	23	118	25
Shāh Shujā'. First reign[2]	—	—	—	—	—	—
Maḥmūd Shāh. At Hirāt .	—	15	—	—	48	—
Maḥmūd Shāh. First reign	—	14	1	7	33	4
Shāh Shujā'. Second reign	4	29	2	10	55	10
Shāh Shujā'. At Pashāwar and Kashmīr . .	—	—	—	—	2	2
Shāh Shujā'. At Pashāwar	—	—	—	—	1	—
Qaiṣar Shāh. At Qandahār	—	1	—	1	1	—
Qaiṣar Shāh. At Kābul and Kashmīr . . .	—	—	—	—	3	—
Maḥmūd Shāh. Second reign	—	24	11	4	87	27
Shāh Nūru-d-dīn. In Kashmīr	2	1	1	2	9	1
Sulṭān 'Alī[2]	—	—	—	—	—	—
Aiyūb Shāh	1	5	3	2	18	5
Kāmrān at Hirāt . .	—	—	—	—	4	—
Shāh Shujā'. Third reign .	—	3	—	3	11	—
Fatḥ Jang	—	1	—	—	5	—
Shahpūr Shāh	—	—	—	—	1	—
Unassigned	—	—	1	—	1	1
Autonomous coins . .	—	—	3	—	—	12
	55	559	59	167	1007	153
		673			1327	

[1] The total includes coins added late. This class is indicated by a letter after the serial number.

[2] No coins known.

INTRODUCTION

Matter introductory to the Catalogue proper is incorporated in the Mint Notes. A brief historical sketch describes the growth of the empire of Nādir and Aḥmad Shāh, its equilibrium under Aḥmad's son Taimūr Shāh and the subsequent decline and fall. The accessions and deaths of kings, the attempts of pretenders, civil wars, foreign expeditions, the capture and loss of towns and territories are mirrored in current coin.

§ 1. HISTORICAL OUTLINE

The Mughal empire of India and the Ṣafavī empire of Persia alike showed signs of disintegration towards the end of the seventeenth century. The tribes of western Afghanistan had come under Ṣafavī rule but they turned the tables by invading Persia and sacking Iṣfahān under the Ghilzai leader Maḥmūd Shāh; Iran was ravaged and laid waste during the brief period of Afghan supremacy, A.D. 1722–9. To the east confusion was growing in the administration of the outlying provinces of the Mughal empire. At this juncture Nādir Shāh appeared on the scene as an instrument of vengeance, a world conqueror. He turned the Afghans out of Persia, drove back the Turks and Russians from the Caspian marches and seized the Persian crown. The timidity and weakness of the Mughal promised easy triumphs in India.

Nādir Qulī, the Slave of the Wonderful One (God), belonged to the Turkmān tribe of Afshārs and was born in Khurāsān about the year 1687. His father made caps and sheepskin coats for a living, while the son was a shepherd boy. Nādir later took to the mountains and became the leader of a brigand band. His strength and daring recommended him to the governor of Khurāsān at a time when the disorders of Persia gave great scope to the ambitions of so able and unscrupulous an adventurer. In 1722 Shāh Ḥusain Ṣafavī was driven from his capital Iṣfahān by the Afghans under Maḥmūd the Ghilzai, whose cruelties filled Persia with blood. The heir-apparent of the Ṣafavīs, Ṭahmāsp Shāh, fled to Māzandarān in the north and his desperate condition compelled him to accept the overtures of Nādir Qulī, who had grown strong enough to capture and hold the mountain stronghold of Kilāt, some fifty miles from Mashhad (Meshed). Nādir's aims were no longer confined to the plunder of defenceless peasants; he was destined to deliver Persia from her foreign enemies and to subvert the reigning dynasty. In 1727 Nādir enlisted under the fugitive Ṭahmāsp who honoured him with the name of Ṭahmāsp Qulī Khān. The new general initiated a series of campaigns which culminated in the triumphant recovery of Iṣfahān from the Afghan usurper Ashraf, son of Maḥmūd, in November, 1729. Subsequent fighting against the Turks carried the victorious Persian arms as far as Tiflīs on the west; the Grand Seigneur was compelled to restore Georgia and Armenia to Iran and a treaty of peace was concluded in the year 1735. Meanwhile Shāh Ṭahmāsp had been deposed and replaced by an infant son named 'Abbās who died early in 1736. Ṭahmāsp Qulī Khān seized the vacant throne and was proclaimed on the 11th March 1736 with the name and titles of *Sulṭānu-s-salāṭīn i Jahān, Shāh i Shāhān, Nādir Shāh, Pādshāh, Ṣāḥibqirān.*[1]

On the 13th October 1736, Nādir Shāh marched out of Iṣfahān bound for Qandahār. This important position fell in the spring of 1738 after a siege of fifteen months. For services rendered the Abdālī tribe of Afghans was restored from exile at Hirāt to its lands in this vicinity, and a new city was built and named Nādirābād. It is recorded that Nādirābād was in occupation by the end of 1738 and proclaimed capital of the province; this is confirmed by the coin date A.H. 1151 which year began in April, 1738. Meanwhile Nādir was advancing to the Indian frontier bent upon the plunder of Hindustan. He had taken into his service an Afghan, Sardār Aḥmad Khān Abdālī, who was destined to be his successor. Ghazni and Kābul fell in turn, the Khyber was forced and Pashāwar taken. With the fall of Pashāwar in October, 1738 passed away the Mughal dominion west of the Indus. The invasion of India occupied the cold weather of A.D. 1738–9, A.H. 1151–2. The Persian marched by the imperial highroad through Lahore and Sarhind and was met by the Mughal emperor Muḥammad Shāh and his army near Karnāl. The battle was fought in February, 1739 and resulted in an easy victory for the invader. At Delhi there followed a great massacre of the defenceless citizens in which 120,000 people are said to have perished, after which the capital was subjected to a systematic and merciless spoliation for the space of fifty days. This terrible visitation put an end to all authority in Northern India. It has been said of Muḥammad Shāh that if his fate had

[1] Sultan of Sultans of the World, King of Kings, Nādir Shāh, Emperor, Lord of the Planetary Conjunctions. The word for emperor is *pādshāh* in Persia, *bādshāh* in India. These titles are written under the portrait which forms the frontispiece of this work. Ṣāḥibqirān was the special epithet of the great Tamerlane, and was used by some of the Mughal emperors of India. Nādir نادر means rare, marvellous; the English nadir has another meaning and is derived from a quite different word نظير [السّمت].

placed him in a region where established laws supply the want of parts in a monarch, he might have slumbered with reputation upon a throne and left behind him the character of a good, though not of a great prince.[1] Opposed to this ease-loving ruler was a captain unsurpassed in personal prowess and powers of command. These qualities were marred by ferocity and an insatiable avarice; in his last years Nādir became a monster of blood and cruelty. He was assassinated in camp by his own officers in June, 1747 (A.H. 1160).

After the death of Nādir Shāh, the Afghan contingent of his forces retreated to Qandahār where one of his ablest officers, the Aḥmad Khān aforesaid, of the Sadozai clan of the Abdālīs, was elected king of Afghanistan in July, 1747; he seized a large treasure which was on its way to Nādir.[2] Aḥmad Khān assumed the style and titles of Aḥmad Shāh, Bādshāh, Durr i Durrān (Pearl of Pearls), and the Abdālīs were henceforth known as the Durrānīs.[3] The Sadozai was already king in July, 1747, and half the year 1160 had yet to run, but I do not know of any coin dated A.H. 1160. Nādir Shāh's successor in Persia was his nephew 'Ādil Shāh. Aḥmad Shāh at once prepared for a descent on India and invaded the Panjab in the autumn of 1747; the Afghans entered Lahore on the 22nd January 1748, first month of A.H. 1161. A general engagement with the imperial troops headed by Aḥmad, son of Muḥammad Shāh, took place near Sarhind and the Afghan forces retreated, demoralized it is said by some war rockets which exploded in the wrong direction. The Mughal army was returning to Delhi when it received the tidings of the death of Muḥammad Shāh; the Durrānī's namesake succeeded as Aḥmad Shāh Bahādur at the end of April, 1748, or the first of the fifth month, A.H. 1161.[4] This news attracted Afghans east of the Indus a second time but they soon retired. Coins were struck by the Durrānī at Lahore and Sarhind in A.H. 1161. In the autumn of the same year 1748, Aḥmad Shāh captured Hirāt and Meshed from the Persians.

[1] A. Dow, *History of Hindostan*, London, 1768, vol. II, p. 45. Jonas Hanway recorded a considered judgment of Nādir Shāh. *Op. cit.*, pp. 265 f.

[2] H. G. Raverty distinguishes between this kingdom dating from the middle of the eighteenth century and the original Afghanistan, the mountain home of the Pathan race, surrounded on all sides by the walls of the Sulaimān Range. The Afghan State of Hirāt, Kābul, Ghazni and Qandahār is a modern conception (*J.A.S.B.*, 1885, p. 143). See also the elaborate description on pp. 453 f. and especially pp. 466 and 467 of *Notes on Afghanistan*, London, 1888. There is a parallel passage on p. 8 of G. B. Malleson's *Herat*, London, 1880; the Afghans proper were the robbers of the mountain.

[3] The correct title درّ درّان is clearly shown on coin Pl. II, 16; these words cannot mean Pearl of the Age. A pearl in the ear was a badge of servitude (*Num. Chron.*, 1929, p. 23). Aḥmad had earned supreme power as chief servant, a pearl of pearls, to Nādir Shāh.

[4] The first money of each emperor is dated 1161, 1, a possible source of confusion.

The gallant Mīr Mannū, son of Muḥammad S͟hāh's Vazir, was made governor of Lahore; he was defeated under the walls of the city by Aḥmad S͟hāh in April, 1752 (A.H. 1165) on the occasion of a third invasion. The imperial filibuster did not advance further; the provinces of Lahore and Multān were annexed to Qandahār. During the next few years things went from bad to worse in Hindustan. Aḥmad S͟hāh Bahādur had been deposed, blinded and murdered, and the Mug͟hal throne was occupied by a puppet king under the grandiloquent style of the second 'Ālamgīr. Another inroad was planned and 'the prospect of a winter campaign in India filled with joy the hearts of the needy Afghan tribesmen. Enough still remained to fill their saddle bags, and their religious fanaticism was glutted with the pillage and massacre of Hindus.' Aḥmad S͟hāh captured Delhi and rode south to Agra. The historian says that not a single straw was left in the capital; the Jumna ran red with blood from the slaughter at Muttra. The Afghan monarch and his son Taimūr married daughters of the imperial house, and Prince Taimūr was appointed Niẓām or governor of Lahore, Multān, Dera and Sind. These events took place in the winter of A.D. 1756–7, A.H. 1170, and money was struck at the Mug͟hal capital in the name of the invader. Aḥmad S͟hāh began the return journey to his capital Qandahār at the end of March. Three months later Robert Clive fought the battle of Plassey.

The affairs of India had been reduced to chaos and the prevailing misery was increased by the advent of the Mahrattas, who swept through Delhi into the Panjab and drove Taimūr out of Lahore over the Frontier. The disorders at Delhi culminated in the murder of the wretched 'Ālamgīr II at the end of November, 1759. In response to the appeal of his fellow Muslims, Aḥmad S͟hāh crossed the Indus at the end of that year. The Mahrattas were expelled from Delhi two months later and the Mug͟hal capital was given over for three days to a general plunder. The devastation had been so thorough that Aḥmad retired eastwards, abandoning Delhi to the Mahrattas, and rested for the rainy season of 1760 at Anūps͟hahr on the Ganges, where he was joined by his allies the Bangas͟h Nawab of Farruk͟hābād, the Rohilla chief Najību-d-daula, and the Nawab Vazir of Oudh.[1] In the autumn the Durrānī moved out to resume the struggle, which by this time had assumed the character of a religious war. The Jumna was crossed in the face of the enemy and finally, on the 7th January 1761, a large Mahratta army was destroyed in the decisive battle of Pānīpat. This disaster put an end to the dreams of supremacy cherished by

[1] Anūps͟hahr is a town on the west bank of the Ganges where several roads converge at an important ferry. From 1773 to 1806 Anūps͟hahr was an outpost of British troops; the garrison was then transferred to Meerut.

the Mahratta race. Aḥmad Shāh reoccupied Delhi but the Afghan troops mutinied and enforced an immediate return to their own country; the Durrānī disappeared from India leaving governors at Sarhind and Lahore. The events of this momentous fifth expedition are reflected in the coinage. There is the little group of mints east of the Jumna. Money was struck at the capital of Hindustan both before and after the battle of Pānīpat; the unique Delhi piece (Pl. III. 14) belongs to the latter period. It is said that after Aḥmad Shāh returned from India crowned with the laurels of Pānīpat, he set himself to build a new capital at Qandahār. But the initial coinage of Aḥmad Shāhī, the Most Noble of Cities, is dated three years before the battle.

During all these changes the Sikhs were growing more numerous and powerful. When the Durrānī retreated through the Panjab with the spoils of Hindustan, he was harassed by the Sikhs and had to abandon much of the heavy baggage including the monster gun named Zamzama; Mirza Taimūr was incompetent to control affairs.[1] Aḥmad Shāh again appeared on the scene and defeated the Sikhs with great slaughter at a place some twenty miles south of Ludhiāna; he did not advance further than Sarhind as he was recalled by disturbances in Afghanistan. These events took place in the spring of A.D. 1762, A.H. 1175. Yet only a year later Zain Khān, the Afghan governor of Sarhind, was defeated and slain by the Sikhs and the town, the hated scene of the immolation of the two sons of Guru Govind Singh, was utterly destroyed.

By this time Aḥmad Shāh's powers were on the wane. A rupee struck in his name at Najībābād by his old ally Najību-d-daula signalizes Aḥmad's last invasion of India in the cold weather of A. D. 1766–7; the Afghan monarch advanced no further than the Sutlej. Lahore had already been lost to the Sikhs but the balance was redressed by a Durrānī advance to the banks of the Oxus. Kashmīr had been annexed in 1762.

Aḥmad Shāh died in October, 1772, A.H. 1186, and was succeeded by Taimūr Shāh. Another son, Mirza Sulaimān, was proclaimed at Qandahār by Aḥmad's Vazir, Shāh Walī Khān; though he was speedily suppressed, money bearing three couplets was issued in the name of this pretender at Aḥmad Shāhī, Pashāwar, Dera, Kābul and Kashmīr. The execution of the Vazir caused great resentment amongst the Durrānīs of Qandahār, so Taimūr Shāh moved his capital to Kābul.[2] It was his custom to winter at Pashāwar. The

[1] *Panjab Notes and Queries*, 1884. Zamzama is of course mentioned in Rudyard Kipling's *Kim*.

[2] For these events see *Wāqi'āt i Durrānī* (Lith. Ed.), p. 20; *Tārīkh i Aḥmad* (Lith. Ed.), p. 13. Also Ferrier's *History of the Afghans*, London, 1858, pp. 97 f.

Sardār Pāyanda Khān was given the title of Sarafrāz Khān and confirmed in the command of the powerful Bārakzai section of the Durrānī tribe. Expeditions were sent to Multān and Sind; Balkh was lost towards the end of the reign. Ferrier says that Taimūr Shāh during his reign of twenty years was only twice at the head of his army to meet his enemies, and holds that this was the result of policy; he commends the intelligence and firmness of the king (*op. cit.*, pp. 99, 105). A different verdict was recorded by a shrewd contemporary, Major William Palmer, British agent with Sindia, in a letter written to Warren Hastings from Agra on the 30th December 1789.[1] 'Timoor Shāh is not of a character to undertake foreign conquest, it is with difficulty he can be stimulated to any personal exertion in defence of his own dominions, which are frequently disturbed by his northern neighbours, and the tribute withheld by the conquered provinces on the east. He can therefore have little or no influence on the transactions of Indostan tho' the bugbear of his approach is annually repeated.'

Taimūr Shāh at his death on the 18th May 1793 left twenty-three sons; they were by different mothers, the usual source of weakness under oriental conditions. Zamān and Shujā' were full brothers; they were opposed by Humāyūn and Maḥmūd. The most influential of the Sardārs was Pāyanda Khān Bārakzai, the father of twenty-two sons. Pāyanda Khān supported Mirza Zamān. Humāyūn, the eldest son of Taimūr, proclaimed himself at Qandahār but was soon defeated and blinded by Zamān, who was acknowledged king at Kābul. Zamān had to deal with the active and determined enmity of Maḥmūd at Hirāt, who was continually stirring up trouble on the Persian side; the Sikhs were predominant in the Panjab. Faced with failing resources and rebellious brothers Shāh Zamān contemplated the resuscitation of the fast fading glory of the Durrānīs by more invasions of India. There was some chance of success because the Afghan monarch was regarded by the Indian Muslims as the champion of Islam.[2] Such was the terror inspired by these savage invaders that their presence in Lahore caused a mobilization in distant Oudh.[3] Zamān twice invaded the Panjab and occupied Lahore without much opposition but was called back each time by threatening developments

[1] British Museum Library, Warren Hastings Papers, vol. XL.

[2] As testified, for example, by a letter addressed to Shāh Zamān by the brother of the Nawab of Dacca. *Lord Valentia's Travels*, London, 1811, vol. I, Appendix II.

[3] S. C. Hill, *The Life of Claud Martin*, Calcutta, 1901, p. 80. Shāh Zamān in 1798 actually launched an ultimatum upon the Nawab of Oudh and the East India Company; the threat from the Frontier was an appreciable factor in bringing about Lord Wellesley's Treaty with Oudh of the 10th November 1801. A recent competent authority is Mr. P. E. Roberts, *India under Wellesley*, London, 1929, pp. 120 f.

towards Hirāt. His troubles were brought to a head by the impolitic execution of Sardār Pāyanda Khān who had been Vazir to both Aḥmad and Taimūr Shāh. This rash act led to Zamān's defeat, deposition and blinding by Maḥmūd. Now began a fight to a finish between the half brothers Maḥmūd Shāh and Shāh Shujā'. Qaiṣar was a son of Shāh Zamān, and Kāmrān of Maḥmūd.

Shujā'u-l-mulk Shāh was obsessed with his kingly birthright; his thoughts seldom strayed from Kābul, Qandahār and his royal prerogative. This indomitable adventurer has left an account of part of his life.[1] Maḥmūd had succeeded Zamān at Kābul on the 25th July A.D. 1801, third month of A.H. 1216; Shujā' was at Pashāwar. In that year Shāh Shujā' at the age of seventeen proclaimed himself king in Pashāwar although he could only command a party of two hundred horse and foot. He must have struck coin for the occasion but no piece can be attributed with certainty to this brief so-called first reign. Maḥmūd was ousted from Kābul two years later and Shāh Shujā' began his second reign in August, 1803, A.H. 1218. Qaiṣar was made governor of Qandahār but rebelled at the instigation of Vazir Fatḥ Khān, the eldest of the Bārakzai brethren. Four years later Qaiṣar again rebelled at Kābul and marched on Pashāwar; Shujā' advanced from Sind and defeated him in March, 1808. Both revolts were signalized by the issue of coin. Maḥmūd Shāh recovered Kābul in the spring of 1809 and defeated Shāh Shujā' at Nīmla in August of that year, A.H. 1224. Shujā' fled to Qandahār, then to the Panjab, where he met Ranjit Singh at Sahiwāl (Cunn., p. 158). The next few years are occupied with various attempts on Pashāwar. In the cold weather of A.D. 1811–2, A.H. 1227, Shujā' expelled the governor Muḥammad 'Aẓīm Khān Bārakzai from Pashāwar and took up his residence in the citadel; this temporary success was commemorated by the issue of coin. Shujā' was taken prisoner in the spring of 1812 by Jahāndād Khān who sent the captive to his brother 'Aṭā Muḥammad Khān Bāmīzai, governor of Kashmīr; the royal hostage, who had with him the Koh i Nūr diamond, was detained in Kashmīr a year. In early 1813 Vazir Fatḥ Khān conquered Kashmīr and left his brother 'Aẓīm Khān Bārakzai governor in place of the defeated 'Aṭā Muḥammad; Shujā' was sent down to Ranjit Singh at Lahore. It was just at this time that anonymous copper coins dated 1228, first regnal year were struck at Kashmīr (Srīnagar) (Coins 1050 and 1051). We are not told that 'Aẓīm proclaimed himself king of Kashmīr; even when the Bārakzais triumphed at Kābul five years later, they struck coin in the name of Sadozai princelings. I

[1] Biographical Sketch of Shah Soojah, ex-King of Cabul, written by himself at Loodianah, in 1826–7. *Calcutta Monthly Journal*, 1839.

think that these pieces embody an assertion of loyalty to Shujā' whom 'Aẓīm had just liberated from the thraldom of 'Aṭā Muḥammad; one coin is called a *sikka*, that is to say, it bears the royal stamp.

The fall of Maḥmūd was the result of the blinding of Vazir Fatḥ Khān Bārakzai early in A.D. 1818. 'Aẓīm Khān, as soon as he heard of the affair, dispatched his younger brother Dost Muḥammad to Kābul; Dost Muḥammad there proclaimed a Sadozai prince Sulṭān 'Alī as king. 'Aẓīm Khān in person proceeded from Kashmīr to Pashāwar. In the first flush of his resentment he made overtures to Shāh Shujā' and undertook on behalf of the Bārakzai brethren to obey Shujā' as his lawful sovereign. Shāh Shujā' advanced from Ludhiāna, entered Pashāwar and took possession of the citadel; it is probable that Coin 1052 was minted on this occasion. But 'Aẓīm had decided to adopt another Sadozai titular Aiyūb as a more pliable tool; Shāh Shujā' was defeated and once more set out on his wanderings, eventually returning to British hospitality at Ludhiāna. 'Aẓīm Khān with his puppet king Aiyūb took the road to Kābul and the ensuing negotiations with Dost Muḥammad terminated in the acknowledgement of 'Aẓīm as Vazir, and of Aiyūb Shāh as nominal sovereign. Shāh Sulṭān 'Alī quietly retired into private life, while Shāh Maḥmūd and his son Kāmrān were allowed to rule on sufferance at Hirāt.[1] Afghanistan was partitioned amongst the Bārakzais. These events took place in A.D. 1818, A.H. 1233–4, and thus came to an end the power of the Sadozais. The royal line of Ṣado, like that of Taimūr, was honoured with the *khuṭba* and the *sikka* long after its power had disappeared. 'The Bārakzai chiefs at first made use of princelets of that family as puppets to conciliate any adherents they might still possess but soon were able to dispense with this pretence, and as not one of these titulars was a man of character or ability, they were allowed to sink into obscurity in their own country, or they drifted away to Ludhiāna'.

In June, 1838 was signed the tripartite treaty between Shāh Shujā', Ranjit Singh and the British Government; it was decided to restore the Afghan monarch. In the autumn of the same year a large British force was dispatched from Bengal through Upper Sind towards the Bolan Pass, while troops from Bombay under Sir John Keane were ordered to effect a junction with the main column by way of the western bank of the Indus. Indian soldiers

[1] Charles Masson has a good account of the early career of Dost Muḥammad and of the events which led to the downfall of the Sadozais. C. Masson's *Narrative*, London, 1842, vol. III, Chapters II to IV. Sulṭān 'Alī was soon murdered. Aiyūb Shāh was more fortunate; he eventually made his way to Lahore and became a pensioner on Ranjit Singh. There is a character sketch of the worthless debauchee Kāmrān in Munshi Mohan Lal's *Journal of a Tour through the Panjab*, &c., Calcutta, 1846, p. 241.

were seen again in southern Afghanistan after the lapse of two centuries. Qandahār and Ghazni fell in turn and the state entry into Kābul took place on the 7th August 1839, A.H. 1255. Dost Muḥammad made good his flight north of the Hindu Kush. The rest of the story is well known. The high command was incapacitated by blundering interference, insurrection was allowed to come to a head, and a British force was destroyed on its retreat from Kābul; Shāh Shujā' was murdered three months later. These events took place in the beginning of A.D. 1842, A.H. 1258. The 'army of retribution' placed Fatḥ Jang, son of Shujā', on the throne, but on the departure of the British troops Fatḥ Jang was wise enough to withdraw; he abandoned Kābul in October, 1842. Dost Muḥammad found his way back and quickly recovered his influence and authority.

One episode in the late Durrānī period requires separate treatment. Coins were struck at Kashmīr from A.H. 1223 to 1228 bearing the name of Shāh Nūru-d-dīn; Shāh is a common appellation for a Muslim *faqīr* and it is clear from the invocation that Nūru-d-dīn was a saint or holy man. Mr. Rodgers merely recorded that the Afghan governors of Kashmīr issued money in the name of the saint Nūru-d-dīn. Mr. Longworth Dames says that Kashmīr had become a perfect hotbed of rebels and pretenders: 'after Qaiṣar Shāh, the governors Nūru-d-dīn and Muḥammad Shāh struck in their own names'. Later Mr. Dames correctly stated that coins issued in the name of the popular saint Nūru-d-dīn, but repeated the misapprehension arising from the alleged Kashmīr coins of 'Muḥammad Shāh'.[1] The Nūru-d-dīn money was issued by 'Aṭā Muḥammad Khān Bāmīzai, grandson of Shāh Walī Khān, Vazir to Aḥmad Shāh, who was appointed governor of Kashmīr in place of 'Abdullah Khān Alakozai by Shāh Shujā' at the end of the year A.H. 1219.[2] 'Aṭā Muḥammad rebelled in the latter half of 1223 and an expedition sent against him under the Vazir Akram Khān was a complete failure. This news reached Pashāwar, the winter capital of Shujā', in the second month of 1224 or April, 1809, just about the time that Maḥmūd Shāh recovered Kābul. Civil war followed and Shujā' was defeated at Nīmla in August, 1809. Maḥmūd became king for the second time with Fatḥ Khān Bārakzai as Vazir. Four years later Fatḥ Khān marched into Kashmīr and defeated 'Aṭā Muḥammad in

[1] See *Encyclopaedia of Islam*, 'Kashmīr', p. 794. The name Muḥammad Shāh is due to an error which I explain in the Mint Note on Kashmīr.

[2] Alakozai, like Popalzai, is a Durrānī tribe. Both Sadozai and Bāmīzai are septs of the Popalzai. R. C. Temple, *Distribution of the Afghan Tribes about Qandahar*, *J.A.S.B.*, 1879.

the second month of 1228, or February, 1813; the Vazir left his brother 'Aẓīm Khān to rule Kashmīr. It is clear that 'Aṭā Muḥammad had made himself independent of Kābul because Shāh Shujā' and Maḥmūd Shāh in turn sent expeditions against him; the period is A.H. 1223 to 1228, precisely that of the Nūru-d-dīn coinage. 'Aṭā Muḥammad would not assume royal honours; he certainly did not wish to acknowledge either Shujā' or Maḥmūd. By way of compromise he struck coin in the name of Shaikh Nūru-d-dīn, the patron saint of rural Kashmīr.[1] The special nature of the occasion is marked by the issue of a handsome silver coin weighing 224 grains, the only piece of this weight in the entire Durrānī series; fine double mohurs of a unique character were struck later.

§ 2. INSCRIPTIONS

The legends on the gold and silver issues of the Durrānīs are generally alike. The obverse contains a Persian couplet of an allusive nature; often, following Indian practice, there is the Hijri date. The reverse exhibits the mint and regnal date, sometimes accompanied by the Mughal formula *sana julūs maimanat mānūs,* Year of Accession associated with Prosperity. Only two rupees, both of Aiyūb Shāh, bear the Kalima, the Muḥammadan Profession of Faith. The copper coins have the royal name and titles, the mint, and date. There is nothing on the mohur or the rupee to denote the denomination; copper currency is merely called فلوس, a vague term meaning 'copper money'. The only exception to this statement is provided by the copper issue of Aḥmad Shāh which bears the words وزن خام رائج الوقت. Neither *laqab* (surname) nor *kuniyat* (patronymic) is found on Durrānī issues except the Kashmīr money of Shāh Nūru-d-dīn. Very few Marks are mint marks in the sense of recurrence through a period of years on the issues of a particular mint. Marks 8 and 22 of Multān mint originated in the reign of Aurangzeb; 48 is characteristic of Bahāwalpūr, and 11 is the lily of Dera. Mark 2 often occurs on the money of Pashāwar, and Kashmīr may be indicated on copper pieces by a sword or crossed swords.

Attention is drawn in the Mint Notes to the frequent aberrations of regnal date exhibited by the coins of the later Durrānīs. The

[1] *The Valley of Kashmir*, W. R. (now Sir Walter) Lawrence, London, 1895, p. 287. The atrocious nature of the Afghan domination is indicated at p. 197. 'Aṭā Muḥammad on his return to Afghanistan joined Prince Kāmrān and made a bold bid for power in the commotions which followed the removal of Vazir Fatḥ Khān Bārakzai. He was quickly outwitted and blinded, a typical Afghan episode (C. Masson, *op. cit.*, vol. III, p. 44).

puzzle of the early Multān issues of Taimūr Shāh is explained by the fact that the Sikhs were in possession just at that time. The second year of Maḥmūd's second reign is 1224 at Kābul, 1226 at Pashāwar, while at Multān the first year is 1227. The power of the Durrānīs was collapsing and their empire was filled with treachery and bloodshed; the times were out of joint and mint masters were liable to lose their heads in more senses than one. In so disturbed a period, the coins cannot be expected to conform with a general scheme of regnal years.

A reference is invited to the Catalogue where the coin couplets are set out and translated as they occur. The couplets bear a family resemblance to those of India and Iran; they are more elaborate than the Mughal inscriptions. Nādir Shāh does not appear to have used the Ṣāḥibqirān distich before his invasion of India. This horoscopic title was probably inspired by his overthrow of the race of Tamerlane who was the Ṣāḥibqirān *par excellence*, though it had already been used by Nādir's predecessor ʿAbbās III (R.S.P., p. 69).

The usual distich of Nādir Shāh is a recital of the titles already given on p. xxii. There is an adequate notice in the Mint Notes of the ephemeral Murshidābād issue with a recently published couplet. The type with Nādir the Sulṭān on the obverse originated in Persia. The ʿAẓīmābād (Patna) rupee is just the normal money of Muḥammad Shāh but Nādir has been substituted for the name of the Mughal. Coin 57 appears to be of Indian mintage and is of unique character. The usual reverse legend is the invocation خلد الله ملکه, 'May God perpetuate his Kingdom', together with the mint and Hijri year but not the regnal date.

The great Aḥmad Shāh remained faithful to one couplet throughout his reign of twenty-five years.[1] Mr. Rodgers' version of the order which proceeded from the Incomparable Creator is 'Strike coin on silver and gold from the Ascension of Pisces to the Moon', translated from the Latin of Marsden. A similar literary trifle occurs in ʿUtbī's Kitāb i Yamīnī where it is said of the fort of Bābātih that 'its top was equal in loftiness to Heaven's height and was parallel to Pisces'. A line in the poetry on Ḥasanābād runs عمارت برآورد براوج ماه (Firishta). The expression is treated by E. G. Browne in his *Literary History of the Persians*, vol. III, p. 113. ماهی is the cosmic Fish; the metaphor is one of universality, both of beauty and location. The couplet is arranged in either three or four lines; the form باحمد is sometimes written به احمد. The word زد occurs instead of زن on early issues of the Bhakhar mint. When Aḥmad Shāh entered the

[1] The rupee *C.J.R.*, 1894, p. 167, No. 1 belongs to the Mughal Aḥmad (*J.A.S.B.*, 1910, p. 670).

Panjab for the last time, he gave the new Sarhind to the Patiāla chief Amar Singh and permitted the use of his coin couplet. This Durrānī couplet appears on the modern money of Patiāla, Jind and Maler Kotla States.

The coinage of Taimūr as his father's Niẓām is monotonous; the couplet is always in three lines. He is already called Shāh and has his own scheme of regnal dates. Sulaimān's brief bid for power is enlivened by three couplets; the Kashmīr couplet will be completed when additional specimens come to light. The tedious distich of Taimūr Shāh embodies the conceit of a revolving sky, alternate day and night, sun and moon, gold and silver, all obedient to the Shāh's command. This legend is arranged in many ways but, for reasons of economy, only a few are reproduced in the Catalogue. The word كند is replaced by زند on the money of Kashmīr. Non-couplet piece 494 is unique.

The claimant Humāyūn approved an elaborate couplet which I cannot elucidate. Shāh Zamān used one couplet in the first half and another in the second half of the reign; on some coins there is an effective arrangement of both couplets. In the second distich the name of the king appears as Zamān Shāh. A form of the first couplet was used at Multān in which the word قرار is replaced by طراز.[1] The Aḥmad Shāhī piece Pl. IX. 5, is a beautiful coin; the arrangement of the mint legend is characteristic of Durrānī money at its best. The expression Right and Left Hand (of the State) is unusual. Possibly a third couplet appears on Coin 759.

Maḥmūd Shāh employs the same couplet on the issues of his first reign and on the abundant silver money struck at Hirāt for thirty years. The distich has affinities with those of the Shāhs of Persia. No couplet can be ascribed with certainty to what is called the first reign of Shāh Shujā'. The normal distich of the second reign is on conventional lines; the Kashmīr couplet is that of the Mughal emperor Farrukhsiyar. Handsome double and single rupees were struck at Bahāwalpūr with a special couplet of the Persian type. I attribute a unique piece (Coin 1052), with a distich so far unread, to a temporary revival of authority at the Shāh's favourite residence Pashāwar (p. xxviii). The rebel Qaiṣar Shāh, like Sulaimān, had three couplets. There is a close resemblance between those of the Qandahār (Aḥmad Shāhī) and Kashmīr mints, the second line being common to both. The Kābul rupee of Qaiṣar, like the Kashmīr coin of Sulaimān, is a solitary specimen.

[1] The Tārīkh i Aḥmad, of which the Daulat i Durrāniya is an Urdu translation, gives this coin couplet, also that of Taimūr as found on the money of Kashmīr. This chronicle also tells us that Humāyūn had the *khuṭba* read and money issued in his own name at Qandahār, but unfortunately the couplet is not given.

There are two couplets used in the second reign of Maḥmūd S͟hāh, that of his first reign and the second of a Persian complexion in which the king is called by a S͟hī'a title, the Second Ḥasan. The distich of S͟hāh Nūru-d-dīn is discussed in the Catalogue. Two couplets were invented for the puppet king Aiyūb; that of Kas͟hmīr contains a punning allusion to Aiyūb's protector Sardār 'Aẓīm K͟hān Bārakzai. The distich of Kāmrān S͟hāh is another couplet partially read; further material is required.

Dost Muḥammad Bārakzai was dethroned and S͟hāh S͟hujā' restored at Kābul by British arms. There is a couplet type of the third reign of S͟hāh S͟hujā'; the first line is identical with that of the couplet quoted by Mr. C. J. Rodgers from the Tārīk͟h i Sulṭānī (L. D., p. 338). The titular Fatḥ Jang is the last of the Sadozais. He appears to have struck a couplet issue (Pl. XIV. 16), but the coin listed exhibits only a part of the legend. I do not know of another specimen.

§ 3. WEIGHTS.

I have incorporated information about weights and standards in the Mint Notes. Only eight of the catalogued coins are on the Persian standard, three silver of Nādir, four gold and one silver of the Durrānīs. Dr. R. Stuart Poole has reproduced the careful Tables of Hanway (R. S. P., pp. lxi f.); he remarked that Nādir's currency includes two unrecorded denominations, the double mohur and the double rupee. Doubtless Jonas Hanway never saw them because they were minted in K͟hurāsān and outside Persia. The only recorded double mohur was struck at Lahore, the double rupees at Qandahār, Pas͟hāwar, Multān, Lahore and Meshed.[1] These double pieces are of Indian weight. The smaller silver coins struck at Qandahār and Nādirābād tally with Hanway's six *s͟hāhī* piece of 108 grains. All the other coins of Nādir in this Catalogue are on the Indian standard. Coin 3 of Aḥmad S͟hāh, the initial gold issue of his new capital Aḥmad S͟hāhī, is an *as͟hrafī* of the Persian denomination. Three other gold coins of Aḥmad S͟hāhī mint in my list are of Persian weight. Coin 930 of Maḥmūd's first reign weighs 54 grains, the equivalent of the old *as͟hrafī*. Coin 974 of the second reign of S͟hujā' is an *as͟hrafī* weighing 47 grains; 1058 of Maḥmūd's second reign only weighs 37·5 grains. The unique thin silver piece of Aḥmad (Coin 172) weighs 62 grains.

The Indian term for the normal weight gold coin of the 168 grain standard is *as͟hrafī* or *muhr* (*Angl.* mohur); the corresponding piece

[1] For double rupees of Meshed see the White King Sale Catalogue.

in silver of the 178 grain standard is the *rupiya* (*Angl.* rupee).[1] Afghanistan was flooded with Indian gold and silver, the hoards of centuries, and the coins are usually of remarkably good metal and full weight. Only in the last years of Maḥmūd S͟hāh at Hirāt, when the Durrānī empire had already fallen, did base metal and small silver appear in Afghanistan. Conditions were of course different in Multān and Kas͟hmīr, where we find comparatively abundant copper issues. Fractions of the Indian weight gold are unknown; fractions of the rupee are extremely rare outside late Kas͟hmīr and Hirāt. There was not a single small silver piece at Bahāwalpūr; my only prize in this line was a half rupee of S͟hāh Zamān of Kābul mint (Coin 815). Coin 109 appears to be a tenth of the rupee.

The Mint Notes contain detailed information about weights. Gold coins of Indian weight are minted to the standard of 168 grains throughout the dynasty. There is a solitary silver piece of the curious weight of 224 grains (Coin 1176). Early silver issues at most mints are on the full standard of 178 grains but deteriorate in weight later. Hirāt silver maintains its weight fairly well till Kāmrān's time; on the other hand, Derajāt and Kas͟hmīr rupees are on a scale of about 170 grains throughout. A critical date is the sixth or seventh year of the second reign of Maḥmūd; the silver standard at Aḥmad S͟hāhī, Pas͟hāwar and Kābul drops from the full weight to about 165 grains. At Bhakhar the weight was maintained till the Afghans were ousted by the Mīrs of K͟hairpūr about the year A.H. 1255. Coin 1218 is a full weight Kābul rupee of the third reign of S͟hāh S͟hujā'; it is exceptional in this respect because the other silver coins of this reign struck at Aḥmad S͟hāhī and Kābul are on a standard of some 145 grains. Mr. Longworth Dames calls this the depreciated Bārakzai standard which, according to Dr. White King, was largely in use all over the North West Frontier at the end of the nineteenth century. Durrānī rupees were still more or less in circulation in the north west Panjab after the Mutiny.[2]

There was little attempt to strike copper money on a uniform scale; the weights vary with local custom and demand. Copper issues of Aḥmad S͟hāh correspond roughly with the *dām* of 320 grains, a Later Mug͟hal standard of some 285 grains (as exemplified in Muḥammad S͟hāh's money of Bhakhar, Elic͟hpūr and Kas͟hmīr) and Aurangzeb's depreciated *dām* of about 215 grains. A favourite weight for Multān copper throughout is some 180 grains; the denomination is lighter in

[1] I think 170 and 180 grains rather high; the definition of the *tola* at just 180 grains belongs to the British period. W. H. Moreland, *Indian Antiquary*, Sept. 1931, p. 161.

[2] 'Table of the Coins of former Governments more or less current in the Bazars of the Goojrat District in 1859', *J.A.S.B.*, 1864.

Kashmīr. Pieces struck by Maḥmūd and Shujā' in Kashmīr centre round 120 and 65 grains.

Two *fulūs* of Aḥmad Shāh in the British Museum are called وزن خام رائج الوقت; there are two more at Berlin. A *khām* or *kachcha* weight is local as distinguished from imperial; these interesting pieces are local weights current at the time of striking, the years 1175 and 1176 respectively. Unfortunately the coins are in poor condition; their weights are 181 and 160 grains. The locality or mint is not given but *fulūs* of this type were struck only at Bhakhar and Dera. The Mughal official maund and *ser* had been based on the weight of a coin, the copper *dām*. In the present case the local *ser* was probably the equivalent of a certain number of copper pieces and the coin under discussion is the local unit of weight.

§ 4. MINT NOTES.

The coins of Nādir Shāh and the Durrānīs of Persian mintage, and anonymous money in general, are omitted. Aḥmad Shāh conquered Khurāsān in A.D. 1748 to 1750 and his son and successor Taimūr Shāh was born at Mashhad (Meshed). Both Aḥmad and Taimūr struck at Mashhad; these issues are represented in the British Museum. Khūī, خوی, is recorded as a mint of Taimūr Shāh on the sole authority of E. Leggett.[1] The place is in western Persia, far outside Taimūr's sphere of influence. The only anonymous pieces listed are copper coins 1050 and 1051, but they exhibit both Hijri and regnal dates.

The totals as given at the beginning of each Mint Note are those from all sources. The pieces actually in the Panjab Museum itself can only be ascertained by reference to the Catalogue proper.

The mints are twenty-seven in number. There are the modern mints of Bahāwalpūr and Aḥmadpūr, and the Camp mint Rikāb which corresponds with the imperial Urdū of the Mughal emperors of Hindustan. The Mughals had struck coin at all the others except Hirāt which was a Persian town till seized by Aḥmad Shāh. Taimūr Shāh issued money at Balkh in Afghan Turkistān, a mint of Shāh Jahān; Qandahār and Kābul are the principal cities of Afghanistan. Kashmīr was taken from the Mughals by Aḥmad Shāh. Bhakhar, Pashāwar, Tatta, Dera, Derajāt and Sind (Ḥaidarābād) are in the territory which was ceded to Nādir Shāh; Atak, Lahore and Multān in the Panjab. Sarhind (Sahrind) stands where Hindustan and the Panjab meet. The remaining nine mints are in Hindustan and the coins commemorate the invasions of India. Both Nādir and Aḥmad issued money at Delhi; the terrified Mughal

[1] *Notes on the Mint Towns and Coins of the Mohamedans*, London, 1885.

officials struck coins in the name of Nādir Shāh at distant Aḥmadābād, Patna ('Aẓīmābād) and Murshidābād. There are five mints of Aḥmad Shāh east of the River Jumna: Ānwala, Barelī, Farrukhābād, Murādābād and Najībābād. They are the towns of Aḥmad's Muslim allies at the battle of Pānīpat.

Half the mints bear honorific epithets. Balkh is the Mother of Cities, Bahāwalpūr the Abode of Pleasure, while Ḥaidarābād in Sind is of Auspicious Foundation. The Camp mint Rikāb is called August or Fortunate, Sarhind is the Seat of Safety, Kashmīr and Hirāt the Resting Place of the Sultanate and Qandahār (Aḥmad Shāhī) the Noblest of Cities. The mountain State is also called the Territory of Kashmīr. Five mints keep the epithets bestowed upon them in happier times. The Mughal capital Shāhjahānābād (Delhi) is the Seat of the Khalifate, Multān the Abode of Security and Farrukhābād in its eponymous form Aḥmadnagar commemorates the Bangash Nawab Aḥmad Khān who fought at Pānīpat. Lahore remains the Seat of the Sultanate. Kābul on the earliest Durrānī coins is called by its Mughal title Abode of Royalty but quickly becomes another Seat of the Sultanate.

It was my intention to omit autonomous coins (pp. xi and xxxv). However at the end of the Catalogue there is a list of these local copper issues from Afghan mints bearing dates which bring them within the period of Durrānī supremacy. Mr. Longworth Dames has included Dera Fatḥ Khān in his list of mints though the so-called 'cat money' is clearly of a local character.[1] His Coin 54 bears the name Taimūr but there is no certain attribution to Dera Fatḥ. Coin 2784 of the White King Sale Catalogue claims to be a Nādir rupee of Dera Fatḥ mint. Dr. White King's Durrānī series, with others, left this country, and it would now be difficult to verify the legends of any particular piece, so I have confined Dera Fatḥ Khān to the autonomous list. Shikārpūr is a mint of the Amirs of Sind. It is represented by a copper piece of year A.H. 1255 (W.K. 2879) struck in the name of Maḥmūd Shāh ten years after his death and twenty-two years after the fall of the Sadozais.

ATAK اٹک

Lat. 33° 53′ Long. 72° 16′

	G.	S.	C.
Aḥmad	2	10	—
Taimūr	1	12	—

Atak (Attock) is the well-known fortified post on the east bank

[1] As illustrated on pp. 195 and 197 of Mr. W. H. Valentine's *Copper Coins of India*, Part 2.

of the Indus, the river which the orthodox Hindu could not cross. The fort was built by the emperor Akbar who struck copper money at Atak Banāras. After Akbar, Atak is represented in the Mughal series by one or two rupees of Muḥammad Shāh.

The north west Panjab was annexed by Aḥmad Shāh Durrānī in A.H. 1165. The rare mint Atak is well represented in the list by gold and silver money of Aḥmad and Taimūr Shāh of normal types and full weight. The latest piece catalogued is of Taimūr's sixteenth year. Subsequently Atak fell to the rising power of the Sikhs.

AḤMADĀBĀD احمداباد

Lat. 23° 1′ Long. 72° 38′

	G.	S.	C.
Nādir	—	2	—

Aḥmadābād, the capital of the Province of Gujarāt, was a splendid city and a prominent mint in the heyday of the Mughal empire. As Nādir Shāh never advanced beyond Delhi, it may well be asked why money should have been struck in the name of the conqueror at a place so remote from the invaded territory. There can be little doubt that, as at Murshidābād, a demand was made for recognition and for tribute and that the Mughal governor did not dare to refuse. Only three or four coins are known, all in silver and of year 1152; Dr. White King had a half rupee. These pieces bear the normal couplet.

AḤMADPŪR احمدپور

Lat. 28° 18′ Long. 70° 7′

	G.	S.	C.
Maḥmūd. Second reign or posthumous	—	4	—

Aḥmadpūr is an old capital of the Bahāwalpūr State. Rupees of an inferior type, probably posthumous, were struck at Aḥmadpūr in the name of Maḥmūd Shāh.

ĀNWALA (AONLA) انوله

Lat. 28° 16′ Long. 79° 12′

	G.	S.	C.
Aḥmad	—	5	—

Aonla is a town in Rohilkhand. Rupees dated 1173 and 1174 were struck here in the name of Aḥmad Shāh by his ally Najību-d-daula. Mahratta successes in the Panjab brought the Durrānī into India for the fifth time. Shāh 'Ālam II had just ascended the Mughal throne but was powerless to influence events. Aḥmad Shāh marched on Delhi by a circuitous route and took it from the Mahrattas in the spring of A.D. 1760, equivalent to A.H. 1173, 14. The unhappy capital and its vicinity had been so devastated that Aḥmad decided to cross the Jumna and to pass the rainy season at Anūpshahr, an important post on the Ganges, now in the Bulandshahr District of the United Provinces. He was joined by the Bangash Nawab of Farrukhābād, the Rohilla chief Najību-d-daula, and Shujā'u-d-daula, the Nawab Vazir of Oudh. The Mahrattas recovered Delhi, but Aḥmad Shāh with his allies crossed the Jumna at the end of October, 1760 and totally defeated a large Mahratta army at Pānīpat on the 7th January, 1761 or A.H. 1174. The Durrānī left Delhi for Afghanistan at the end of March, 1761. During this invasion money was struck by his allies in the name of the Afghan conqueror at the mints of Aonla, Barelī, Farrukhābād, and Murādābād. Aonla rupees are listed countermarked with dates 1188 and 1191; Aḥmad Shāh died in 1186.

BARELĪ بریلی

Lat. 28° 22′ Long. 79° 26′

	G.	S.	C.
Aḥmad	—	2	—

Barelī is the principal town of Rohilkhand. Rupees dated 1173 and 1174 were struck here in the name of Aḥmad Shāh by his ally Najību-d-daula. A reference is invited to the collective Note under Aonla.

BALKH بلخ

Lat. 36° 36′ Long. 67° 10′

	G.	S.	C.
Taimūr	—	2	4

Balkh in Afghan Turkistān, once the capital of ancient Bactria, was a mint of Shāh Jahān. In A.D. 1764–5 Aḥmad Shāh Durrānī conducted a campaign against the Amir of Bukhāra and the Oxus was fixed as the boundary between the two States. Taimūr Shāh struck silver coins at the Mother of Cities, as Balkh was called; copper pieces are listed of dates A.H. 1202, 1205, and 1206. Copper coins of what appear to be the first two dates were published at p. 387 of C. M. Fraehn's *Opusculorum Postumorum, Pars Prima*, Petropoli, 1855. Balkh was recovered by the Uzbegs in or about the year A.H. 1206.

BAHĀWALPŪR بهاولپور

Lat. 29° 24′ Long. 71° 47′

		G.	S.	C.
Maḥmūd.	First reign	5	7	—
Shujā'	Second reign	3	10	—
Maḥmūd.	Second reign	1	13	—

There is a notice of Bahāwalpūr in the Preface; it was a succession State of the Mughal empire. Bahāwalpūr town possessed some commercial importance. Imports for Hindustan were conveyed in camel caravans from Kābul to Delhi by way of Multān, Bahāwalpūr, Sūratgaṛh and Bhatner; if intended for Sind, they diverged south from Bahāwalpūr.[1] In the year A.D. 1788 Taimūr Shāh in person subdued the Nawab of Bahāwalpūr and the desert stronghold of Derāwar was taken after a three months' siege. The Nawab paid an indemnity and agreed to remit a yearly tribute to Kābul. Bahāwalpūr came early into contact with the British; the Political Mission under Mountstuart Elphinstone halted here in December, 1808 on its way to Pashāwar. Durrānī suzerainty ceased with the fall of Maḥmūd Shāh in 1818. The State was an active ally of the British in the First Afghan War.

Gold and silver coins were struck at Bahāwalpūr in both reigns of Maḥmūd Shāh and in the second reign of Shāh Shujā'; these pieces usually exhibit a rough oblique milling, a tribute to British influence. I saw some thousands of handsome double pieces in both metals; they had never been in circulation. The mint opened in the year 1217 of Maḥmūd's first reign with double and single pieces in gold, the edge being obliquely milled.[2] I found only two unmilled specimens out of many hundred double mohurs like 932; Pl. X. 7 is one of the two and was in my Cabinet. The initial silver issue is unmilled and bears the name of the mint attended by an epithet *Dāru-s-surūr*, Abode of Pleasure (Pl. X. 8). At the beginning of the second reign of Shujā', double and single pieces were struck in silver with a special couplet. There are no double pieces of the second reign of Maḥmūd Shāh. The issue of inferior silver coin continues in the name of Maḥmūd not only after his deposition in A.H. 1233, but also after his decease in the year 1245.

[1] On Tabular Returns of the N. W. Frontier Trade with Afghanistan. *J.A.S.B.*, 1841, pp. 251, 484.

[2] The milling is coarse and seems to have been done by hand after the coins had left the dies.

These coins of Maḥmūd are succeeded by autonomous silver coins of Bahāwalpūr State. The legends are: *Sikka i mubārak Dāru-l-Islām*, and the Hijri date: *Ẓarb Dāru-s-surūr Bahāwalpūr*. An early date in the Indian Museum is 1251.

BHAKHAR بهکهر

Lat. 31° 37′ Long. 71° 5′

		G.	S.	C.
Nādir		1	8	3
Aḥmad		2	27	4
Taimūr as Niẓām		—	9	—
Taimūr Shāh		3	40	3
Zamān		1	3	1
Maḥmūd.	First reign	—	1	—
Shujā'.	Second reign	—	3	1
Maḥmūd.	Second reign and posthumous	—	13	—

Planted in mid-stream between Sakhar (Sukkur) and Rohrī is the island-stronghold of Bhakhar; it is one of the few pretty spots on the Indus and in old days was the key of Sind. Bhakhar was founded in early Muhammadan times and played an important part in the history of the Province. In Akbar's reign it was a *sarkār* in the *ṣūba* of Multān. Sind was ceded to Nādir Shāh. The Persian conqueror after his return from Delhi stayed in Kābul only six days. Then, sending his treasure to Hirāt, he went to Sind by way of Bangash and the Derajāt in order to compel the surrender of the governor of Bhakhar. Nādir arrived in Dera Ghāzī Khān on the 15th Shawwāl, 1152; he left Lārkāna on his return from Sind in the first month of the year 1153.

The gold and silver pieces of Nādir Shāh struck at Bhakhar mint are couplet coins of the full imperial Indian weight. Bhakhar gold of Nādir is very rare; I note two dates only, 1155 and 1158. Silver is comparatively abundant and the sequence of years from 1153 to 1160 inclusive is complete. Bhakhar is the only Indian mint at which Nādir struck copper money of the *fulūs* type. There is a copper coin of Muḥammad Shāh in the British Museum dated 1160 which points to a temporary revival of Mughal influence at Bhakhar on the death of Nādir.

Gold coins of Aḥmad are very scarce, indeed gold was sparingly struck at Bhakhar throughout the dynasty. I give two examples, both from the Bahāwalpūr Toshakhāna. The first is of the normal couplet type, dates 1168, 8; the second has احمد شاه دُرّ دُرّان in a central area surrounded by the couplet, date 1177. There is a full and interesting sequence of rupees. The earliest coin is a dumpy piece of year three with an unusual arrangement of the couplet in which زد replaces the normal زن; the Hijri date being in small figures on the extreme right is generally off the *flan*. Standard pieces of the seventh and eighth years are replaced in the latter year by a central area type; the couplet is arranged around a foliated closed figure containing the words احمد شاه درّ دران, Aḥmad Shāh, Pearl of Pearls. This effective type of the eighth year was also adopted by the mints of Dera, Derajāt, Kābul and Multān. In the case of Bhakhar mint it continues with variations of the reverse legend till the end of the reign, the latest example listed being of year 1184. Gold and silver throughout are of the full imperial Indian weight. Copper coin 262 is a heavy piece resembling the Mughal *dām*; the other examples approximate to the Later Mughal standards of about 285 and 215 grains.

The Bhakhar mint is found on the coins of Taimūr, first as Niẓām or governor for his father Aḥmad, and subsequently as king in succession to Aḥmad Shāh. Gold coins of Taimūr Shāh Niẓām from Bhakhar have yet to be found. In some years the rupees of Aḥmad as king and of his son as governor overlap. On coins of Dera, Lahore and Multān mints, 1170 is called the first year of the Niẓāmat yet at Bhakhar 1173 is the second year and 1177–78 is the third year. Perhaps the governorship at Bhakhar was one of broken periods; Aḥmad himself struck there in 1174 and 1175. Niẓāmat rupees of Bhakhar mint appear in each year from 1182 to 1186 inclusive, of a type without regnal date.

Gold coins of Taimūr Shāh as king are extremely rare. I give three examples, two from the Bahāwalpūr Toshakhāna and the third in the British Museum (from my Cabinet). The last belongs to a late and inferior type with the mint name written Bakhar at the top of the coin. Silver is abundant and I list an excellent series, almost every year of the reign being represented. The first year reverse type is the same as that of years 1182 and 1183 of the Niẓāmaṭ. Speaking generally, the obverse is of a central area kind, the last three words of the couplet being surrounded by the remainder. In the year 1195 there is a change, the last two words only—تیمور شاه—of the couplet remaining in the central area, and this obverse type continues to the end of the reign. In certain years the couplet is presented in its conventional four line form. There is no fixed model for the reverse legend, but the Hijri year invariably appears on this side and the regnal date is not given. The type changes in an arbitrary fashion; the list contains four different items for each of the years 1196 and 1197. The weight throughout remains well up to the theoretical maximum of 178 grains. A few copper coins are known of Bhakhar mint and appear to have been struck to a standard of 250 grains.

In my Notes I find a reference to one gold coin of Shāh Zamān from this mint. It is at Bahāwalpūr; the mint name is written Bakhar. Silver coin 759 is unique, and remarkable in two ways. I do not know of any other coin of Zamān of a central area type; also the legend is different from the two known couplets of Shāh Zamān but cannot be read without the aid of other specimens. Items 760 and 761 exhibit the inferior Bakhar reverse derived from the Taimūr type (Pl. V. 14). I catalogue one copper coin of Shāh Zamān on which the mint name is written Bhakkar.

Silver coin 949 is of the Bakhar type; I attribute it, though dateless, to Maḥmūd's first reign because the legends are about as good as the inscriptions on similar coins of Shāh Zamān, and better than those of certain coins which I have placed in Maḥmūd's second reign.

Both silver and copper are known of Shujā'u-l-mulk Shāh's second reign. The former are again of the Bakhar type; 995 bears date 1218. A few Bhakhar copper pieces exist like 1038.

As regards Maḥmūd's second reign, silver coin 1078, like 949, is of the Bakhar type, but the obverse legend is differently arranged, the style is debased and the Hijri year appears at the top of the obverse. The central area rupee dated 1245 was struck in the year of Maḥmūd's death and is full weight. Its successors of 1255 and subsequent years are light pieces weighing 152 or 153 grains, and must have been coined by the Mīrs of Khairpūr who captured Bhakhar from the Afghans. The first issue of 1258 exhibits a bird, peafowl or pigeon, on the obverse, while the reverse bears a peafowl with a cobra in its beak. Other coins of the same year have a hare on the obverse. This hare again appears on issues of 1259 and 1261, corresponding with A.D. 1843 and 1845, but on the reverse is a lion. Sir Charles Napier had arrived in Sind, and Bhakhar with other places was ceded by a treaty signed in February, 1843. The battle of Miāni was fought on the 17th February of that year and Sind became a Province of British India.

PASHĀWAR پشاور

Lat. 34° 0′ Long. 71° 38′

		G.	S.	C.
Nādir		4	7	1
Aḥmad		2	20	1
Sulaimān		—	1	—
Taimūr Shāh		9	24	7
Zamān		3	18	—
Maḥmūd.	First reign	—	3	—
Shujā'.	Second reign	—	10	—
Maḥmūd.	Second reign	—	11	1
Aiyūb		2	12	2

The ancient frontier city of Pashāwar was the winter capital of the Durrānīs and the favourite residence of Shāh Shujā'. Nādir Shāh on his way to India took Pashāwar from the Mughals in October, A.D. 1738, A.H. 1151. Coins of Muḥammad Shāh are known of this year (*P. M. Cat.*, p. 330). The only Nādir pieces of this mint dated 1151 seem to be the double rupee in the Cabinet de France of the نادر السلطان type and W. K. 2780. The earliest listed specimen of Indian type is dated 1153 and there are examples in either gold or silver of each year till 1160, with the exception of 1156; they are of the full Indian weight. Coin 66 is a solitary piece in copper of date 1160; it formerly belonged to Mr. Longworth Dames. The mint name is written پشاور, not پیشاور, and appears in this form on the Durrānī issues.

The coins of Aḥmad Shāh are on the Mughal model; their style is neat and effective and the legends are well centred. The coin illustrated at Pl. III, 9 is a fractional piece and appears to be a tenth of the rupee. Copper money is known which by legend and regnal year might belong either to the Mughal Aḥmad Shāh Bahādur or to the Durrānī Aḥmad Shāh. In my Panjab Museum Catalogue I attributed them to the Mughal (*P. M. Cat.*, p. 361) but Pashāwar was ceded by Muḥammad Shāh to Nādir Shāh and belonged to the Durrānī empire.

Coin 345 is a unique rupee of the pretender Sulaimān; I found it at Bahāwalpūr.

The gold and silver issues of Taimūr Shāh continue in the style of Aḥmad and Sulaimān till and including the seventeenth year. From 1197 to 1199 there are aberrations of regnal year. In year 18 the four line arrangement of the couplet is replaced by one in three lines and the reverse inscription appears in a characteristic flowing style (Pl. V. 16). The latter is differently arranged in year 19 (Pl. VII. 2) and so remains till the end of the reign. A posthumous specimen in gold is dated 1209, 21. All these coins are well struck and of full weight. The Catalogue describes several copper coins. Specimens of years 1, 4 and 8 are of the Later Mughal model in legend and weight. On other coins of lighter weight the reverse inscription surrounds a lobed figure.

The reverse of Taimūr's latest Pashāwar currency is found on the gold and silver coins of Shāh Zamān. Zamān's first couplet is used till the fourth year—1211 and 1212. It is displaced by the second couplet in year 4. In 1215, 8 appears a type on which the first couplet is surrounded by the second; this is also found of dates 1215, 9 and 1216, 9. All these coins are of remarkably full weight. I am not acquainted with a Pashāwar issue of Zamān in copper.

Rupees are listed of all three years of Maḥmūd's first reign—1216, 1217 and 1218. The reverse of the first year is that of Shāh Zamān's currency (Pl. X, 9) but something quite different appears in the second year (Pl. X, 11); the words *julūs maimanat mānūs* are dropped. I have not found a copper coin which can be attributed with certainty to Maḥmūd's first reign. It is safer to place the piece illustrated at Pl. X, 17 in the second reign because a specimen in the British Museum is dated 123–.

The Pashāwar rupees of Shāh Shujā' are discussed in the Introduction. All are well struck, of good metal and full weight. The Pashāwar rupees of Maḥmūd's second reign are handsome coins bearing the حسن دیگر couplet. The list shows that these are full weight till year 4; from year 6 the standard is about 165 grains. In year 8 appears a central area type of obverse; the area contains سلطان محمود and the Hijri date and the remainder of the couplet is arranged in the four marginal compartments. The latest coin is dated 1233, 10.

In 1233 Aiyūb Shāh, a son of Taimūr Shāh, was proclaimed king at Pashāwar by the Bārakzai chief Muḥammad 'Aẓīm Khān, elder brother of Dost Muḥammad. Coins of all three metals were struck in the name of this puppet king. The gold pieces are of poor metal and light weight, a great contrast with the lordly money of the opulent past. There is an interesting series of rupees bearing regnal dates from 1 to 12; the couplet is exhibited in different ways. Copper coins are procurable; a piece similar to 1203 was published by Colonel von Zambaur in the *Numismatische Zeitschrift*, 1904.

Pashāwar was taken by the Sikhs in A.H. 1250, A.D. 1834.

TATTA تتہ

Lat. 24° 44′ Long. 68° 0′

	G.	S.	C.
Nādir	—	1	—
Aḥmad	—	2	—
Taimūr	—	2	—

Tatta, as the name is written on the coins of the Mug͟hal dynasty, is an old capital and port of Sind. According to Major H. G. Raverty it was founded when the Sammahs rose to power shortly before Muḥammad bin Tug͟hlaq, Sultan of Delhi, died in A.H. 752, A.D. 1351 ('The Mihrān of Sind', *J.A.S.B.*, 1892, pp. 272, 329). Captain Walter Paynton, writing about the year 1612, mentions Diul (Dewal) near the mouth of the Indus, and says, 'Tatta is one of the most celebrated marts of India; Loor Bander (Lahrī Bandar) is the port of it'. Later in the seventeenth century Tavernier described Tatta as one of the greatest cities of India. Tatta now stands at the apex of the Indus delta, the navigable channels are silted up, and its old glories have departed. Mr. H. Cousens calls it Dewal-Ṭhaṭhah, and believes that the place approximately occupies the site of Debal or Dewal, an ancient port and one of the first towns in Sind to be attacked by the Arab invaders of the eighth century (*The Antiquities of Sind*, Calcutta, 1929, pp. 124 f.). M. R. Haig places Dewal some twenty miles south west of Tatta (*Indus Delta Country*, London, 1894, p. 47), but Cousens points out that the Tatta site was probably only half its present distance from the sea at the time of the Arab conquest. The view that Dewal, Lahrī Bandar and Tatta were different places is supported by the fact that Akbar struck coin at all three, probably in the same year (*P. M. Cat.*, Mint Notes).

Tatta was a prominent silver mint of the Mug͟hal emperors; the latest coin of that series is a rupee of Aḥmad S͟hāh Bahādur. Owing to its remote situation, the money of this mint town is apt to display pleasing deviations from the uniformity of type prevailing elsewhere. Examples of this tendency are cited in my Mint Note on Tatta (*P. M. Cat.*, p. lxiv). The Bahāwalpūr hoard was rich in coins of Tatta mint, and I discovered specimens of all the great rarities, the most interesting being the first known couplet piece of Rafī'u-d-daula, S͟hāh Jahān II.

The rupee of Nādir S͟hāh of Tatta mint is new and unique; it is of the normal type and came from Bahāwalpūr. No date is visible but the issue was probably struck in the cold weather of 1152–3 while Nādir was campaigning in Sind. A few inferior silver coins are known of Aḥmad S͟hāh and Taimūr S͟hāh.

ḤAIDARĀBĀD. *See* SIND.

DERA ديره

Lat. 34° 24′ Long. 72° 59′

		G.	S.	C.
Aḥmad		7	31	7
Taimūr as Niẓām		2	4	1
Sulaimān		—	2	—
Taimūr Shāh		3	27	3
Zamān		3	10	1
Maḥmūd.	First reign	—	2	—
Shujā'.	Second reign	1	3	—

The mint of Dera was at the frontier town of Dera Ghāzī Khān, west of the Indus. Its rise is described in the Note on Derajāt. Coins of Nādir Shāh are not known of Dera mint although he struck at Derajāt.

Dera was an important mint of Aḥmad, Taimūr and Zamān Shāh; their issues were found in great abundance at Bahāwalpūr. A rupee is listed of Aḥmad Shāh's first year; its reverse bears the lily which is characteristic of Dera mint. Coin 127 interrupts the series with an unusual three line arrangement of the couplet. In year 8 appears the effective central area type of obverse which at Dera is repeated in year 9. The same year sees a return to the normal couplet type and to the abbreviated reverse formula which omits the words *julūs maimanat mānūs*; this type continues to the end of the reign, year 26. The Catalogue records a fine series of rupees. Both gold and silver coins are in good style and of full weight. There are seven entries of copper. The same type persists from the first to the tenth year, but the weight varies considerably. There seems to have been no accurate striking to definite standards.

Dera is a mint of Taimūr as deputy for his father Aḥmad Shāh but only for the first three years of the Niẓāmat. The coin sequence appears to be as follows. Aḥmad himself issued gold and silver at Dera in 1170; this date is not only called regnal year 10, which is quite correct, but also 12 and 13. Then comes the money of the first three years of Taimūr Shāh Niẓām. All three years are listed in silver but the second year is missing in gold. Coin 342 is the only copper coin of the Niẓāmat known to me; it is piece *C.J.R.*, 1891, p. 118, No. 27. Prince Taimūr's coinage now ceases to issue from the Dera mint and is replaced by that of his imperial father.

Silver coins were struck at Dera in the name of the pretender Sulaimān. I found a score of rupees of the couplet type at Bahāwalpūr but only one of a non-couplet type (Pl. V. 11).

Dera was one of the principal mints of Taimūr Shāh though I list only three different dates in gold. Coin 372 is a handsome piece; several hundreds of this issue were in a bag at Bahāwalpūr. The series of rupees must be almost complete. It begins with a non-couplet piece of year 1186, 1, modelled on the coin of Sulaimān of this type (Pl. VII. 4). There follows a coin, also of 1186, 1, on which the couplet is quite unusual both in arrangement and style (Pl. VII. 5). Then comes the normal series from the first to the nineteenth year; the style of the reverse changes slightly about year 9. In 1204, 19 appears the counterpart in silver of the fine gold coin mentioned above and illustrated at Pl. VI. 1. This type continues till the end of the reign, 1207, 21; to 1207 also belongs the exceptional piece shown at Pl. VII. 6. I only list three copper coins.

There are three gold coins of Zamān Shāh dated regnal years 1, 2, and 3; they bear his first couplet. The legends on the silver pieces are in a coarse, bold style and the first couplet persists from 1208, 1 to 1215, 7. This series is followed in 1215 by an issue in different style with a new arrangement of the reverse legend; there is no regnal date and the weight is five grains less. The copper coin has the same date as the specimen described by Mr. Longworth Dames (*Num. Chron.*, 1888).

The mint is represented in Maḥmūd's first reign by silver issues of the first and second years.

A gold coin is listed of Shujā'u-l-mulk Shāh's second reign, date 1218, 1, also silver issues of regnal years 1, 4, and 5. The rupees of Maḥmūd and Shujā' are good metal and full weight.

Dera was taken by the Sikhs in A.H. 1235.

DERAJĀT ديرجات

Lat. 32° 2′ Long. 72° 4′

		G.	S.	C.
Nādir		2	3	—
Aḥmad		3	6	—
Taimūr Shāh		—	24	—
Zamān		1	14	—
Maḥmūd.	First reign	—	2	—
Shujā'.	Second reign	—	9	—
Maḥmūd.	Second reign	—	19	—

The Derajāt is the alluvial tract between the Sulaimān Range and the Indus; the region takes its name from the three Deras or settlements of Dera Ghāzī Khān in the Lower Derajāt, and of Dera Ismā'īl Khān and Dera Fatḥ Khān in the Upper Derajāt. All three were founded towards the end of the fifteenth century, Dera Ghāzī Khān by the Baloch Mirāni chieftain Ghāzī Khān, and Dera Ismā'īl Khān and Dera Fatḥ Khān by the Baloch Hot leaders Ismā'īl Khān and Fatḥ Khān. Autonomous copper money issued from Dera Fatḥ Khān, and the White King Sale Catalogue mentions a rupee of Nādir Shāh, legends and type not described. The mint of Derajāt, so-called, was situated in the town of Dera Ismā'īl Khān, now in the North West Frontier Province. Gold coins of this mint are very scarce and copper not listed.

Nādir Shāh struck at Derajāt in gold and silver towards the end of his reign; the dates listed are 1158, 1159, and 1160. Nādir was assassinated in June, 1747, half way through the year 1160, and within a month Aḥmad, the Sadozai Afghan, was elected king at Qandahār. But Aḥmad Shāh did not strike money till 1161. In the period of confusion between Nādir's unexpected death and the consolidation of Aḥmad's power, coins issued at Derajāt in the name of the Mughal emperors Muḥammad Shāh (1160, 30) and Aḥmad Shāh Bahādur (1161, 1) (*P. M. Cat.*, pp. 331, 351).

Derajāt coins of Aḥmad Shāh are rare and are usually of inferior execution and style. Examples are the two gold coins illustrated at Pl. II. 10 and 11. The central area obverse type is known in both gold and silver. The mint name is written Derajāt and Derahjāt and there is diversity of reverse legend. Coins 160 to 162 are light weight. The last mentioned piece is of exceptionally good style for this mint (Pl. III. 15).

Gold of Taimūr Shāh is wanting but silver is common and a long series of rupees ranges from 1192 to the end of the reign. As with Aḥmad Shāh there are various arrangements of the reverse legend and the mint name is written both Derajāt and Derahjāt. Some coins exhibit inaccuracies of regnal date. The weight conforms with a standard of about 171 grains, seven less than the full Mughal weight of 178 grains. The general style is up to the average of Taimūr Shāh.

There is a handsome full weight gold coin of Zamān Shāh. The date is 1211 which on this specimen is called the second regnal year; it should be either 3 or 4. Silver entries number no less than fourteen. The weight standard of about 171 grains continues from Taimūr's reign; the first couplet is used throughout. Dates 1209, 1210, 1211, and 1212 are all called regnal year two. The mint is written Derahjāt till it becomes Derajāt in 1212, 2, and so remains till the end of the reign. Late coins of years 6, 7, and 8 exhibit the proper regnal years.

Mr. Longworth Dames has recorded 1212, 6, 1213, 7, and 1215, 8. The reverse of the later coins with mint name Derahjāt contains the pious ejaculation هو, 'He', the name of God.

Derahjāt rupees of Maḥmūd's first reign weigh 170 grains or so, and are dated 1216, 1 and 1217, 2. Mr. Longworth Dames has 1218, 2.

The second reigns of Shujā' and Maḥmūd are well represented but once more only in silver weighing up to 170 or 171 grains. The mint name is written Derahjāt throughout.

The Derajāt was annexed by Ranjit Singh in A.H. 1236.

RIKĀB رکاب

		G.	S.	C.
Aḥmad.	Rikāb i Mubārak	1	—	—
Taimūr.	Rikāb	1	1	—
„	Rikāb i Mubārak	—	1	—
Shujā'. (Second reign)	„ „	1	—	—

The August Stirrup is the camp mint of the Durrānīs corresponding with the Urdū or Urdū i Ẓafar Qarīn, the Camp associated with Victory of the Mughal emperors.[1] The name Rikāb occurs alone, also as Rikāb i Mubārak; it is a very rare mint.

The gold coin of Aḥmad Shāh is remarkable and unique; it is the only piece in the entire series which bears the name of the month and must have been struck to commemorate the New Year's Day of the year A.H. 1173; Aḥmad was not in India at the time. The gold coin of Taimūr Shāh is also a solitary specimen and was bought at the Da Cunha Sale in 1889; its style indicates Pashāwar or its vicinity. Pashāwar was the winter capital where Taimūr spent much of his time. Coin 545 is on the Mughal model; the Rikāb rupee 546 is of Persian style. A Rikāb coin of Taimūr, year 1187, is mentioned on p. 386 of C. M. Fraehn's *Opusculorum Postumorum, Pars Prima*, Petropoli, 1855. A dozen gold coins of Shujā' like 979 were in a small wash-leather bag at Bahāwalpūr; no others are known to me.

[1] The term Rikāb was also used in and before Mughal times, e.g. *Ṭabaqāt i Nāṣirī*, H. G. Raverty, London, 1881, p. 811. *Tūzuk i Jahāngīrī*, Rogers and Beveridge, London, 1914, vol. II, p. 131.

SIND

Lat. 25° 23′ Long. 68° 25′

	G.	S.	C.
Nādir	1	7	—
Taimūr as Niẕām	—	1	—
Taimūr Shāh	—	6	—
,, Ḥaidarābād Sind	—	1	—
,, Ḥaidarābād	—	1	—

Sind was ceded to Nādir Shāh together with the trans-Indus territory of the Mughal empire and the Persian invaded the Province in person during the winter of A.H. 1152–3 to exact tribute from its Kalhora rulers. Full weight rupees of Sind mintage are known from 1153 to the end of the reign in 1160 and were fairly numerous at Bahāwalpūr. The date is at the bottom of the obverse and is usually off the flan; a fine specimen is R. S. P., Pl. VII. 263. The only piece known to me in gold is at Vienna. Aḥmad Shāh Durrānī exercised absolute authority over Sind but did not strike coin there. The territory appears to have been administered by his son Taimūr as governor but Coin 300 is a single specimen. The modern capital Ḥaidarābād was founded by Ghulām Shāh Kalhora in A.H. 1182, A.D. 1768; older coins must have been struck at Tatta.

There was an invasion of Sind by Taimūr's general Madad Khān, and Taimūr Shāh on another occasion advanced in person as far as Shikārpūr. The Kalhoras were replaced by the Talpurs in A.D. 1786 and were confirmed as feudatories of Sind by Taimūr Shāh. Zamān Shāh determined to exact in person the arrears of tribute but penetrated no further than Multān. In A.H. 1218 Shujā' invaded Sind with a large army as far as Lārkāna. The later Durrānīs could not control this remote Province and no coins are known after Taimūr Shāh.

The Sind money of Taimūr is silver only and falls into three classes. There is a central area type struck at Sind and a similar issue with the double name Ḥaidarābād Sind. All are inferior in style, especially the light weight money of late date. Coin 492 is a unique specimen, undoubtedly of Taimūr's own striking, on which the mint name Ḥaidarābād is attended by the honorific epithet *Khujista Bunyād*, 'of auspicious foundation'. This epithet on Mughal coins is confined to Aurangābād in the Dekkan.

SAHRIND (SARHIND)

Lat. 30° 38′ Long. 76° 27′

	G.	S.	C.
Nādir	—	1	—
Aḥmad	4	7	—

The old town of Sarhind (Sahrind on these coins) occupied an important strategical position where Hindustan and the Panjab meet, on the royal road from Lahore to Delhi. The disintegration of the Mughal empire exposed it to continual attack. Nādir Shāh struck a silver coin at Sahrind on his return journey from Delhi which bears a new epithet *Dāru-l-aman*, Abode of Security. Sahrind was repeatedly occupied by Aḥmad Shāh; an issue of his first year testifies to a battle fought in this vicinity within ten months of the assassination of Nādir Shāh. The year 1161 was also the first regnal year of the Mughal emperor Aḥmad Shāh Bahādur who struck money at Sahrind in this and each of the five following years (*P. M. Cat.*, p. 356; *I. M. Cat.*, p. 253). This temporary revival of imperial influence terminated in the reign of ʿĀlamgīr II. The Durrānī issues of 1174, 14 and 1174, 15 were struck during the memorable fifth invasion, before and after the battle of Pānīpat. There is also money of 1176 testifying to the sixth invasion. A year later Zain Khān, the Durrānī governor of Sahrind, was defeated by the Sikhs and the town was utterly destroyed. The modern town of Sarhind is in Patiāla State, the coinage of which still exhibits the couplet of Aḥmad Shāh. It is said that the Sadozai in person, on the occasion of his last invasion, allowed the use of his coin legend to the Patiāla chief Amar Singh at Sarhind (*J.A.S.B.*, 1885, Pl. II. 17).

SHĀHJAHĀNĀBĀD (DELHI)

Lat. 28° 39′ Long. 77° 15′

	G.	S.	C.
Nādir	—	2	—
Aḥmad	7	5	—

After his easily won victory near Karnāl, Nādir Shāh entered Shāhjahānābād on the 9th of the twelfth month, A.H. 1151 or the 20th March, A.D. 1739. The general massacre took place there three days later and was followed by a systematic spoliation of the surviving citizens. Delhi was evacuated on the 7th of the second month, A.D. 1152. The conqueror authorized an issue of coin in the Mughal capital, in fact Jonas Hanway states that payments to the troops were made in Nādir's own coin.[1] This seems unlikely because Nādir

[1] *Hanway's Travels*, London, 1753, vol. IV, p. 183.

Shāh's silver money of Shāhjahānābād mint is scarce and gold unknown. Mr. C. J. Rodgers at the time he wrote an article on this subject only knew of three specimens, all silver and of year 1152.[1] I have seen perhaps forty rupees in all, of dates 1151 and 1152, but gold is still missing.

The issues of Aḥmad Shāh are the results of the two expeditions to Delhi which completed the ruin of that unfortunate city. The first took place in the cold weather of A.D. 1756–7, A.H. 1170; the second led to a longer occupation. The Mahrattas were driven out of Delhi in February, 1760 (middle of A.H. 1173) and Aḥmad Shāh passed the summer at Anūpshahr, some thirty miles to the east, temporarily losing control of the capital. A large Mahratta army was routed at Pānīpat on the 7th January, 1761 and Aḥmad Shāh retook Shāhjahānābād. The Afghan troops had been more than a year in the plains of India and a serious mutiny frustrated the designs of their leader. He withdrew from Delhi on the 22nd March 1761 (A.H. 1174) never to return.

Pieces in gold and silver with legends in the imperial Delhi style are found of date 1170, 11. The issues of the second occupation, also in both metals, are dated 1173, 14 and 1174, 15. The former were struck in the spring of the year A.D. 1760 and the latter early in 1761 after the battle of Pānīpat. There are two arrangements of the obverse inscription, two styles (Durrānī and Mughal) and the size may be as much as 1·5 inches. Coin 172 is a single specimen of unique character (Pl. III. 14). It weighs only 62 grains and must be a presentation piece. The White King Sale Catalogue records a one-eighth of a rupee, date 11 (W. K., 2820).

‘AẒĪMĀBĀD (PATNA)

Lat. 25° 37′ Long. 85° 12′

	G.	S.	C.
Nādir	—	1	—

Patna in the eighteenth century was the capital of Bihar Province. It was renamed ‘Aẓīmābād in honour of ‘Aẓīmu-sh-shān, second son of prince Mu‘aẓẓam (afterwards Shāh ‘Ālam Bahādur), who was appointed governor of Bengal and Bihar during the last years of the reign of his grandfather Aurangzeb. Money was struck at Patna and Murshidābād in the name of Nādir Shāh for identical reasons; I invite a reference to the Note on Murshidābād mint. The silver coin in the Guthrie Collection at Berlin is unique. The date is 1151

[1] ‘On some Coins of Nādir Shāh struck in India’, *Num. Chron.*, 1882, p. 324.

and the legend is that of the money of Muḥammad Shāh struck at Patna; the name Nādir is substituted for Muḥammad (Pl. I. 11). There is a rupee of the latter emperor dated 1152 in the Indian Museum, Calcutta (*I. M. Cat.*, No. 1891).

FARRUKHĀBĀD

Lat. 27° 24′ Long. 79° 34′

	G.	S.	C.
Aḥmad	1	2	—

Farrukhābād took its name from Farrukhsiyar and is now the head-quarters of a District in the Province of Agra. It was one of the succession States of the Mughal empire and as such was founded by Nawab Muḥammad Khān, Ghaẓanfar Jang, a Pathan of the Bangash tribe who now live near Kohāt in the North West Frontier Province (W. Irvine, 'The Bangash Nawabs of Farrukhābād', *J.A.S.B.*, 1878 and 1879). Muḥammad Khān died in A.H. 1156. His second son Nawab Aḥmad Khān, Ghālib Jang, who ruled the territory from 1163 to his death in 1185, gave his name to Aḥmadnagar-Farrukhābād. Aḥmad Khān fought at Pānīpat and issued coin in the name of Aḥmad Shāh Durrānī. A reference is invited to the collective Note under Aonla. On the money of 1176, 15 the regnal year is not correct. The coins are broad handsome pieces in characteristic style.

QANDAHĀR. *Also* NĀDIRĀBĀD *and* AḤMAD SHĀHĪ

Lat. 31° 37′ Long. 65° 43′

			G.	S.	C.
Nādir		Qandahār	—	3	—
		Nādirābād	—	3	—
Aḥmad		Aḥmad Shāhī	4	13	—
Sulaimān		,,	—	1	—
Taimūr		,,	6	20	—
Humāyūn		,,	1	1	—
Zamān		Qandahār	1	—	—
		Aḥmad Shāhī	—	19	—
Maḥmūd.	First reign	Aḥmad Shāhī	2	6	—
Qaiṣar		,,	1	1	—
Shujā'.	Second reign	,,	2	12	—
Maḥmūd.	Second reign	,,	1	12	—
Aiyūb		,,	—	1	—
Shujā'.	Third reign	,,	—	3	—
Fatḥ Jang		,,	—	1	—

Qandahār dominates southern Afghanistan and is a position of great strategic importance. The practical road to India is by way of the fertile tracts of Hirāt and Qandahār, not through the sterile and difficult passes between Kābul and Pashāwar. The Persians had held Qandahār since its capture from the Mughal Shāh Jahān in A.D. 1648, but the growing weakness of the Ṣafavī dynasty became unequal to the task of controlling this distant Province, and Qandahār fell to the Ghilzais about the year 1709. It was captured and destroyed in 1738 by Nādir Shāh after a prolonged resistance. During the course of the siege Nādir had chosen a site for a new city which he called Nādirābād. He restored the Abdālīs from exile at Hirāt to their original lands near Qandahār. Aḥmad Shāh Abdālī or Durrānī was crowned at Qandahār and later built a capital there, which he named Aḥmad Shāhī, the Most Noble of Cities. His successor Taimūr moved the capital to Kābul.

Qandahār is one of the principal Afghan mints. The coins are well struck, artistic, of full weight and good metal. There are autonomous issues in copper.

Nādir Shāh struck silver money at Qandahār in the year 1150. Coin 44 is a double rupee of Indian weight while 45 and 46 are of Nādir's Persian standard; all are of the نادر السلطان type. Nādirābād silver coins dated 1151 and 1152 are of similar type and denominations.

Few examples of Aḥmad's Aḥmad Shāhī currency are described in earlier Catalogues but there was no lack of them in the Bahāwalpūr Toshakhāna. The name of the mint is attended by its honorific epithet *Ashrafu-l-bilād*, Most Noble of Cities. Qandahār is the scene of Aḥmad's coronation, he built his new capital and was buried there, yet he did not issue coin from Qandahār till he could inscribe the name Aḥmad Shāhī upon his money ten years after his accession. The earliest issue is dated 1171, 11 three years before the battle of Pānīpat. The initial gold coinage consists of a thin broad piece equivalent to the Persian *ashrafī* in weight; other dates listed in gold are 22 and 23. The silver coins are of the full Indian rupee standard and run from the eleventh year to the end of the reign. From the seventeenth year the coins exhibit the *julūs maimanat mānūs*, Regnal Year associated with Prosperity formula derived from the Mughal currency.

'After Aḥmad Shāh's funeral, the Vazir Shāh Walī Khān seated his son-in-law Sulaimān Shāh, half brother of Taimūr Shāh, on the throne at Aḥmad Shāhī, and had the *khuṭba* read in his name', (*Wāqi'āt i Durrānī*). As we are specifically informed that the ephemeral king Sulaimān acceded at Aḥmad Shāhī I was specially pleased to find rupee 344 at Bahāwalpūr, one of two known specimens. It contains the مهر و ماه couplet and the reverse is similar to that of Aḥmad's last year. The form سنه ۱ instead of the usual سنه احد is unusual.

Aḥmad Shāhī is one of Taimūr's principal mints; gold and silver were struck here throughout the reign. The reverse of the first year money reproduces Sulaimān's mint side inscription. The year 1204 witnesses the introduction of an arrangement of the reverse legend characteristic of this mint (Coin 356). This continues with modifications till the end of the reign. The coins are good broad pieces of full weight.

Aḥmad Shāhī is the only known mint of the claimant Humāyūn who disputed the succession with Shāh Zamān. Gold and silver of the same type have come to light. I discovered two gold pieces and a score of rupees at Bahāwalpūr and do not know of any other source.

Shāh Zamān struck abundantly at Aḥmad Shāhī in gold and silver. These issues are broad good pieces of full weight and are about the best of the dynasty. That of the first year reproduces the reverse of Humāyūn's coinage, derived in its turn from the reverse type of the last years of Taimūr Shāh. The obverse is first occupied by what I call couplet Z1. In the year 1212 this is replaced by couplet Z2 without change either in the reverse legend or in style. A type of the seventh and eighth years exhibits both couplets; couplet Z1 occupies the obverse and couplet Z2 is arranged in a circular margin around the normal reverse legend. The foregoing remarks hold good for both metals. Two double rupees, once the property of Mr. Longworth Dames and now belonging to Mr. P. Thorburn, require special notice. Each piece is a single specimen. Coin 756 is of the eighth year type just mentioned. Coin 751 has both couplets on the obverse, an arrangement found on the double rupees of Kābul mint (Pl. IX. 14). Gold coin Pl. IX. 1 is the only piece known to me of the entire Durrānī series on which Aḥmad Shāhī is given its old name of Qandahār.

Maḥmūd Shāh struck rupees at Aḥmad Shāhī in all three years of his first reign; probably gold also of similar types though only 1218 is exemplified in the nobler metal. Coin 930 is of the same Persian denomination as 3 of Aḥmad Shāh. In 1217 appeared a broad well-executed piece with the invocation یا محمود as an addition to the reverse inscription.[1] The type continues into the next year; sometimes یا محمود is replaced by یا عزیز, O Mighty One.[2]

[1] One of the three names of the Prophet—Muḥammad, Aḥmad, Maḥmūd.

[2] One of the ninety and nine Excellent Names of God.

In the year 1218 coins in gold and silver were struck at Aḥmad Shāhī by prince Qaiṣar, son of Shāh Zamān; in style they are much like those just described and are broad well struck pieces of full weight. The gold coin is a single specimen. I found quite a number of rupees at Bahāwalpūr, their only source as far as I know.

The beautiful coins of the second reign of Shujā' correspond closely in form and style with those of Maḥmūd, of which they are a continuation. Coin 974 is a thin broad piece in gold weighing 47 grains. All seven years of the second reign are represented in silver; there is a quarter rupee of 1218. The arrangement of the couplet changes in 1222.

Maḥmūd Shāh regained Aḥmad Shāhī in the year 1224; the earlier coins of his second reign repeat the couplet of the first reign. Coin 1066 of year 1222 shows that there was some overlapping with Shujā'. The only gold piece listed is a thin broad coin weighing 37·5 grains; the date is not certain. The silver series is quite representative. Maḥmūd's first reign couplet is employed till 1226; the invocation یا محمود reappears on Coin 1068 of year 1224. In the year 1226 the obverse legend changes to the حسن دیگر (Second Ḥasan) distich peculiar to the second reign. Coin 1073 is of full weight, but later pieces as exemplified by specimens of years 1229, 1230, 1231 and 1233 are light weight coins conforming to a standard of about 160 grains.

The Aḥmad Shāhī rupee of Aiyūb Shāh is a single specimen (Pl. XIII. 16). This coin and 1201, also of this puppet king, are the only Durrānī pieces known to me which contain the Kalima, the Muḥammadan Profession of Faith.

Shujā' struck silver coins at Aḥmad Shāhī in the year 1255 on a reduced standard of 140–150 grains. They bear a couplet peculiar to his third reign which is found on Kābul rupees of the same date and weight.

Coin Pl. XIV. 15 is an Aḥmad Shāhī rupee of Fatḥ Jang, date 1258, weight 141 grains. It, like the Aiyūb rupee of this mint, is a single specimen. Both coins came from my Cabinet.

KĀBUL

Lat. 34° 30′ Long. 69° 13′

	G.	S.	C.
Nādir	1	2	—
Aḥmad	5	27	—
Sulaimān	1	2	—
Taimūr	9	33	—

Zamān		6	21	—
Maḥmūd.	First reign	—	5	—
Qaiṣar		—	1	—
Shujā'.	Second reign	1	2	—
Maḥmūd.	Second reign	2	5	—
Aiyūb		—	1	—
Shujā'.	Third reign	3	7	—
Fatḥ Jang		—	4	—

At the beginning of the eighteenth century the territory of Kābul still remained an Indian province, but the Mughal authority was on the wane and the administration had fallen into confusion. After the capture of Qandahār, Nādir Shāh marched by Ghazni to Kābul; the place could offer little resistance and the citadel surrendered on the 22nd May 1738. Taimūr Shāh removed the seat of government from Qandahār to Kābul.

The Kābul money, like that of Aḥmad Shāhī, consists of well-executed pieces in good metal exhibiting the entire legends. As a rule they are of the full Mughal weight standard. Again, as at Aḥmad Shāhī, there is no copper issue apart from autonomous pieces.

It is unexpected to find that Nādir Shāh struck at Kābul in one year only, 1157; both metals are represented. Kābul is called by its Mughal title *Dāru-l-mulk,* Seat of Royalty. Other dates ought to come to light because Kābul remained firmly in Nādir's hands from the time of its capture early in 1151 till his death. Probably Coin 48 dated 1159, 7, is of Kābul mint but the name is written قابل, a version I have not seen elsewhere, attended by the honorific title *Dāru-s-salṭanat,* Seat of the Sultanate.

The currency of Aḥmad Shāh begins with a piece of unusual character dated 1161, 1, exemplified in both metals (Pl. II. 19). The obverse contains a three line arrangement of the couplet. The reverse inscription is a reproduction of that found on Muḥammad Shāh's coins (*P. M. Cat.*, Nos. 2329, 2530); Kābul is called *Dāru-l-mulk.* This reverse type is found in silver of the third year but the couplet is now of the more usual four line form. On coins of the fifth year Kābul is called *Dāru-s-salṭanat* and so remains for the rest of the Durrānī régime. Attention is invited to Coin 179 of year 8 (Pl. III. 17). A central area type of this date is characteristic of Dera, Derajāt and Multān mints but the Kābul piece is a single specimen. I acquired it at Lahore. The Mughal formula *julūs maimanat mānūs,* Regnal Year associated with Prosperity, reappears on this occasion. The gold coin of the tenth year illustrated at Pl. II. 17 is a fine piece of true Durrānī type. There is an excellent series of rupees from the year 1170, 10 to the end of the reign; date 1172 is missing. The arrangement of the reverse legend changes; Pl. III. 20 is quite unusual. The word سنة may or may not be present. Finally in 1175, 15 (Coin 189) the reverse inscription (Pl. II. 18) becomes static; as a rule both Hijri and regnal dates appear on this side. The Kābul coins of Aḥmad Shāh are full of variety and interest. There were hundreds of them at Bahāwalpūr. The series catalogued is quite representative.

The pretender Sulaimān struck at Kābul in both metals. There is a long couplet on the obverse; the reverse legend is similar to that on the coins of Aḥmad Shāh's last year. I found two or three gold coins (Pl. V. 7) and some twenty rupees at Bahāwalpūr. The silver coins exhibit two arrangements of the couplet.

Taimūr Shāh struck gold and silver at Kābul in 1186, the year of Aḥmad's death and Sulaimān's suppression. The reverse is that of Sulaimān's coins and the obverse is occupied by a three line version of Taimūr's ingenious but tedious couplet. This type continues till and including 1189, 3. In 1189, 3 appears a four line arrangement of the couplet with the Hijri year on the obverse together with an exceptional presentment of the reverse legend; this outstanding type exists in both metals (Pl. VI. 2). But the same year 1189, 3 sees a reversion to something more ordinary (Coin 560). The latter type continues with modifications of the obverse till the year 1204; the series is interrupted by Coin 572 of 1201. Coin 577 of 1204, 18 revives the reverse arrangement of 572 and this type runs to the end of the reign in 1207, 21.

Shāh Zamān began in great style with the fine broad pieces illustrated at Pl. VIII. 14. They contain his first couplet Z 1; the arrangement of the reverse is symmetrical and effective. The second couplet Z 2 appears on a coin of 1212, 4 and continues till the end of the reign, latest date 1215, 8; there is some overlapping as the first couplet is found on a specimen of year 5 (Coin 813). A half and a quarter rupee are listed; fractional denominations are extremely rare. Handsome double rupees were issued in years 1212 and 1213; the obverse exhibits both couplets. The specimen illustrated at Pl. IX. 14 is a fine broad coin with ample margins; it is in the Fitzwilliam Museum, Cambridge. The issue of these double rupees must have been large because a fair number have survived; there were none at Bahāwalpūr. Coin 824 is a posthumous issue of light weight, date 1258. The Kābul coins of Taimūr Shāh and Shāh Zamān, like those of Aḥmad, were found in abundance at Bahāwalpūr.

Gold of Maḥmūd's first reign is not represented. There are rupees of all three years.

The rupee of Sulṭān Qaiṣar illustrated at Pl. XII. 10 is unique;

it was in my Cabinet. The couplet is clearly different from those on the Aḥmad Shāhī and Kashmīr coins but cannot be read without the aid of other specimens.

Kābul coins of Shujā'u-l-mulk Shāh's second reign appear to be quite rare. I have catalogued one in gold and two in silver, all three British Museum specimens. The obverse legend is a four line arrangement of the normal couplet.

The coins of Maḥmūd's second reign exhibit a couplet in which he is called Sulṭān Maḥmūd, the second Ḥasan. The gold piece of the eighth year in the British Museum is a broad handsome coin; the lettering of the reverse legend is expanded in a bold decorative style known as *ṭughrā* (Pl. XII. 14). The rupees of the second and fifth years are full weight; that of year eight conforms to a standard of about 165 grains.

The Kābul currency of Aiyūb appears to be very scarce; one specimen, a rupee, is catalogued. It is on the reduced standard of some 165 grains and exhibits the usual couplet.

Shujā'u-l-mulk Shāh was restored at Kābul by British arms in A.H. 1255, A.D. 1839. Coins were freely struck in both gold and silver and are listed in one or the other metal of years 1255, 56, 58, and 59; date 1257 is missing. Kābul was evacuated by the British garrison on the 6th January 1842 and Shujā' was murdered three months later. The Hijri year 1258 began on the 12th February 1842; the money of year 1259 is posthumous. The only type catalogued in gold is Pl. XIV. 10; all three coins listed are full weight. The rupee illustrated at Pl. XIV. 12 is a broad coin weighing 177 grains. It was followed in the same year, 1255, by a similar piece but of the normal diameter and weight some thirty grains less. During the remainder of the dynasty the rupees conform to this Bārakzai standard of about 145 grains. Coin 1220 of 1255 is a couplet piece; the couplet is elucidated for the first time. The same distich is found on the silver money of Aḥmad Shāhī mint. On a rupee of year 1259 the title *Durr i Durrān* is revived.

Rupees of Fatḥ Jang are known on the weight standard of about 145 grains, and of year 1258. A few specimens of type Pl. XIV. 17 exist. The solitary couplet coin cannot be read without the aid of other specimens. A third type exhibits the title *Durr i Durrān.*

KASHMĪR

Lat. 34° 5′ Long. 74° 50′

		G.	S.	C.
Aḥmad		1	13	2
Sulaimān		—	1	—
Taimūr Shāh		2	22	11
Zamān		—	15	16
Maḥmūd.	First reign	—	5	4
Qaiṣar		—	2	—
Shujā'.	Second reign	—	7	6
Shāh Nūru-d-dīn		2	9	1
Maḥmūd.	Second reign	—	9	7
Aiyūb		—	2	—

Coins bearing the mint name Kashmīr were struck at Srīnagar, the capital of the Province. Kashmīr is in a different category from such Indian mints as Sind. It was not ceded by the Mughals to Nādir Shāh but was taken from them by Aḥmad Shāh Durrānī. This outlying mountain valley, remote and difficult of access, was in the times of the later Durrānīs a refuge for rebels and pretenders and a bone of contention between Afghans and Sikhs. The coins of Kashmīr mint, as might be expected, are apt to differ from the general Durrānī issues. Gold is very rare; only five coins of this metal are listed and all are up to the full Mughal weight standard. On the other hand, copper is unusually abundant. The silver currency of Taimūr Shāh and his successors is struck to a reduced standard of about 170 grains; the metal is often debased though the style is up to the average. G. Forster visited Kashmīr in 1783 during the reign of Taimūr Shāh and has something to say about the coinage. 'The rupee is the current coin of Kashmire, and that struck at Moradabad in Rohilcund is held in the greatest estimation. From the baseness of the silver a large discount is allowed on that of Kashmire. Copper money of the value of a halfpenny and cowreys, a small marine shell, compose the other currency of this province.' (*Journey from Bengal*, &c., London, 1808.)

There are aberrations of regnal date which may or may not be significant. The copper coins are sometimes just lumps of metal and the weights differ so much that it is difficult to deduce definite standards.

The solitary gold piece of Aḥmad Shāh Durrānī, dated 1167, 6 is the sole numismatic memorial of the Afghan invasion of the Happy Valley in A.D. 1753–54. There was an interlude marked by an issue of coin in the name of 'Ālamgīr II.' Kashmīr was annexed to the

Durrānī empire in A.D. 1762, A.H. 1176, and a silver currency was established in the same year. Rupees of Aḥmad Shāh are by no means common; even the best specimens weigh three or four grains less than the full Mughal standard of 178 grains. There are different arrangements of the legends. Copper is very scarce. The specimens catalogued belonged to Mr. R. Sutcliffe and have been described by Mr. Valentine. They were collected in Kashmīr fifty years ago by a missionary, the Rev. J. Doxie.

A rupee struck in the name of the pretender Sulaimān was an unexpected and pleasing discovery; I found the coin in Srīnagar itself.

Taimūr Shāh coined extensively in silver and copper but the two gold coins in the Rodgers Collection at Lahore are the only specimens in this metal known to me. On one of them Kashmīr is called *Dāru-s-salṭanat*, 'Seat of the Sultanate', an epithet which is found on no other coin of this mint.[1] The second gold coin is a fine broad piece which exhibits a deviation from the normal couplet, the word کند, 'may make', being displaced by زند, 'may strike'.

Rupees with the زند couplet appeared regularly throughout the reign. The style is good and characteristic of the mint but the metal is apt to be inferior and the weight standard is only about 170 grains. This reduced standard is retained till the end of the dynasty. As at other mints there are aberrations of regnal date. Taimūr Shāh began to reign in 1186, so his first year is 1186–7 and year 10 is 1195–6. But according to the Kashmīr rupees this tenth regnal year is 1197–8. Similarly year 12 is 1199–1200, year 17 is 1204–5, and year 19 is 1206–7; on these data the first regnal year should be 1188–9. All the catalogued rupees on which both Hijri and regnal dates are legible support this inference except the earliest coin of all, which is dated 1187, 1. I cannot say if the matter has any significance. Copper coins of Taimūr are common to this day in the Srīnagar bazar. The year 13 is 1200–1 as on the rupees.

Zamān Shāh also struck abundantly in silver and copper at Kashmīr. The earliest listed rupee is dated 1208, 2 (Pl. IX. 8). This type runs till 1212, 5. In the same year the words *julūs maimanat mānūs* are dropped from the reverse legend and the mint is called Khiṭṭa Kashmīr, the territory or district of Kashmīr (Pl. IX. 9). The new style is repeated in 1213, 6 but that year sees another arrangement of the same reverse legend surrounded by an ample margin (Pl. IX. 10). This recurs in 1213, 7 and 1214, 7. Finally in 1214, 7 the epithet Khiṭṭa is omitted and this last type continues into the eighth

[1] Entry 75 of Longworth Dames' *Coins of the Durrānīs* is incorrect.

year (Pl. IX. 11). The rupees of Zamān Shāh are well struck and exhibit the entire legends but the metal is inferior and the weight standard is about 170 grains as already remarked. The regnal dates are correct. Kashmīr is the only common copper mint of Zamān. A sword appears sometimes as the mint mark; the weights vary considerably. It is possible to deduce heavy, medium and light denominations of say 210, 170, and 120 grains respectively, but one piece of 267 grains is far heavier than the rest and corresponds to the heavy copper coins of Taimūr.

The silver currency of Maḥmūd's first reign bears his general couplet. It includes a quarter rupee of date 1217, 2 (Pl. X. 13). The reverse type changes in 1218, 3 to that illustrated at Pl. X. 14. Copper coins are catalogued of years one and two.

Silver coins were struck at Khiṭṭa Kashmīr in the name of Qaiṣar Shāh; the dates are 1222, 1 and 1223, 2.

The rupees of the second reign of Shujā' bear a couplet peculiar to Kashmīr mint (p. xxxii). All years are recorded from 1218 to 1223 inclusive. The reverse of some of the copper coins merely bears the regnal year and a sword or swords.

Handsome double mohurs, on the full Mughal standard of 168 grains, were struck at Khiṭṭa Kashmīr bearing the name of the country's patron saint Shāh Nūru-d-dīn (pp. xxix–xxx). Two or three specimens are known of date 1225, 2 with a square area obverse (Pl. XIII. 10). The companion piece of 1225, 3 (Pl. XIII. 11) is the only specimen known to me. The silver coins of Nūru-d-dīn range from 1223, 1 to 1228, 5. The handsome and unique piece illustrated at Pl. XIII. 12 weighs 224 grains, the only silver coin of this weight throughout the Durrānī series. I found several copper coins in the Srīnagar bazar; they are lumps of metal weighing from 115 to 120 grains. A legible Hijri date is 1225.

The Kashmīr coins of Maḥmūd's second reign are difficult to interpret. Shujā' (1218–24) was defeated by Maḥmūd in 1224 and Maḥmūd's precarious tenure of power ended in his ejection from Kābul by the Bārakzais in 1233. Thereupon Maḥmūd retired to Hirāt. Maḥmūd's rupees are of Khiṭṭa Kashmīr and bear the legends found on the last issue of his first reign (Pl. X. 14) with different arrangement and style. The earliest piece on the list is dated regnal year 6, but the unit figure of the Hijri date is illegible; the piece of the seventh year has the full date 1225. It is plain that these regnal years count from the first reign.

Four Kashmīr rupees are recorded on p. 357 of Mr. Longworth Dames' *Coins of the Durrānīs* under the name of Muḥammad Shāh, with dates 1227, 28, 30, and 32. There is no word of explanation beyond the reference to Mr. W. Theobald. I do not know of any Durrānī Muḥammad Shāh who struck coin. The mystery is explained by an entry in the Theobald Sale Catalogue, 1901, 'Durrani or Afghan rupees of Nuruddin Muhammad Shah of Kashmir (4).' The rupees appear to be either of Shāh Nūru-d-dīn or of Maḥmūd Shāh.

The name of the Sadozai princeling Aiyūb Shāh, who held his court under sufferance at Pashāwar, is found on Kashmīr rupees of dates 1234, 1 and 1234, 2. On the issues of 1234, 1 the mint is called Khiṭṭa Kashmīr. The couplet contains a punning allusion to Aiyūb's protector, the Bārakzai chief Muḥammad 'Aẓīm Khān.

Kashmīr was annexed by Ranjit Singh in A.H. 1234, A.D. 1819.

LĀHOR.

Lat. 31° 35′ Long. 74° 20′

	G.	S.	C.
Nādir	1	2	—
Aḥmad	2	18	—
Taimūr Shāh Niẓām	2	3	—
Zamān	1	2	—

Nādir Shāh, in his advance upon Shāhjahānābād, occupied the capital of the Panjab in December, A.D. 1738 (ninth month of year A.H. 1151). He returned by Lāhor at the end of the following May, or early in A.H. 1152, which year began on April 10th, A.D. 1739. Coins of Lāhor are very rare; four specimens are known. The mint name is attended by its epithet Seat of the Sultanate. The only piece of date 1151 is the double mohur of the نادر السلطان type in the British Museum. Its poor style and abnormal weight are suspicious but it is probably genuine.[1] There is a fine double rupee dated 1152 at Berlin. The couplet type is exemplified by two rupees; that catalogued was in my Cabinet, while the second is Coin 2782 in the Third Part of the White King Sale Catalogue.

Aḥmad Shāh invaded India soon after his accession, and Afghan troops entered Lāhor on the 22nd January 1748; this was also the first month of A.H. 1161 which commenced on the 2nd January. The Durrānī retired to Qandahār at the end of that cold weather and Lāhor was reoccupied by the Mughals at the beginning of April. Aḥmad again took Lāhor in April, 1752 (A.H. 1165), and annexed the

[1] The coin was acquired by the British Museum from Mr. C. J. Rodgers. It is the piece illustrated at *Num. Chron.*, 1882, Pl. XV and R. S. P., Pl. VII. 215.

north west Panjab. Five years later he deputed his son Taimūr to govern the Panjab, the Derajāt and Sind. These events are reflected in the coinage. Gold and silver were struck at Lāhor in the year 1161. The initial type bears the usual couplet on the obverse while the reverse has the words 'Aḥmad S͟hāh, Emperor, Pearl of Pearls' in addition to the normal legend. There is a gap between 1161 and 1165 according to expectation and the Mug͟hal emperor Aḥmad S͟hāh Bahādur was issuing money in these years (*P. M. Cat.*, p. 359). The Durrānī coinage recommences in 1165, 5 but there is another hiatus till the tenth year with the Mug͟hal 'Ālamgīr II striking in 1168, 1169, 1171, and 1172 (*P. M. Cat.*, p. 374). The coins of Taimūr S͟hāh as governor are dated 1170, 1171 and 1173. It was a very disturbed time and the currency reflects the prevailing confusion. 'Ālamgīr II was assassinated in 1173 and Mug͟hal coins cease with the end of his reign. Durrānī rupees continued to issue from 1173 till 1180 when Lāhor was taken by the Sikhs. A Sikh rupee of Lāhor mintage dated *Sambat* 1823 or A.D. 1766, equivalent to A.H. 1179–80, inaugurates a regular issue by the Sikh commonwealth.

Taimūr S͟hāh took no steps to enforce his claims in the central Panjab. S͟hāh Zamān invaded India and occupied Lāhor without serious opposition on two separate occasions. He entered that city at the beginning of A.D. 1797 but was compelled to retire by the rebellion of his half brother Maḥmūd at Hirāt. Zamān again penetrated as far as Lāhor in November, 1798, but once more had to beat a hasty retreat owing to the invasion of K͟hurāsān by a Persian army. There are numismatic memorials of both Indian adventures. I found several pieces at Bahāwalpūr in gold and silver of an issue struck at Lāhor in 1211, 4 by S͟hāh Zamān. These coins exhibit the first couplet. Coin 840 is a broad handsome rupee dated 1213, 6 of the second couplet type. It is a solitary specimen and was collected by me in Lāhor itself.

MURĀDĀBĀD.

Lat. 28° 49′ Long. 78° 49′

	G.	S.	C.
Aḥmad	—	1	—

Murādābād is a town in Rohilkhand. Rupees dated 1173 were struck here in the name of Aḥmad S͟hāh by his ally Najību-d-daula. A reference is invited to the collective Note under Aonla.

MURSHIDĀBĀD

Lat. 24° 11′ Long. 88° 18′

	G.	S.	C.
Nādir	—	6	—

The issue of money in the name of Nādir Shāh so far afield as Murshidābād, the capital of Bengal, is explained in a passage from Gladwin's Bengal Narrative; it was due to the fear inspired by the deeds of the ferocious tyrant and to the pusillanimity of the Mughal governor. 'When Nādir Shāh plundered Dehly, every part of Hindostan was filled with the dread of a visitation by the merciless invader. Sirafrāz Khān (deputy governor of Bengal) ordered coin to be struck and the *khuṭba* to be read in the name of Nādir Shāh, and remitted to him the revenues of Bengal. After Nādir Shāh's departure, these actions were used by his enemies to injure Sirafrāz Khān with Muḥammad Shāh'. (F. Gladwin, *Bengal Narrative,* Calcutta, 1788, p. 155.)

Nādir Shāh's coins of Murshidābād mint are very scarce, and are known only in silver. A rupee of date A.H. 1152 was illustrated by J. D. Koehler in 1746 but it does not exhibit enough of the legend to ensure a satisfactory reading.[1] O. G. Tychsen embodied the reference on p. 212 of his *Introductio in Rem Numariam Muhammedanorum,* Rostock, 1794. The Christ Church coin, dated 1151, is by far the best I have seen and is the only specimen which shows enough of the inscription to make the reading practically certain. The legend is found on no other issue. The Ashmolean Museum, Oxford, has a rupee of year 1152 together with the half, quarter, eighth and sixteenth, a unique feature. All were struck from dies much too large and the legends are fragmentary. The Kaiser Friedrich Museum, Berlin, possesses all the denominations of year 1152 except the half and the sixteenth. No other fractional piece of Nādir Shāh is known.[2]

Attention is invited to the unique rupee 57 (Pl. I. 18). There is only a vestige of the mint name which may possibly be Murshidābād; the date is 1152. The legends on both faces differ from all the rest; the reverse presents the ampler invocation: 'May God perpetuate his kingdom and his autocracy'.

[1] J. D. Koehler, *Historische Münz-Belustigung,* Nürnberg, 1746, vol. 18, p. 105.

[2] I repeat the substance of the relevant part of my paper 'Some Notable Coins of the Mughal Emperors of India', *Num. Chron.,* 1930.

MULTĀN

Lat. 30° 12′ Long. 71° 30′

		G.	S.	C.
Nādir		—	1	—
Aḥmad		8	19	2
Taimūr as Niẓām		5	37	—
Taimūr S͟hāh		2	19	13
Zamān		1	6	7
Maḥmūd.	First reign	—	2	—
S͟hujā'.	Second reign	2	2	1
Maḥmūd.	Second reign	—	—	19
Aiyūb		—	1	—

The ancient and historic city of Multān was a regular mint of the Mug͟hal emperors. It was annexed by Aḥmad S͟hāh Durrānī in A.H. 1165.

I did not know that Nādir S͟hāh had coined at Multān till I found two or three rupees at Bahāwalpūr. The issue is limited to 1152, the year of his return from Delhi; Muḥammad S͟hāh also struck at Multān in this year (*P. M. Cat.*, p. 348). The mint name is accompanied by the epithet *Dāru-l-amān*, Abode of Security; this occurs on the Mug͟hal pieces of the first four years of Aurangzeb. There is a double rupee of Nādir in the Hunterian Collection, Glasgow.

Aḥmad S͟hāh Bahādur issued money at Multān till 1164, 4 (*P. M. Cat.*, p. 361); the first issue of Aḥmad S͟hāh Durrānī is dated 1165, 5 and is found in both gold and silver (Pl. IV. 5). The tulip mint mark, so characteristic of the Multān money, appears on the second issue of 1165, 5; like the epithet, it dates from Aurangzeb's reign. The epithet itself comes into use on the central area coins of the eighth year. This central area type of year 8 is common to Multān, Dera, Derajāt and Kābul mints, and at Multān is repeated in 1169, 9; this ninth year sees a reversion to the usual four line arrangement of the couplet. There are several models of 1170, 10; on the last issue of this date the mint name is found without the epithet. Some copper coins are known, usually in poor condition. The dates listed are 1170, 10 and 1172, 12. It is surprising to find the latter year because Taimūr was in full possession of the mint from 1170 as his father's governor.

The striking of money at Multān is continued without a break from 1170, 1 to 1185, 16 by Taimūr S͟hāh as governor for his father, with his own sequence of regnal dates. The series of rupees in the Panjab Museum is almost complete. The three line arrangement of the couplet does not change but the Hijri year may occur in the first, the second or the third line, all illustrated on Pl. V. As on Aḥmad's latest coin, the mint name on the first issue of Taimūr Shāh Niẓām is without the epithet. The date is 1170, 1 and it is listed in both gold and silver of the same type. In 1172, 2 the epithet appears and continues for the rest of the reign except on an issue of 1173, 2 (Coin 311). There are no less than five entries for the year 1173, 2. The Mahrattas held Multān in parts of 1172 and 1173 and struck rupees there in the name of 'Ālamgīr II (N. S. XLII, p. 70 N). The last Durrānī issue of 1173, 2 (Coin 315) exhibits a different arrangement of the reverse from that illustrated at Pl. V. 4 and this variety with modifications is minted till 1178, 9. In 1179, 9 the words *julūs maimanat mānūs* are dropped from the reverse and type Pl. IV. 17 continues till the end of the reign. All Taimūr Shāh Niẓām's coins of Multān mint are good pieces of the full Indian weight standard.

Multān gold of Taimūr Shāh is scarce; only two specimens are listed, both of 1203, regnal dates 9 and 10. The silver coins confirm the supposition that the early regnal dates at Multān do not count from 1186, the year of accession. The earliest date catalogued in silver is 1194, 3; at other mints 1194 is the eighth year. The year 1198 is 5, 6, and 7. Time stands still in the seventh year which is the regnal equivalent of 1198, 1199, 1200 and 1201. This confusion is due to the fact that Multān was taken by the Sikhs in 1185 and not recovered by the Afghans till 1194 (Cunn., pp. 122, 123). I found at Bahāwalpūr Sikh rupees of Multān mint which cover the period of occupation (*Sambats* 1829 to 1836 inclusive). There are rupees of Taimūr Shāh of 1203, 9 and 1203, 10 which resemble the gold coins, also of 1204, 10 of the same rather inferior type. But now there is a sudden change for the better. In the same year 1204 appeared a broad coin in good style and of the correct regnal date 18 (Pl. VII. 17); this type continues to the end of the reign, the latest piece in the list being of 1207, 20. The gold and silver coins throughout are of full weight; the mint name is always attended with the epithet. There was an abundant copper issue. Coin 702 bears Taimūr Shāh's imperial titles but appears to be of 1181, the period of the Niẓāmat; the coin may have been restruck. Apart from this anomalous piece, the earliest copper coin, as in silver, is dated 1194, 3. The series exhibits the abnormal regnal dates of the rupees till, as in the case of the silver coins, the type changes and we get the correct issues of 1205, 19 and 1206, 20. The standard appears to be about 185 grains.

The only gold coin of Shāh Zamān described in the Catalogue is a piece at Bahāwalpūr of date 1210 and first regnal year (instead of 3 or 4). Coin 841 is a fine rupee of the first year (Pl. IX. 13). The couplet differs from that of other mints; the word قرار 'permanency', is replaced by طراز 'adornment'. There are silver coins of 1207, 1208, 1209 and 1210, all described as the first year, abnormalities of regnal date comparable with those of Taimūr Shāh. A gap occurs till 1215 which is correctly designated year 8. Copper, as of Taimūr, is fairly plentiful and of the same type and weight standard. The regnal dates are correct.

The first reign of Maḥmūd Shāh is represented by two rupees only, dates 1216 and 1218, both termed first regnal year.

Coins of the second reign of Shāh Shujā' are rare but specimens are listed in all three metals. The copper piece resembles those of Taimūr and Zamān.

The issues of Maḥmūd's second reign are restricted to copper. Coins in this metal are plentiful and cover a long series of dates. Multān was taken by the Sikhs in June, A.D. 1818, A.H. 1233, and subsequent money in the name of Maḥmūd Shāh must have been authorized by them.

The reading Multān on a rupee of Aiyūb Shāh is not certain; the date 1239 is equivalent to A.D. 1823–24. Like the silver coin of Aḥmad Shāhī, date illegible, this rupee bears the Kalima and is a single specimen.

NAJĪBĀBĀD

Lat. 29° 36′ Long. 78° 23′

	G.	S.	C.
Aḥmad	1	1	—

Najībābād is a town in the Bijnor District of the Province of Agra; it took its name from the Rohilla chief Najību-d-daula. Coins dated 1180 were struck here by Najību-d-daula in the name of Aḥmad Shāh. This issue must have been occasioned by the Durrānī's last invasion of India, although the Afghan did not advance beyond the Sutlej. At this time Najību-d-daula was Vazir at Delhi and coins were being struck at Najībābād in the name of Shāh 'Ālam II, including an issue of year 1180.

HIRĀT

Lat. 34° 29′ Long. 62° 8′

	G.	S.	C.
Aḥmad	1	5	—
Taimūr Shāh	7	45	—
Zamān	2	10	—
Maḥmūd (continuous at Hirāt)	—	48	—
Kāmrān	—	4	—

Hirāt is the principal city in the valley of the Harī Rūd River in the north west corner of Afghanistan. The strategic and commercial importance of Hirāt are due to its situation where roads from India, Persia, and Bukhāra converge; the locality is so fertile that the place has been called 'the granary and garden of Central Asia' (G. B. Malleson's *Herat*, London, 1880). Ibn Hauqal recorded a glowing description of Hirāt in the tenth century and Ibn Batuta, who visited the place about the year A.D. 1340, wrote of it as the most important city of Khurāsān. Hirāt was taken by the Persians in A.D. 1510 and remained in their hands till it surrendered to the Afghan Abdālīs in 1717; it was recovered for Persia by Nādir Shāh early in the year 1738.

Aḥmad Shāh took Hirāt from the Persians in the autumn of A.D. 1748, A.H. 1161, and this important frontier stronghold remained in Durrānī hands till the end of the dynasty. Aḥmad can only have struck spasmodically at Hirāt as his money of this mint is quite rare. Coins are known of both gold and silver. They are usually dateless and inferior in style but are up to the full Indian weight standards. The only legible date recorded is 1171. The name of the mint is generally attended by its epithet *Dāru-s-salṭanat*, Seat of the Sultanate.

Taimūr Shāh struck abundantly at Hirāt in gold and silver on the full Indian standards. There is a long series of rupees which exhibits frequent and capricious changes in the arrangement of the legends and in the position of the dates. As a rule the earlier coins omit and the later pieces show the epithet *Dāru-s-salṭanat*. The initial issues bear the pre-accession date 1184. The year 1192 has three different settings of the couplet, one in gold and two in silver. In 1204 commence the characteristic broad issues illustrated at Pl. VII. 20 and Pl. VIII. 1 which continue to the end of the reign. Coin 667 is a small piece weighing only 14 grains. Posthumous issues were minted for ten years after the death of Taimūr Shāh.

Hirāt was governed by Maḥmūd, and Shāh Zamān did not strike money there till the time of his expedition against Hirāt where he arrived on the 14th October, 1797 (fourth month of A.H. 1212). Gold and silver coins issued in 1212 with the second couplet; this type continued to the end of the reign.

Maḥmūd Shāh maintained a hold on Hirāt throughout the vicissitudes of his career and I have listed his Hirāt silver separately. I do not know of any gold issue bearing the name of Maḥmūd Shāh. The silver coins must have been struck in great abundance. They are common in the bazars and fifty thousand lie at Bahāwalpūr. Every year is represented in the Catalogue from 1216 to 1238 inclusive. The rupee of 1242 is accompanied by a half and a quarter. There are two halves of 1243; one reverse has the interpolation يا هو, 'O He (God)'. This long series is monotonous and without distinction; the striking is shallow. The coins become dumpy and debased though the weight is fairly well maintained; the metal quality deteriorates after 1232 and the striking of fractions of the rupee in Maḥmūd's closing years also points to a growing scarcity of bullion.

Kāmrān became master of Hirāt after the death of his father Maḥmūd and a few reduced weight silver coins of Kāmrān are known. Pieces of a couplet and of a non couplet type are listed. The latter appear to be quarter rupees while the couplet type is known in the rupee and half rupee size. Dates catalogued are 1248 and 1252; L. White-King had a rupee of year 1254 (W.K. 2895). Kāmrān was expelled from Hirāt by Yār Muḥammad Bārakzai in A.H. 1258.

COINS OF NĀDIR SHĀH AND OF THE DURRĀNĪ DYNASTY STRUCK IN AFGHANISTAN AND INDIA

NĀDIR SHĀH

(from the capture of Qandahār to his death)

A.H. 1150–1160. A.D. 1738–1747.

Metal No.	Mint	Date	Obverse	Reverse
AV 1	بهکهر Bhakhar	1158	Within double circle containing one of dots نادر حبقرا شاهان صا ن شـــــــــاه بر سلاطین جهان هـــست سلطان **W.** 167. **S.** ·75. Date 1155 in York Museum. The couplet is سلطان هست بر سلاطینِ جهان شاهِ شاهان نادر صاحب قِران 'Is Sultan over the Sultans of the world, The king of kings Nādir, the Ṣāḥibqirān.'	Contained as obverse الله ملکه خـــــلد ۱۱۵۸ بهـــــکهر ضرب
2	پشاور Pashāwar	1154	As 1. **W.** 168. **S.** ·8.	In circle of dots الله ملکه خـــــلد سنه ۱۱۵۴ ضرب پشاور
3 B.M.	"	1155	" Also I.M.	" ۱۱۵۵
4 B.M.	"	1157	"	" ۱۱۵۷

Metal No.	Mint	Date	Obverse	Reverse
AV				
5 Paris	پشاور Pashāwar	1159	As 1. Cabinet de France, Bibliothèque Nationale.	As 2. ١١٥٩
6 B.M.	ديرجات Derajāt	1159	نادر حبقرا شاهان صا ن شـــــــاه بر سلاطين جها سلطان ن هست **W.** 169. **S.** ·85.	خلد الله ملكه ت ١١٥٩ ديرجا ضرب M. 1. Pl. I. 2.
7 I.M.	„	1160	As 6.	As. 6. ١١٦٠
8 Vienna	سند Sind	—	As 6. Kunsthistorisches Museum, Vienna.	In circle on floral field سند ضرب
9 B.M.	كابل Kābul *Dāru-l-mulk*	1157	As 1. **W.** 167. **S.** ·8.	الله ملكه خـــــــلد ١١٥٧ كابل سنة ضرب دار الملك
10 B.M.	لاهور Lāhor *Dāru-s-salṭanat*	1151	In double circle containing one of dots در نا السلطا ن **W.** 366·3. **S.** 1·1. A double mohur of inferior style.	خلد الله ملكه لاهور دار السلطنة ضرب ١١٥١ Pl. I. 1.

Metal No.	Mint	Date	Obverse	Reverse
AR 11 B.M.	احمداباد Aḥmad-ābād	1152	نادر صا قران حب جهان شاه شاهان هست سلطان بر سلاطین W. 177. S. 1·0. Also in Ashmolean Museum, Oxford.	خلد الله ملکه احمداباد ضرب ۱۱۵۲ سنه Pl. I. 3.
12 W.K.	,,	,,	,, Half-rupee. White King Sale Catalogue, Part III, No. 2781.	,,
13 B.M.	بهکهر Bhakhar	1153	As 1, but no circle. W. 176. S. ·8.	As 1, but no circle. ۱۱۵۳ Pl. I. 4.
14	,,	1154	,,	,, ۱۱۵۴
15 B.M.	,,	1155	,, W. 178.	,, ۱۱۵۵
16 B.M.	,,	1156	,,	,, ۱۱۵۶
17	,,	1157	,,	,, ۱۱۵۷
18	,,	1158	,,	,, ۱۱۵۸
19	,,	1159	,,	,, ۱۱۵۹
20	,,	1160	,, W. 175. S. ·85.	,, ۱۱۶۰

Metal No.	Mint	Date	Obverse	Reverse
AR 21 Paris	پشاور Pashāwar	1151	در نا السلطا ن **W.** 350. **S.** 1·0. Double rupee. Also W.K.	خلد الله ملکه پشاور ب ضر ١١٥١
22	,,	1153	As 1. **W.** 172. **S.** ·8.	As 2. ١١٥٣
23	,,	1154	,, **W.** 173.	,, ١١٥٤
24	,,	1157	,, **W.** 174.	,, ١١٥٧
25 B.M.	,,	1158	,, **W.** 176.	,, ١١٥٨
26 B.M.	,,	1159	,, **W.** 175.	,, ١١٥٩
27	,,	1160	,, **W.** 175.	,, ١١٦٠
28 B.M.	,,	—	,, **W.** 173. **S.** ·9.	خلد الله ملکه ضرب پشاور Pl. I. 5.
29 B M.	تته Tatta	—	As 11. **W.** 175. **S.** ·8.	خلد الله ملکه ضرب تته Pl. I. 7.
30	دیرجات Derajāt	1158	As 6. **W.** 174. **S.** ·9.	As 6. ١١٥٨ M. 1.

Metal No.	Mint	Date	Obverse	Reverse
Æ 31	ديرجات Derajāt	1159	As 6.	As 6. ١١٥٩
32	”	1160	” **W.** 176.	” ١١٦٠
33	سند Sind	—	As 6. **W.** 178.	As 8.
34 B.M.	”	1153	As 1. **W.** 177. **S.** ·85.	سند ١١٥٣ ب ضر Pl. I. 8.
35 B.M.	”	1155	As 6, but date ١١٥٥ below legend. **W.** 176. **S.** ·8.	As 8.
36 B.M.	”	1156	” ١١٥٦ **W.** 177.	”
37 B.M.	”	1157	” ١١٥٧ **W.** 177.	” Pl. I. 6.
38 B.M.	”	1158	” ١١٥٨ **W.** 177.	”
39 B.M.	”	1160	As 1, but date ١١٦٠ to l. of last line. **W.** 176.	”
40 B.M.	سهرند Sahrind *Dāru-l-aman*	1152	As 1. **W.** 176. **S.** ·85.	الله ملكه خلد دارالامن ١١٥٢ ضرب سهرند Pl. I. 9.

Metal No.	Mint	Date	Obverse	Reverse
Æ 41	شاه جهان اباد Shābjahānābād *Dāru-l-khilāfat*	1151	As 1. **W.** 176. **S.** ·9.	الله ملکه خـــلد ١١٥١ شاه جهان اباد ضرب دار الخلافة
42	„	1152	„ **W.** 176.	„ ١١٥٢ Pl. I. 10.
43 Berlin	عظیم اباد 'Aẓīmābād	1151	نادر شاه م بادشاه غاز ســـكه مبارك ١١٥١ **W.** 172. Kaiser Friedrich Museum, Berlin.	عظیم اباد ضرب میمنت مانوس جلوس احد سنه M. 2. Pl. I. 11
44 B.M.	قندهار Qandahār	1150	In dotted circle در نا السلطا ن **W.** 350·8. **S.** 1·1. Double rupee.	الله خـــلد ملکه قندهار ب ضر ١١٥٠
45 B.M.	„	„	Contained in elaborate circular border as 44; broad and thin. **W.** 103. **S.** ·95.	„ Pl. I. 12.

Metal No.	Mint	Date	Obverse	Reverse
Æ **46**	قندهار Qandahār	1150	As 44; dumpy piece. **W.** 104. **S.** ·75.	As 44.
47	کابل Kābul *Dāru-l-mulk*	1157	As 9. **W.** 175. **S.** ·85.	As 9.
48	قابل Kābul (written Qābul) *Dāru-s-salṭanat*	1159 7	As 6; also in B.M. Both specimens came from Bahâwalpūr. **W.** 175. **S.** ·S.	قابل السلطنة ۱۱۵۹ دار ۷ ضرب
49 B.M.	لاهور Lāhor *Dāru-s-salṭanat*	1152	Legend complete in circle. نادر حبقران شاهان صا شـــــــاه بر سلاطين جهان هست سلطان **W.** 172. **S.** ·95 (rubbed). Also W.K.	In circle الله ملكه خـــلـــد دار السلطنة لاهور ب ضر ۱۱۵۲ Pl. I. 14.
50 Berlin	„	1152	In triple circle در نا السلطا ن **W.** 352. **S.** 1·05. Double rupee.	الله خلد ملكه دار لاهور السلطنة ب ضر ۱۱۵۲ Pl. I. 13.

Metal No.	Mint	Date	Obverse	Reverse
Æ 51[1] Ch.Ch.	مرشداباد Murshid-ābād	1151 1	از نادر شه گیتی پناه رو بر مهر و ماه سکه ۱۱۵۱ داده زیب تازه **W.** 176. **S.** ·85. Christ Church Library, Oxford. The couplet is:— داده زیب تازه رو بر مهر و ماه از سکه نادر شه گیتی پناه 'Given beauty fresh of face on the sun and moon (gold and silver) By the stamp of Nādir Shah, Asylum of the Universe.'	مانوس میمنت احد سنه جلوس ضرب مرشد اباد
52 Ashmolean Berlin	,,	1152 1	As 51, but larger characters. ۱۱۵۲ **S.** ·95.	As 51. Pl. I. 15.
53 Ashmolean	,,	,,	As 52. **W.** 88. Half rupee.	,, Pl. I. 16.
54 Ashmolean Berlin	,,	,,	,, **W.** 43. Quarter rupee.	,, Pl. I. 17.
55 Ashmolean Berlin	,,	,,	,, **W.** 22. Eighth rupee.	,,

[1] Described and illustrated in my paper 'Some Notable Coins of the Mughal Emperors of India', Part III, *Num. Chron.*, 1930.

Metal No.	Mint	Date	Obverse	Reverse
Æ **56** Ashmo-lean	مرشداباد Murshid-ābād	1152 1	As 52. **W.** 11. Sixteenth rupee.	As 51.
57 B.M.	Murshid-ābād (?)	„	نادر شاه بادشاه صاحب قران کـــــــــــــــــ سکه مبار ١١٥٢ **W.** 175. **S.** ·85.	الله ملکه خلد و سلطانه سنه احد ضرب مر شـــ Pl. I. 18.
58 B.M.	ملتان Multān *Dāru-l-amān*	1152	نادر حبقران شاهان صا شـــــــــــاه بر سلاطین جهان هست سلطان **W.** 175. **S.** ·95.	الله ملکه خلد دارالامان ١١٥٢ ضرب ملتان Pl. II. 1.
59 Glas-gow	„	1152	As 58. **W.** 352. **S.** 1·1. Double rupee. Hunterian Collection, Glasgow.	As 58.
60 B.M.	نادراباد Nādir-ābād	1151	In dotted circle, as 10. **W.** 353. **S.** 1·05. Double rupee.	In dotted circle الله خلد ملکه نادراباد ب ضر ١١٥١ Pl. II. 2.
61 B.M.	„	1151	„ **W.** 105. **S.** ·75.	As 60.

Metal No.	Mint	Date	Obverse	Reverse
ÆR 62	نادراباد Nādirā- bād	1152	In dotted circle, as 10. **W.** 352. **S.** 1·0. Double rupee.	As 60. ١١٥٢
Æ 63 B.M.	بهکهر Bhakhar	1156	نادر شاهی فلوس **W.** 291. **S.** ·85. Dates 1151 in Eugene Leggett Coin Catalogue, Karachi, and 1157 (W.K.).	بهکهر ١١٥٦ ضرب
64 B.M.	,,	1158	,, **W.** 287. **S.** ·85.	,, ١١٥٨
65 B.M.	,,	1158	,, **W.** 243. **S.** ·95.	,, ١١٥٨
66 B.M.	پشاور Pashāwar	1160	نادر السلطا ن **W.** 192. **S.** ·75.	خلد الله ملکه سنه ١١٦٠ ضرب پشاور

Pl. II. 3.

Coin 2784 in the White King Sale Catalogue is a rupee of Dera Fatḥ mint, date 1154, weight 176 grains—see Mint Note on Derajāt. I know nothing further about this piece.

I

AḤMAD SHĀH

A.H. 1160–1186. A.D. 1747–1772.

<table>
<tr><th>Metal
No.</th><th>Mint</th><th>Date</th><th>Obverse</th><th>Reverse</th></tr>
<tr><td>AV
1
I.M.</td><td>اتك
Atak
(Attock)</td><td>—
15</td><td>The following couplet arranged in four lines
از قادر بیچون
شد
باحمد بادشاه
حکم
سکه زن بر سیم و زر هم
از اوج ما تا بماه
W. 167. S. ·73.
Date 17 (W.K. 2818).</td><td>مانوس
میمنت
جلوس
ضرب
۱۵
اتك سنه</td></tr>
<tr><td></td><td></td><td></td><td colspan="2">The couplet is :—
حکم شد از قادر بیچون باحمد بادشاه
سکه زن برسیم و زر از اوج ماهی تا بماه
‘ The command issued from the Incomparable Creator to Aḥmad the emperor,
“ Strike coin on silver and gold from the height of the Fish to the Moon.” ’</td></tr>
<tr><td>2
B.M.</td><td>”</td><td>1181
21</td><td>As 1.
To l. of second line ۱۱۸۱
W. 168. S. ·8.</td><td>As 1.
۲۱
M. 1.
Pl. II. 4.</td></tr>
<tr><td>3
B.M.
•</td><td>احمد شاهی
Aḥmad
Shāhī
Ashrafu-l-bilād</td><td>1171
11</td><td>On dotted field
از قادر بیچون
شد
باحمد بادشاه ۷۱
۱۱ حکم
زن بر سیم و زر از
سکه
اوج ماهی تا بماه
W. 53·5. S. ·95.
In weight equivalent to the Persian ashrafī.</td><td>On dotted field
احمد شاهی
اشرف البلاد
ب
۱۱
ضر سنه</td></tr>
</table>

Metal No.	Mint	Date	Obverse	Reverse
AV 4	احمد شاهی Aḥmad Shāhī *Ashrafu-* *l-bilād*	— 22	As 3. **W.** 168. **S.** ·76.	احمد شاه اشرف البلاد میمنت جلوس مانوس ضرب سنه ۲۲
5 I.M.	,,	— 22	As 3, but without و between زر and سیم	,, ۲۲
5 A Bah.	,,	— 23	As 5.	As 4.
6 Bah.	بهکهر Bhakhar	1168 8	As 3. ۱۱۶۸	مانوس میمنت جلوس ۸ ضرب بهکهر
7 Bah.	,,	1177	Within central foliation احمد در شــــا دران ء Surrounding the area couplet starting and ending at the top of the coin, reading outwards.	In foliation مانوس میمنت جلوس ۷۷ بهکهر ۱۱ ضرب
8 I.M.	پشاور Pashāwar	1161 1	As 3, but احمد بد; ۱۱۶۱ l. second line. **W.** 169. **S.** ·78.	مانوس میمنت جلوس احد ضرب پشاور M. 2.
9	,,	— 9	As 3. **W.** 168. Date 21 (W.K. 2819).	,, ۹

Metal No.	Mint	Date	Obverse	Reverse
AV 10 B.M.	دیره Dera	1166 5	As 3, but بہ احمد ; date ۱۱۶۶ over third line. **W.** 169. **S.** ·85.	مانوس میمنت ٥ سنہ جلوس ب ضر دیرہ M. 3.
11 B.M. I.M.	„	8	As 7. **W.** 170. **S.** ·8.	Within foliated central area on dotted field, all surrounded by a circle and then by a circle of dots مانوس میمنت ٨ سنہ جلوس ضرب دیرہ Pl. II. 5.
12	„	9	As 3. **W.** 170. **S.** ·75.	On dotted field as 10; no mark ۹ Pl. II. 7.
13 B.M.	„	1170 10	As 10; above second line ۱۱۷۰ **W.** 169.	In circle of dots ۱۰ سنہ ب ضر دیرہ M. 4. Pl. II. 8.
14	„	1175 15	As 10. ۱۱۷۵ **W.** 170. **S.** ·7.	As 13. ۱۵

Metal No.	Mint	Date	Obverse	Reverse
AV 15 I.M.	ديرة Dera	1175 16	As 10. ١١٧٥ **W.** 170. **S.** ·7.	As 13. ١٦
16 I.M.	"	1184 25	" ١١٨٤ **W.** 169. **S.** ·75.	" ٢٥
17 B.M. I.M.	ديرجات Derajāt	1161	As 10, but different style. **W.** 167. **S.** ·78.	١١٦١ ت ديرجا ب ضر ١١٦١ Pl. II. 10.
18 B.M.	"	1180	As 7; rude style. **W.** 168. **S.** ·75.	مانوس ميمنت جلوس ديرجا ت ضرب ١١٨٠
19	"	— 23	As 10. **W.** 167. **S.** ·78. Also in I.M.	Within double circle, poor style سنه ٢٣ ب ضر ت ديرجا Pl. II. 11.
20 B.M.	ركاب Rikāb *Mubārak*	1173 Month Muḥarram (New Year's Day)	On flowered field as 5. **W.** 169. **S.** ·88.	Within rayed and dotted border on flowered field مبارك ماه محرم ب ضرب ر ٣ كا ١١٧ Pl. II. 6.

Metal No.	Mint	Date	Obverse	Reverse
AV 21 I.M.	سهرند Sahrind	— 1	حکم شد از قادر بیچون شاه باحمد باد زن بر سیم و زر سکه از اوج ماهی تا بماه **W.** 168. **S.** ·8.	مانوس میمنت احد سنه جلوس ضرب سهرند
22	,,	— 1	As 21, but differently arranged.	As 21. Pl. II. 14.
23 I.M.	,,	1172 —	As 21. **W.** 168. **S.** ·75.	مانوس میمنت ۱۱۷۲ سنه جلوس ضرب سهرند
24 B.M.	,,	— 16	,,	,, ۱۶
25	شاه جهان اباد Shāhja- hānābād *Dāru-l-* *khilāfat*	1170 11	As 3; ۱۱۷۰ to l. of second line. A broad coin with legends in the imperial Delhi style. **W.** 167. **S.** 1·03.	فة جهاا اباد دار الخلا شاه ن ضرب جلوس میمنت مانوس ۱۱ سنه
26	,,	1173 14	As 25. ۱۱۷۳ **W.** 168. **S.** ·85.	As 25. ۱۴
27	,,	1173 14	As 25 but broader; ringed. **W.** 166. **S.** 1·25.	,,
28 B.M.	,,	1173 14	As 25; broad thin coin, ringed. **W.** 171. **S.** 1·45.	,,

Metal No.	Mint	Date	Obverse	Reverse
AV 29 I.M.	شاه جهان اباد Shāhjahānābād *Dāru-l-khilāfat*	1173 **14**	As 26, but Durrānī style. **W.** 165. **S.** ·85.	As 26.
30 B.M.	,,	1173 **14**	In triple circle on dotted field. شد از قادر بیچون حکم باحمد بادشاه ۱۱۷۳ سکه زن بر سیم و زر از بماه اوج ماهی تا **W.** 167. **S.** 1·35. A fine broad piece.	,, Pl. II. 9.
31 I.M.	,,	1174 **15**	As 29; Durrānī style. ۱۱۷۴	As 29. ۱۵ Pl. II. 12.
32 B.M.	فرخ اباد Farrukhābād *Aḥmadnagar*	1176 **15**	As 3, but large bold characters; date ۱۱۷۶ to l. of second line. **W.** 167. **S.** 1·1.	مانوس میمنت ۱۵ سنه جلوس ضرب احمدنگر فرخ اباد M. 5. Pl. II. 13.
33 B.M.	کابل Kābul *Dāru-l-mulk*	1161 **1**	Three-line form of couplet; date ۱۱۶۱ **W.** 168. **S.** ·85.	جلوس میمنت مانوس دارالملک ضرب کابل احد Pl. II. 19.

Metal No.	Mint	Date	Obverse	Reverse
AV 34 B.M. I.M.	Kābul *Dāru-s-salṯanat*	1170 **10**	As 5; date ١١٧٠ to l. of second line. **W.** 167. **S.** ·85.	On flowered field ١٠ سنه لسلطنة بل دار ا کا ب ضر Pl. II. 17.
35	,,	1181 **21**	As 5, but both dates on reverse. **W.** 168.	In double circle لسلطنة دار ا کابل ١١٨١ ضرب ٢١ سنه Pl. II. 18.
36 B.M.	,,	1185 **25**	,, **W.** 168. **S.** ·8.	,, ١١٨٥ ٢٥
37	,,	1186 **25**	,, **W.** 168.	,, ١١٨٦ ٢٥
38 B.M.	کشمیر Kashmīr	1167 **6**	As 203; ١١٦٧ to l. of third line. **W.** 168. **S.** ·82.	In triple circle مانوس میمنت ٦ سنه جلوس ب ضر کشمیر To l. of last line M. 6. Pl. II. 15.

Metal No.	Mint	Date	Obverse	Reverse
AV 39 I.M.	لاهور Lāhor *Dāru-s-saltanat*	1161 1	از قادر بیچون به شـــــــــد ۱۱۶۱ حکم احمد بادشاه ســـــــــکه زن بر سیم و زر از اوج ماهی تا بماه **W.** 168. **S.** ·9.	احمد شاه بادشـــــاه درّ درّان احد ضرب دار السلطنة لاهور میمنت جلوس مانوس Pl. II. 16.
40 I.M.	„	1175 15	In circle as 3; date ۱۱۷۵ to l. of second line. **W.** 165. **S.** ·85.	In circle لاهور دار السلطنة ضرب جلوس میمنت مانوس ۱۵ سنه
41 I.M.	ملتان Multān	1165 5	As 8; ۱۱۶۵ above third line. **W.** 169. **S.** ·8.	مانوس میمنت ۵ جلوس ضرب ملتان M. 7 in loop of س of جلوس.
42 I.M.	„	1166 5	As 41 but ۱۱۶۶. **W.** 169. **S.** ·8.	مانوس میمنت ۵ سنه جلوس ضرب ملتان M. 8.
43	„	1167 6	As 41; broad coin in good style. Date ۱۱۶۷ to l. of second line. **W.** 171. **S.** ·9.	As 42. ۶

Metal No.	Mint	Date	Obverse	Reverse
AV 44 I.M.	Multān *Dāru-l-amān*	8	In double circle as 7; no Hijri year. W. 169. S. ·87.	In foliation surrounded by double circle. مانوس میمنت سنه ٨ جلوس ملتان دار الامان ضرب
45 B.M. I.M.	"	1169 9	As 44. Date ١١٦٩ reading outwards at eight o'clock. W. 171. S. ·8.	As 44, but different style. Date ٩ in loop of س of جلوس without word سنه. Pl. III. 1.
46	"	1170 9	Couplet in four lines as 5, but ١١٧٠ above third line. W. 171. S. ·83.	مانوس میمنت ٩ سنه جلوس ضرب دار الامان ملتان M. 8.
47	"	1170 10	As 46.	As 46. ١٠
48	Multān	1170 10	"	As 42. ١٠
49 Bah.	نجیب اباد Najīb-ābād	1180 21	Couplet; date ١١٨٠ l. second line.	اباد نجیب ضرب جلوس میمنت مانوس ٢١ سنه
50 I.M.	هرات Hirāt	—	As 5; dates off the coin. W. 169. S. ·8.	On flowered field in triple circle; whole surrounded by one of dots. ما هر ت نوس ا میمنت ضرب جلوس Pl. III. 2.

Metal No.	Mint	Date	Obverse	Reverse
Æ 51	اتك Atak	— 9	As 1. **W.** 176. **S.** ·85.	مانوس میمنت ۹ سنہ جلوس ضرب اتك
52	,,	1170 11	As 1; ۱۱۷۰ l. of second line.	مانوس میمنت جلوس ضرب ۱۱ اتك سنہ To r. of جلوس M. 9.
53	,,	1171 11	As 1, but ۱۱۷۱ l. third line and no و between سیم and زر.	As 52. ۱۱
54 I.M.	,,	— 13	As 1.	,, ۱۳
55 B.M.	,,	— 14	,,	,, ۱۴
56 I.M.	,,	— ۱۱۷-	,,	مانوس میمنت ۱۱۷- سنہ جلوس ضرب اتك
57[1]	,,	— 19	,,	As 52. ۱۹
58	,,	— 21	**W.** 172. ,,	,, ۲۱

[1] A specimen in the British Museum is countermarked with رائج and an illegible date.

Metal No.	Mint	Date	Obverse	Reverse
Æ 58 A Bah.	اتك Atak	1181	As 1.	Like 56, but ۸۱ سنه to l. of اتك.
59 I.M.	,,	— 22	,, **W**. 169. **S**. ·9.	As 52. ۲۲
60	احمد شاهی Aḥmad Shāhī *Ashrafu-l-bilād*	1171 11	In triple circle, as 5. Date ۱۱۷۱ l. second line. **W**. 177. **S**. ·9.	In double circle, outer one of dots احمد شاهی اشرف البلاد ضرب سنه ۱۱
61	,,	— 11	As 60, but سیم و زر. **W**. 176. **S**. ·9.	As 60.
62 B.M.	,,	1172 12	As 61. Date ۱۱۷۲ at nine o'clock. **W**. 180. **S**. ·9.	احمد شاهی ۱۲ البلاد سنه ف ضرب اشر Pl. III. 4.
63 B.M.	,,	1172 12	,, **W**. 178. **S**. ·95.	شاهی احمد البلاد ۱۲ اشرف سنه ضرب Pl. III. 3.
64	,,	— 16	,, **W**. 175. **S**. ·8.	As 60. ۱۶

Metal No.	Mint	Date	Obverse	Reverse
Æ 65[1] B.M.	احمد شاهی Aḥmad Shāhī *Ashrafu-l-bilād*	— 17	As 61. **W.** 177. **S.** ·9.	احمد شاه اشرف البلاد میمنت جلوس مانوس ضرب سنة ١٧
66	"	1178 18	" ٧٨ ١١ at 9 o'clock.	As 65. ١٨
67	"	1180 20	As 66. ١١٨٠	" ٢٠
68 I.M.	"	1182 22	" ١١٨٢	" ٢٢
69 I.M.	"	1182 23	" ١١٨٢	" ٢٣
70	"	1184 23	" ١١٨٤	" ٢٣
71 I.M.	"	— 25	"	" ٢٥
72	"	— 26	" **W.** 175. **S.** ·85.	" ٢٦ Pl. III. 5.
73 B.M.	انوله Ānwala (Aonla)	1173 14	In double circle couplet; date ١١٧٣. **W.** 172. **S.** ·9.	مانوس میمنت ١٤ جلوس سنة ضرب انوله M. 10. Pl. III. 6.

[1] Other dates of this type at Bahāwalpūr 1174, 13 and —, 16. I have seen a specimen of date —, 19 surcharged رائج ١١٨٤.

Metal No.	Mint	Date	Obverse	Reverse
AR 74	انوله Ānwala (Aonla)	— 14	As 73, but باحمد and date off coin. **W.** 171.	As 73. ۱۴
75 B.M.	„	1174 14	As 73; باحمد and date ۱۱۷۴ to l. of second line. **W.** 172. **S.** ·9.	As 73.
76 B.M.	„	— 14 Counter-struck 1188	As 73. **W.** 171.	As 73; countermarked with ۱۱۸۸ رائج in lozenge.
77 B.M.	„	— 14 Counter-struck 1191	„ **W.** 171.	As 73; countermarked with ۱۱۹۱ رائج in cartouche.
78	بریلی Barelī	1173 14	As 73, but باحمد. ۱۱۷۳ **W.** 171.	On dotted field مانوس میمنت ۱۴ جلوس سنه یلی ضرب بر
79 B.M.	„	1174 14	As 78. ۱۱۷۴ **W.** 172.	As 78. Pl. III. 7.
80 I.M. B.M.	بهکهر Bhakhar	— 3	قادر بیچون شاه از بہ احمد باد حکم شد سیم و زر از اوج ما تا سکہ هی بماه زد بر **W.** 176. **S.** ·75. An unusual arrangement in small neat lettering; زد instead of زن.	جلوس مانوس میمنت ۳ بهکهر ضرب Pl. III. 8.

Metal No.	Mint	Date	Obverse	Reverse
AR 81	بهکهر Bhakhar	116- 4	As 80; date ١١٦- in tiny figures under the word سیم. Also I.M.	As 80. ۴
82 B.M.	,,	1165 5	As 81. ١١٦٥ **W.** 175.	,, ۵
83	,,	1166 7	Couplet in three lines. **W.** 175.	مانوس میمنت ۷ جلوس سنه ب ضر بهکهر
84 B.M.	,,	1166 7	In triple circle as 3. ١١٦٦ **W.** 174. **S.** ·9.	In triple circle مانوس میمنت جلوس ۷ ضرب بهکهر
85	,,	— 8	As 3. **W.** 177. **S.** ·9.	As 84. ۸ Pl. III. 10.
86 B.M.	,,	8	As 7. **W.** 176. **S.** ·85.	In foliation مانوس میمنت ۸ جلوس سنه بهکهر ضرب
86A Bah.	Bhakkar	9	,,	As 86. Mint name written بهکر. ۹

Metal No.	Mint	Date	Obverse	Reverse
Æ 87	Bhakhar	1169	As 7. W. 177·5.	As 86, but ١١٦٩ and no regnal date, ١٩ over سنه and ١١ l. of ضرب.
87 A Bah.	„	1170	„	جلوس میمنت بهکهر ١١٧٠ ضرب
88	„	1170	„ W. 177.	As 87, but word سنه omitted; date ١١٧٠ l. جلوس
89	„	1171	„ W. 178.	As 88. ١١٧١
90	„	1172	„	„ ١١٧٢
91	„	1173	„	„ ١١٧٣
92	„	1174	„ W. 177. S. ·95.	„ ١١٧٤
93	„	1175	„	„ ١١٧٥
94 I.M.	„	1177	„	„ ١١٧٧
95 B.M. I.M.	„	1178	„	„ ١١٧٨ Pl. III. 12.
96 B.M.	„	1178	„ W. 178. S. ·9.	In foliated area جلوس میمنت مانوس بهکهر ب ضر ١١٧٨ Pl. III. 11.

Metal No.	Mint	Date	Obverse	Reverse
Æ 96 A Bah.	Bhakhar	20	As 7.	As 96, but ۲۰ to l. of ضر.
97	„	1179	„ W. 178. S. ·95.	In foliated area as 88, but date arranged differently.
98	„	1179	„ W. 178. S. ·95.	As 96. ۱۱۷۹
99 I.M.	„	1180	„	„ ۱۱۸۰
100	„	1180	„ W. 175.	In eight-foil area جلوس میمنت مانوس ۱۱۸۰ بهکهر ضرب
101	„	1183	„ W. 176.	As 96. ۱۱۸۳
102 B.M.	„	1183	Couplet in three lines. W. 175. S. ·7. A thick dumpy coin interrupting the series.	As 96. ۱۱۸۳
103	„	1184	As 7. W. 175. S. ·95. Also B.M.	As 96. ۱۱۸۴
104	پشاور Pashāwar	1161 1	As 8. ۱۱۶۱ W. 175. S. ·85.	As 8. احد To l. of mint name M. 2.

Metal No.	Mint	Date	Obverse	Reverse
Æ 105	پشاور Pashāwar	1161 2	As 8. ١١٦١	As 104. ٢
106	,,	1162 2	,, ١١٦٢	,, ٢
107 I.M.	,,	1164 3	,, ١١٦۴	,, ٣
108 I.M.	,,	— 4	,, Date off coin.	,, ۴
109 B.M.	,,	1167 7	In double circle ٧ احمد شـــاه در دران **W.** 17·3. **S.** ·45.	In dotted circle ١١٦٧ ضرب پشاور Pl. III. 9.
110	,,	1170 10	As 8, but باحمد ١١٧٠	As 8. ١٠
111	,,	1171 11	As 110. ١١٧١	,, ١١
112 I.M.	,,	— 12	,,	,, ١٢
113 B.M.	,,	— 14	,,	,, ١۴
114 I.M.	,,	— 15	,,	,, ١٥
115	,,	1176 16	,, ١١٧٦	,, ١٦
116	,,	1177 17	,, ١١٧٧	,, ١٧
117	,,	— 18	,,	,, ١٨

Metal No.	Mint	Date	Obverse	Reverse
Æ 118 I.M.	پشاور Pashāwar	— 19	As 110.	As 8. ١٩
119 I.M.	„	— 22	„	„ ٢٢
120	„	1183 23	„ ١١٨٣ **W.** 175. **S.** ·9.	„ ٢٣
121	„	1184 24	„ ١١٨۴	„ ٢۴
122	„	1185 25	„ ١١٨٥	„ ٢٥
123	„	1186 26	„ ١١٨٦ **W.** 176. **S.** ·9.	„ ٢٦ Pl. III. 13.
124 B.M.	تته Tatta	1171 —	Couplet in three lines. **W.** 176. **S.** ·75.	مانوس میمنت سنه جلوس ب ضر تته ٧١--
125 I.M.	„	— 14	As 124. **W.** 177.	As 124, but ١۴ over سنه.
126 B.M.	دیره Dera	— 1	As 3. **W.** 175. **S.** ·8.	In double circle, outer one of dots احد سنه ب ضر دیره L. top line M. 11.

Metal No.	Mint	Date	Obverse	Reverse
Æ 127 B.M.	دیره Dera	1166 5	As 33; date ۱۱۶۶. **W.** 175. **S.** ·85.	مانوس میمنت ۵ سنه جلوس ب ضر دیره M. 12.
128	,,	1166 5	As 3, but بہ احمد ; ۱۱۶۶ over third line. **W.** 175. **S.** ·85.	As 127. M. 12 in loop of س of جلوس.
129	,,	1167 6	As 128. ۱۱۶۷	As 128. ۶
130	,,	1167 7	,, ۱۱۶۷	,, ۷
131	,,	1168 7	,, ۱۱۶۸	,, ۷
132	,,	1168 8	,, ۱۱۶۸	,, ۸
133	,,	8	As 7. **W.** 176. **S.** ·85.	As 11.
134	,,	9	,,	,, ۹
135	,,	1169 9	As 3; ۱۱۶۹ l. of second line. **W.** 175. **S.** ·85.	In double circle, outer one of dots ۹ سنه ب ضر دیره To l. of top line M. 13.

Metal No.	Mint	Date	Obverse	Reverse
Æ 136	دیره Dera	1170 10	As 8. ١١٧٠	As 135. ١٠
137 B.M.	”	1170 10	As 8, but date ١١٧٠ above second line.	” ١٠
138	”	1170 12 *sic*	As 137. ١١٧٠	” ١٢
139	”	1170 13 *sic*	” ١١٧٠	” ١٣
140	”	1173 13	As 137, but larger characters. ١١٧٣	” ١٣
141	”	1173 14	As 140. ١١٧٣	” ١٤
142	”	1174 14	” ١١٧٤	” ١٤
143	”	1175 15	As 137. ١١٧٥	” ١٥
144	”	1175 16	” ١١٧٥	” ١٦
145	”	1176 16	” ١١٧٦	” ١٦
146	”	1177 17	” ١١٧٧	” ١٧
147	”	1178 18	” ١١٧٨	” ١٨
148	”	1179 19	” ١١٧٩	” ١٩

Metal No.	Mint	Date	Obverse	Reverse
Æ 149 B.M.	دیرة Dera	1180 **20**	As 137. ١١٨٠ **W.** 175.	As 135. ٢٠ Pl. III, 18.
150	"	1180 **21**	" ١١٨٠	" ٢١
151	"	1180 *sic* **22**	" ١١٨٠ **W.** 175. **S.** ·85.	" ٢٢
152	"	1182 **23**	" ١١٨٢	" ٢٣
153	"	1182 **24**	" ١١٨٢	" ٢٤
154 I.M.	"	1184 **24**	" ١١٨٤	" ٢٤
155	"	1185 **25**	" ١١٨٥	" ٢٥
156	"	1185 **26**	" ١١٨٥ **W.** 176.	" ٢٦
157	دیرجات Derajāt	1168	As 7. **W.** 178. **S.** ·9.	In foliated area مانوس میمنت جلوس دیرجا ت ١١٦٨ ضرب
158 B.M.	Derahjāt	1173	As 3; very poor style. **W.** 177. **S.** ·85.	In double circle ١١٧٣ جات ب ضر دیرة

Metal No.	Mint	Date	Obverse	Reverse
Æ 159 B.M.	ديرجات Derajāt	1180	As 7 ; very poor style. **W.** 175.	As 157. ١١٨٠
160	„	118–?	As 7. **W.** 168.	In foliated area مانوس ميمنت جلوس جات ضرب دير ١١٨– سنه
161	„	— 23	As 3. **W.** 167. **S.** ·8. Also B.M.	٢٣ سنه ب ضر ت ديرجا To l. of top line M. 14.
162 B.M.	„	1183 23	As 3; date ١١٨٣ over second line. **W.** 170. **S.** ·9.	In triple circle سنه ٢٣ ت ضر ديرجا ب ١١٨٣ R. top line, star. Pl. III. 15.
163	سهرند Sahrind	— 1	As 21. **W.** 173. **S.** ·85. Also I.M.	As 21.
164 B.M.	„	1164 4	Couplet in three lines. ١١٦٤	مانوس ميمنت ٤ سنه جلوس ضرب سهرند

Metal No.	Mint	Date	Obverse	Reverse
AR 165	سهرند Sahrind	1174 14	As 164. ١١٧٤ W. 173.	As 164. ١٤
166 B.M.	"	1174 15	" ١١٧٤	" ١٥
167 B.M.	"	— 15	"	مانوس میمنت ١٥ جلوس سنه ضرب سهرند
168	"	1175 16	As 164. ١١٧٥	As 164. ١٦
169	"	1176 —	" ١١٧٦ W. 172. S. ·85.	"
170	شاه جهان اباد Shāhjahānābād *Dāru-l-khilāfat*	1170 11	As 25. W. 175. S. ·95. One-eighth rupee of this date—W.K. 2820.	As 25.
171	"	1173 14	" ١١٧٣	" ١٤
171 A R.B.	"	1173 14	As 28; a thin broad coin. Collection of Sir Richard Burn. W. 174. S. 1·5.	" ١٤

Metal No.	Mint	Date	Obverse	Reverse
Æ 172 B.M.	شاه جهان اباد Shāhja-hānābād *Dāru-l-khilāfat*	14	In small central area bounded by triple circle احمد Around it the couplet beginning at one o'clock and reading inwards against the hands of a watch. Whole contained in an elaborate five-fold circular border. **W.** 62. **S.** 1·1.	In elaborate circular border, as 25 ۱۴ Pl. III. 14.
173	"	1174 15	As 25. ۱۱۷۴ **W.** 176. **S.** ·9.	As 25. ۱۵
174	فرخ اباد Farrukh-ābād *Aḥmad-nagar*	1174 14	As 32. ۱۱۷۴ **W.** 175. **S.** 1·1.	As 32. ۱۴
175 B.M.	"	1176 15	" ۱۱۷۶	" ۱۵
176	کابل Kābul *Dāru-l-mulk*	— 1	As 33, but date off coin. **W.** 175. **S.** ·95.	As 33.
177 B.M.	"	— 3	As 3; date illegible. **W.** 175.	" ۳
178 B.M.	Kābul *Dāru-s-salṭanat*	— 5	As 5. **W.** 176.	In dotted circle دار السلطنة ب ۵ ضر کابل سنه

Metal No.	Mint	Date	Obverse	Reverse
AR 179 B.M.	کابل Kābul *Dāru-s-salṭanat*	8	As 7. **W.** 176. **S.** 1·0.	In foliated area مانوس میمنت جلوس کابل ۸ دار السلطنة ضرب Pl. III. 17.
180	,,	1170	As 5; ۱۱۷۰ to l. of second line. **W.** 175.	دار ضرب السلطنة کابل ۱۱۷۰
181 B.M.	,,	1171	As 5; date not visible.	As 180. ۱۱۷۱ Pl. III. 20.
182	,,	1171	As 5; dateless. **W.** 176. **S.** ·9.	In double circle لسلطنة ۱۱۷۱ دار ا کابل سنه ضر ب
183 B.M.	,,	1173	As 182.	As 182. ۱۱۷۳
184	,,	1173	,, **W.** 176. **S.** ·9.	In double circle السلطنة دار کابل ۱۱۷۳ ضرب
185 B.M.	,,	1173	,, **W.** 176. **S.** ·9.	In double circle کابل ۱۱۷۳ لسلطنة ضر دار ا ب Pl. III. 21.

Metal No.	Mint	Date	Obverse	Reverse
Æ 186	کابل Kābul *Dāru-s-salṭanat*	1174	As 182.	As 184. ١١٧٤
187 B.M.	„	1175	„	„ ١١٧٥
188 I.M.	„	15	„	لسلطنة دار ا کابل ضرب ١٥ سنة
189 B.M.	„	1175 15	„	لسلطنة دار ا کابل ١١٧٥ ضرب ١٥ سنة
190 B.M.	„	1176 16	„	As 189. ١١٧٦ ١٦
191	„	1177 17	„	„ ١١٧٧ ١٧
192	„	1178 18	„	„ ١١٧٨ ١٨
193 I.M.	„	1180 20	„	„ ١١٨٠ ٢٠
194	„	1181	„ Also B.M.	„ ١١٨١; no regnal date.
195	„	1182 22	„	„ ١١٨٢; ٢٢ written ٣٢.
196	„	1183 23	„	„ ١١٨٣; ٢٣ written ٣٣.

Metal No.	Mint	Date	Obverse	Reverse
Æ 197	كابل Kābul *Dāru-s-salṭanat*	1183	As 182.	As 189. ١١٨٣ ; no regnal date.
198	,,	1184	,,	,, ١١٨٤ ; no regnal date.
199 B.M.	,,	1184 23	,, **W.** 174. **S.** ·9.	,, ١١٨٤ ٢٣
200	,,	1184 24	,,	,, ١١٨٤ ٢٤
201	,,	1185 24	,,	,, ١١٨٥ ٢٤
202	,,	1186 25	,, **W.** 176. **S.** ·85.	,, ١١٨٦ ٢٥
203	كشمير Kashmīr	1176 14	In triple circle شد از قادر بیچون حکم باحمد بادشاه سکه زن بر سیم و زر هـ ٦[١١٧] از اوج ما تا بماه **W.** 174. **S.** ·95.	مانوس میمنت ١٤ سنه جلوس ب ضر کشمیر
204	,,	1176 15	As 203.	As 203. ١٥
205 Edin.	,,	1177 15	,, ١١٧٧ Royal Scottish Museum, Edinburgh.	,, ١٥
206	,,	1177 16	,, ١١٧٧	,, ١٦

Metal No.	Mint	Date	Obverse	Reverse
AR 207 B.M.	کشمیر Kashmīr	— 17	As 203, but از قادر بیچون شـــــاه حکم شد باحمد باد **W.** 173. **S.** ·9.	مانوس میمنت س ١٧ سنه جلو کشمیر ضرب
208 Edin.	„	1178 17	As 207. ١١٧٨	As 207. ١٧
209 R.S.	„	— 18	„ Collection of the late Mr. R. Sutcliffe, Burnley.	„ ١٨
210	„	— 21	„	„ ٢١
211	„	— 22	As 203, but حکم از قادر بیچون شـــــد **W.** 173. **S.** ·95.	٢٢ جلوس سنه مانوس میمنت کشمیر ضرب Pl. III. 19.
212	„	1182 22	As 203, but از قادر بیچون شـــــد حکم باحمد بادشاه **W.** 173. **S.** ·95.	مانوس میمنت ٢٢ سنه جلوس کشمیر ضرب Pl. III. 16.
213 B.M.	„	1184 23	As 212. ١١٨٤	As 212. ٢٣

Metal No.	Mint	Date	Obverse	Reverse
Æ 214 Edin.	كشمير Kashmīr	1184 24	As 212. ١١٨٤	As 212. ٢٤
215 Fitz.	,,	1185 24	,, ١١٨٥ Fitzwilliam Museum, Cambridge.	,, ٢٤
216	لاهور Lāhor *Dāru-s-salṭanat*	116– 1	As 39, but date cut. **W.** 174. **S.** ·8.	As 39.
217 B.M.	,,	1165 5	In circle, as 3. ١١٦٥ **W.** 175. **S.** ·85.	In circle لاهور دار السلطنة ضرب سنة ٥ ميمنت جلوس مانوس Pl. III. 22.
218	,,	10	As 3, but apparently no Hijri date. M. 15.	As 217. ١٠ In loop of س of جلوس M. 15.
219	,,	1170 11	As 3; ٧٠ ١١ to middle l.	In double circle as 217, with mark as 218. ١١
220	,,	1173 13	,, ١١٧٣	,, ١٣
221	,,	1173 14	,, ١١٧٣	,, ١٤
222 B.M.	,,	1173 14	As 219; broad coin in good style. **W.** 173. **S.** 1·0.	,, ١٤

Metal No.	Mint	Date	Obverse	Reverse
Æ 223 B.M.	لاهور Lāhor *Dāru-s-salṭanat*	1174 15	As 219. ١١٧٤	As 219. ١٥
224	"	1175 15	" ١١٧٥	" ١٥
225	"	1175 15	As 219, but date ١١٧٥ over ش of شاه in second line. W. 174. S. ·85.	" ١٥
226	"	1175 16	As 225. ١١٧٥	" ١٦
227	"	1176 16	" ١١٧٦	" ١٦
228	"	1176 17	" ١١٧٦	" ١٧
229	"	1177 17	" ١١٧٧	" ١٧
230	"	1177 18	As 225, but شاه written شاه. ١١٧٧ W. 174.	" ١٨ Pl. IV. 1.
231	"	1178 18	As 230. ١١٧٨	" ١٨
232	"	1178 19	" ١١٧٨	" ١٩
233	"	1180 21	" ١١٨٠ W. 174. S. ·8.	" ٢١

Metal No.	Mint	Date	Obverse	Reverse
Æ 234[1] B.M.	مراداباد Murād- ābād	1173 14	As 3. ١١٧٣ **W.** 174. **S.** ·85.	مانوس میمنت ١٤ جلوس سنه ضرب مراداباد M. 16. Pl. IV. 4.
235	ملتان Multān	1165 5	As 8, but date above third line. ١١٦٥ **W.** 176. **S.** ·85.	As 41. ٥ Pl. IV. 5.
236	,,	1165 5	As 235. ١١٦٥	As 42. M. 8.
237	,,	1166 5	As 235. ١١٦٦ **W.** 175. **S.** ·85.	As 236.
238 B.M.	,,	1166 6	In rayed double circle as 235, but ١١٦٦ l. of second line. **W.** 174. **S.** 1·0.	,, ٦ Pl. IV. 2.
239	,,	1167 6	As 238. ١١٦٧	,, ٦
240	,,	— 6	As 238, but باحمد. Also in B.M.	,, ٦
241	,,	1167 7	As 238. ١١٦٧	,, ٧

[1] I have noted a specimen surcharged رائج ١١٩١.

Metal No.	Mint	Date	Obverse	Reverse
Æ 242	ملتان Multān	1168 7	As 238. ١١٦٨	As 236. ٧
243	„	1168 8	„ ١١٦٨ **W.** 175.	„ ٨
244	Multān *Dāru-l-amān*	1168 8	In triple circle as 7; date ١١٦٨ at nine o'clock. **W.** 176. **S.** ·9.	In foliated area and triple circle as 44.
245	„	1169 8	As 7, but in rayed circle; date at ten o'clock. ١١٦٩	As 44. ٨ Pl. IV. 3.
246	„	1169 9	As 245. ١١٦٩ **W.** 177. Different style; date at nine o'clock.	As 45. ٩
247	„	1170 9	In rayed circle, as 5. ١١٧٠ **W.** 176. **S.** ·9.	In triple circle as 46, but دار الآمان. M. 8.
248 B.M.	„	1170 9	As 3. ١١٧٠ **W.** 177.	As 46. Pl. IV. 6.
249	„	1170 10	As 5, but بد احمد. ١١٧٠	As 248. ١٠
250 B.M.	„	1170 10	As 3. ١١٧٠ **W.** 177. **S.** ·9.	As 247. ١٠

Metal No.	Mint	Date	Obverse	Reverse
Æ 251 B.M.	ملتان Multān *Dāru-l-amān*	1170 10	As 249. ١١٧٠ W. 176.	مانوس ميمنت ١٠ جلوس دار الامان ب ضر ملتان Pl. IV. 7.
252	Multān	1170 10	As 247. ١١٧٠ W. 177. S. ·9.	مانوس ميمنت ١٠ سنه جلوس ب ضر ملتان M. 8.
253 B.M.	"	1170 10	As 249. ١١٧٠ W. 177.	As 252. ١٠
254 B.M.	نجيب اباد Najīb-ābād	1180 21	As 49. ١١٨٠ W. 172. S. ·8.	As 49. ٢١ M. 17. Pl. IV. 8.
255 B.M.	هرات Hirāt *Dāru-s-salṭanat*	1171	As 5. W. 175. S. ·9.	In double circle, outer one of dots, on dotted field جلوس مانوس ميمنت دار السلطنة ١١٧١ ضرب هرات Pl. IV. 10.
256 I.M. B.M.	"	—	As 5.	As 255, but date off the coin.

Metal No.	Mint	Date	Obverse	Reverse
Æ 257 B.M.	هرات Hirāt *Dāru-s-salṭanat*	—	As 5. **W.** 176. **S.** ·85.	In circle on dotted field surrounded by broad margin هرات لسلطنة دار ضرب Pl. IV. 9.
258	"	—	" **W.** 175.	In circle هر ا ت السلطنة دار ضرب
259 B.M.	Hirāt	—	" **W.** 175. **S.** ·85.	In triple circle on dotted field هر ت نوس ا میمنت ضر جلوس ما ب Pl. IV. 11.
Æ 260 B.M.	بهکهر Bhakhar	1162 1	In triple circle احمد شاه فلوس ١١٦٢ **W.** 257. **S.** 1·1.	In triple circle بهکهر احد ضرب
261 B.M.	"	1163 3	As 260. ١١٦٣ **W.** 233.	As 260. ٣
262 B.M.	"	1168 8	" ١١٦٨ **W.** 302. **S.** ·9.	" ٨ Pl. IV. 13.

Metal No.	Mint	Date	Obverse	Reverse
Æ 263 B.M.	بهکهر Bhakbar	1169 8	As 260. ۱۱٦۹ **W.** 257.	As 260. ۸
264	پشاور Pashāwar	— 7	احمد شاه ح -- شاه غاز ------ **W.** 180. **S.** ·8. Also known of year 4: p. xliii and *P.M. Cat.*, p. 361.	فلوس ضرب پشاور ۷
265 B.M.	دیره Dera	1161 1	As 260. ۱۱٦۱ **W.** 237. **S.** 1·15.	In triple circle دیره ب ضر سنه احد
266 B.M.	,,	1162 1	,, ۱۱٦۲ **W.** 238. **S.** ·8. Date 3 — W.K. 2835.	As 265.
267 B.M.	,,	1165 5	,, ۱۱٦۵ **W.** 217. **S.** ·9.	,, ۵
268	,,	1167 7	,, ۱۱٦۷ **W.** 284. **S.** 1·1.	,, ۷
269 B.M.	,,	1168 7	,, ۱۱٦۸ **W.** 267. **S.** 1.	,, ۷
270	,,	— 10	,, **W.** 201. **S.** ·9.	دیره ب ۱۰ ضر سنه

Metal No.	Mint	Date	Obverse	Reverse
Æ 271 B.M.	دیرہ Dera	117–	As 260. **W.** 183. **S.** ·8. Poor condition.	In circle ۱۱۷– سنہ ب ضر دیرہ
272 R.S.	کشمیر Kashmīr	— 23	احمد نی شاہ درا سس سکہ فلو For R.S., *see* 209.	۲۳ سنہ کشمیر ضرب
273 R.S.	„	1187 *sic* —	As 272, but ۱۱۸۷ above top line.	As 272; date off coin.
274	ملتان Multān	1170 10	In circle احمد شاہ بادشاہ در درانی فلوس ۱۱۷۰ **W.** 213. **S.** ·9.	In circle ملتان ضرب جلوس مبارک ۱۰ Pl. IV. 12.
275 B.M.	„	1172 12	As 274. ۱۱۷۲ **W.** 210.	As 274. ۱۲
276 B.M.		1175 15	احمد شاهی فلوس ۱۱۷۵ **W.** 181. **S.** ·85.	وزن‌خام قمت رائج الو ۱۵ Pl. IV. 14.
277 B.M.		1176 16	As 276. ۱۱۷۶ **W.** 160. **S.** ·85. See p. xxxv; two of these remarkable coins are in the Guthrie Collection at Berlin.	وزن خام قمت رائج الو ۱۶ Pl. IV. 15.

TAIMŪR SHĀH NIẒĀM

Appointed Niẓām (Governor) of the Panjab, Sind and the Derajāt by Aḥmad Shāh.

A.H 1170–1186. A.D. 1757–1772.

Metal No.	Mint	Date	Obverse	Reverse
AV 278	ديرة Dera	1170 1	خدا و رسول انام ۱۱۷۰ بحكم تيمور شاه نظام سكه بعالم يافت **W.** 170. **S.** ·8. The couplet is :— بعالم يافت سكه تيمور شاه نظام بحكم خدا و رسول انام 'The stamp of Taimūr Shāh gained rule in the world By command of God and of the Prophet of Mankind.'[1]	In dotted circle احد سنه ب ضر ديرة M. 13. Pl. IV. 16.
279 I.M.	,,	117– 3	As 278. ۱۱۷– **W.** 170. **S.** ·75.	In double circle as 278. ۳
280	لاهور Lāhor *Dāru-s-salṭanat*	1170 1	In triple circle as 278; date ۱۱۷۰ to left of bottom line. **W.** 167. **S.** ·85.	As 217. احد Pl. IV. 18.
281 B.M.	,,	1171 1	As 280. ۱۱۷۱ **W.** 168.	As 280.

[1] There is a play on the meanings of the word نظام.

Metal No.	Mint	Date	Obverse	Reverse
AV 282 B.M.	ملتان Multān	1170 1	As 278, but date ١١٧٠ is above second line. **W.** 169·5. **S.** ·8.	مانوس میمنت احد سنه جلوس ضرب ملتان M. 8.
283 I.M.	Multān *Dāru-l-amān*	1173 2	As 282. ١١٧٣ **W.** 170. **S.** ·75.	As 247. ٢ M. 8.
284	,,	1176 6	,, ١١٧٦ **W.** 168. **S.** ·8.	As 283; additional mark M. 18 above ج of جلوس.
285 I.M.	,,	— 9	As 278; date is off this specimen. **W.** 169. **S.** ·75.	In foliated lozenge enclosed in double circle ملتان ضرب ٩ دار الامان سنه
286	,,	1182 12	As 282. ١١٨٢ **W.** 168. **S.** ·75.	As 285. ١٢ M. 19. Pl. IV. 17.
AR 287 B.M.	بهکهر Bhakhar	1173 2	خدا و رسول انام بحکم تیمور شاه ١١٧٣ سکه یافت بعالم نظام **W.** 175. **S.** ·9.	جلوس میمنت ٢ مانوس سنه ب ضر بهکهر Pl. IV. 19.

Metal No.	Mint	Date	Obverse	Reverse
Æ **288**	بهکهر Bhakbar	1177 **3**	خدا و رسول انام بحکم تیمور شاه نظام سکه یافت بعالم ۱۱۷۷ **W.** 177. **S.** ·95.	As 287. ۳ Pl. IV. 20.
289 B.M.	"	1178 **3** *sic*	As 288. ۱۱ l. second line and ۷۸ l. third line.	" ۳
290 B.M.	"	1181 **7?**	" ۱۱۸۱ to l. of third line.	On dotted field as 287; word سنه omitted.
291 B.M.	"	1182	As 287, but no date. **W.** 177. **S.** ·85.	On dotted field جلوس میمنت مانوس بهکهر ب ضر ۱۱۸۲ Pl. IV. 22.
292	"	1183	As 291.	As 291. ۱۱۸۳
293	"	1184	" **W.** 176. **S.** ·9.	In triple circle بهکهر ضرب ۱۱۸۴
294	"	1185	"	As 293. ۱۱۸۵ Pl. IV. 21.
295 B.M.	"	1186	" **W.** 176. **S.** ·9.	" ۱۱۸۶

Metal No.	Mint	Date	Obverse	Reverse
Æ 296	ديره Dera	1170 1	As 278. **W**. 177. **S**. ·85.	As 278.
297 I.M.	„	1170 1	„ **W**. 178.	„ Slightly different style.
298 I.M.	„	— 2	„ Date illegible.	„ ٢
299	„	— 3	„ Date illegible.	„ ٣
300 B.M.	سند Sind	1170 1	In triple circle as 278, but date ١١٧٠ below نظام. **W**. 176. **S**. ·9.	In triple circle مانوس میمنت احد جلوس سنه ب ضر سند Pl. V. 1.
301	لاهور Lāhor *Dāru-s-salṭanat*	1170 1	As 280. ١١٧٠ **W**. 175. **S**. ·9.	As 280. احد
302	„	1171 1	„ ١١٧١	„ احد
303	„	1173 3	„ ١١٧٣	„ ٣
304	ملتان Multān	1170 1	As 282. **W**. 176. **S**. ·9.	As 282.
305	„	1170 1	As 282, but date ١١٧٠ above ت of يانت.	As 282.

Metal No.	Mint	Date	Obverse	Reverse
AR 306 I.M.	ملتان Multān	1170 1	As 305. **W.** 177. **S.** ·95.	As 252. احد M. 8.
307 I.M.	„	1171 1	As 282, but date ۱۱۷۱ is under first line.	As 282.
308	„	1171 1	As 282. ۱۱۷۱ **W.** 177.	As 252. احد Pl. V. 2.
309	„	1172 2	As 282. ۱۱۷۲	As 282. ۲
310	Multān *Dāru-l-amān*	1172 2	As 307. ۱۱۷۲ **W.** 176. **S.** .85.	مانوس میمنت دار الأمان ۲ جلوس سنه ضرب ملتان M. 20.
311	Multān	1173 2	As 282. ۱۱۷۳ **W.** 176. **S.** ·8.	As 282. ۲
312	Multān *Dāru-l-amān*	1173 2	As 307. ۱۱۷۳ **W.** 176. **S.** ·85.	As 310. Pl. V. 3.
313	„	1173 2	As 282. ۱۱۷۳	„
314	„	1173 2	As 305.	„ but M. 21. Pl. V. 4.

Metal No.	Mint	Date	Obverse	Reverse
AR 315	Multān *Dāru-l-amān*	1173 2	As 282. ١١٧٣ **W.** 176. **S.** ·9.	As 283. M. 22.
316	,,	1173 3	,, ١١٧٣	As 283. ٣
317	,,	1174 3	,, ١١٧٤	As 319. ٣
318	,,	1174 3	,, ١١٧٤	As 283. ٣
319	,,	1174 4	,, ١١٧٤	,, ٤ Additional mark M. 23.
320	,,	1175 4	,, ١١٧٥	As 319. ٤ but M. 24 instead of M. 23.
321	,,	1175 5	,, ١١٧٥	As 320. ٥
322	,,	1176 5	,, ١١٧٦	,, ٥
323	,,	1176 6	,, ١١٧٦	As 319. ٦ but M. 18 instead of M. 23.
324	,,	1177 7	,, ١١٧٧ **W.** 176.	As 323. ٧
325	,,	1177 8	,, ١١٧٧	,, ٨

Metal No.	Mint	Date	Obverse	Reverse
Æ 326	Multān *Dāru-l-amān*	1178 8	As 282. ١١٧٨	As 323. ٨
327	,,	1178 9	,, ١١٧٨	,, ٩
328	,,	1179 9	As 278; date ١١٧٩ at top of coin. W. 176. S. ·85.	As 285. ٩
329	,,	1179 10	As 278. ١١٧٩	,, ١٠
330	,,	1180 10	As 328. ١١٨٠ W. 176.	,, ١٠
331	,,	1181 11	As 282. ١١٨١	,, ١١
332	,,	1181 12	,, ١١٨١	,, ١٢
333 I.M.	,,	1182 12	,, ١١٨٢	,, ١٢
334	,,	1182 13	,, ١١٨٢	,, ١٣
335	,,	1183 13	,, ١١٨٣	,, ١٣
336	,,	1183 14	,, ١١٨٣	,, ١٤
337 I.M.	,,	1184 14	,, ١١٨٤	,, ١٤
338	,,	1184 15	,, ١١٨٤	,, ١٥

Metal No.	Mint	Date	Obverse	Reverse
AR 339	Multān *Dāru-l-amān*	1185 15	As 282. ١١٨٥	As 285. ١٥
340	„	1185 16	„ ١١٨٥ W. 177.	„ ١٦
341	?	— 3	Portions of the couplet; unusual style. W. 176. S. ·75.	مانوس میمنت ٣ جلوس سنه ب ضر - - - - - - Pl. V. 5.
Æ 342	دیرہ Dera	1172 3	شا تیمور هم فلوس ١١٧٢ W. 186. S. ·85.	٣ سنه ب ضر دیرہ Pl. V. 6.

SULAIMĀN

A.H. 1186. A.D. 1772.

AV 343 B.M.	کابل Kābul *Dāru-s-salṭanat*	1186 1	دران وارث شاهنشه شاه سلیمان باد سیم و زر را سرفرازی داد چون خورشید و ماه W. 167·5. S. ·8. The couplet is:— سیم و زر را سرفرازی داد چون خورشید و ماه وارث شاهنشه دران سلیمان بادشاه 'Gave exaltation to silver and gold like the sun and moon, The emperor Sulaimān, heir of the Durrān king of kings.'	لسلطنة دار ١ کابل ١١٨٦ ضرب احد سنه Pl. V. 7.

Metal No.	Mint	Date	Obverse	Reverse
AR **344** B.M.	احمد شاهی Aḥmad Shāhī *Ashrafu-l-bilād*	— 1	On flowered field احمد شه شـــاه مهر و ماه سليما باد چون ابن ن سـکه زد برسيم و زر **W.** 176. **S.** ·85. The couplet is:— سکه زد برسیم و زر چون مهر و ماه سلیمان بادشاه ابن احمد شه 'Struck coin on silver and gold like the sun and moon, The emperor Sulaimān, son of Aḥmad Shah.'	On flowered field احمد شاهی اشرف البلاد میمنت جلوس مانوس ضرب سنه ۱ Pl. V. 9.
345 B.M.	پشاور Pashāwar	— 1	The couplet of 343. **W.** 176. **S.** ·9.	مانوس میمنت جلوس احد ضرب پشاور To l. of last line M. 2. Pl. V. 10.
346	دیره Dera	1186 1	In triple circle ۱۱۸۶ احمد شه شـــاه مهر و ماه ابن سلیمان باد سـکه زد برسیم و زر چون **W.** 176. **S.** ·75. The couplet is the same as that of 344.	In triple circle احد سنه ب ضر دیره To l. of top line M. 13. Pl. V. 8.
347 B.M.	,,	1186 1	سلیمان شـــاه در دران سـکه ۱۱۸۶ سکه مبار **W.** 177. **S.** ·8.	In dotted circle احد سنه ب ضر دیره M. 11. Pl. V. 11.

Metal No.	Mint	Date	Obverse	Reverse
AR 348 B.M.	کابل Kābul *Dāru-s-salṯanat*	1186 1	As 343. **W.** 175. **S.** ·85.	In triple circle as 343.
349	„	1186 1	In circle دران وارث شاهنشه شـــــاه سلیمان باد سیم بے زر را سرفراز داد شـــــید چون خور ماه **W.** 177. **S.** ·85. The couplet is that of 343 differently arranged and with the two conjunctions و omitted.	In triple circle as 343. Pl. V. 12.
350 B.M.	کشمیر Kashmīr	1186 1	اله -- در -- شـــــاه درانی سلیمان باد از فضل و الطاف ســـــکه زد بر سیم و زر ۲(۱۱۸) **W.** 169. **S.** ·95. The top line of the legend is illegible. The couplet must be on these lines:— سکه زد بر سیم و زر از فضل و الطاف اله شاه درانی ----- سلیمان بادشاه 'Struck coin on silver and gold through the grace and loving-kindness of God, The Durrānī king, the · · · ·, the emperor Sulaimān.'	In triple circle مانوس میمنت احد سنه جلوس کشمیر ضرب Pl. V. 13.

II

TAIMŪR SHĀH

A.H. 1186–1207. A.D. 1772–1793.

Metal No.	Mint	Date	Obverse	Reverse
AV 351 I.M.	اتك Atak (Attock)	1188 2	سکه تیمور شاه نقـــــشـــــں و ماه تا کند بر چهره شـــــــــید چرخ می ارد طلا و نقره از خور Date ١١٨٨ over second line. **W.** 168. **S.** ·8. The couplet is:— چرخ می آرد طلا و نقره از خورشید و ماه تا کند بر چهره نقش سکه تیمور شاه 'The revolution (of the heavens) brings gold and silver from the sun and moon, In order that it may make on the face (of the metal) the design of the stamp of Taimūr Shāh.'	مانوس میمنت جلوس ضرب ٢ اتك سنه
352	احمد شاهی Aḥmad Shāhī *Ashrafu-l-bilād*	1186 1	چرخ می آرد طــــــــلا و نقره از خور و ماه شــــــــید نقش سکه تیمور شاه کـــــــند تا بر چهره ١١٨٦ **W.** 168. **S.** ·9.	In dotted circle on flowered field احمد شاهی اشرف البلاد میمنت جلوس مانوس ضرب سنه ١
353 B.M.	,,	1190	از خور و ماه شــــــــید چرخ می ارد طلا و نقره شــــــــاه بر چهره نقش سکه تیمور تا کــــــــند ١١٩٠ **W.** 167. **S.** ·8.	In double circle, outer one of dots احمد شاهی اشر البلاد ف ضرب

Metal No.	Mint	Date	Obverse	Reverse
AV **354** B.M.	احمد شاهی Aḥmad Shāhī *Ashrafu-l-bilād*	1197 **12**	چرخ می ارد طـــــلا و نقرهٔ از خور و ماه شـــــید چهرهٔ نقش سکهٔ تیمور شاه کـــــنـــــد تا بر ۱۱۹۷ **W.** 167. **S.** ·85.	In double circle البلا احمد اشرف د ا شـــــا ۱۲ نو جلوس ماس هی سنه میمنت ضرب
355 I.M.	,,	— **14**	As 353. **W.** 168. **S.** ·85.	As 352. ۱۴
356	,,	1204 **18**	In double circle از خورشید و ماه تا کند چهـــــرهٔ بر نقش سکهٔ تیمور شاه نقـــــرهٔ چرخ می آرد طلا و **W.** 165.	احمد هم ا د ف البلا شاه ۱۲۰۴ ب ضر شر ۱۸
357	,,	1207 **21** (written **12**)	As 356. **W.** 168. **S.** ·9.	In double circle شاهم ف د البلا احمد ا ا ۱۲۰۷ ب ضر شر ۱۲
358 Bah.	بهکهر Bhakhar	1196 —	Couplet in four lines.	As 291. ۱۱۹۶
359 Bah.	,,	1204 —	,,	مانوس میمنت جلوس ۱۲۰۴ بهکهر ضرب

Metal No.	Mint	Date	Obverse	Reverse
AV **360** B.M.	Bakhar	1204 **18**	In triple circle از خورشید و ماه چهره بر نقش سکه تیمور شاه نقره چرخ می ارد طلا و تا کند ۱۲۰۴ **W.** 169. **S.** 1.	In triple circle بکهر میمنت ب ضر س ما س جلو نو ۱۸ Pl. V. 14.
361 B.M.	پشاور Pashāwar	1186 **1**	تیمور شاه سکه بر چهره نقش ۱۱۸۶ کند از خورشید و ماه تا نقره چرخ می ارد طلا و **W.** 168. **S.** ·8.	مانوس میمنت جلوس احد ضرب پشاور M. 2.
362 I.M.	,,	1194 **8**	As 361. ۱۱۹۴	As 361. ۸
363 B.M.	,,	1196 **11**	,, ۱۱۹۶	,, ۱۱
364	,,	— **12**	,, Date off coin.	,, ۱۲
365 I.M.	,,	1202 **15**	,, ۱۲۰۲ **W.** 168. **S.** ·8.	,, ۱۵
366	,,	1204 **17**	,, ۱۲۰۴	,, ۱۷

Metal No.	Mint	Date	Obverse	Reverse
AV 367 B.M.	پشاور Pashāwar	1204 18	As 356, but ۱۲۰۴ above second line and بر at end of first line. W. 168. S. ·9.	In flowing style with letters of uniform thickness, on dotted field جلوس میمنت مانوس ۱۸ ضرب پشاور Pl. V. 16.
368 B.M.	„	1205 18	As 367. ۱۲۰۵	As 367. ۱۸
369 I.M.	„	1209 *sic* 21	„ ۱۲۰۹ W. 168. S. ·9.	In style as 367. ضرب میمنت س س ور جلو ما پشا ۲۱ نو
370 I.M.	دیرہ Dera	— 1	Couplet in four lines. W. 168. S. ·8.	In double circle as 347. احد
371 I.M.	„	1202 17	As 370, but in much larger characters. Date ۱۲۰۲ beneath word نقش. W. 168. S. ·8. Struck in high relief.	As 370. ۱۷
372	„	1204 19	As 367. ۱۲۰۴ W. 168. S. ·9.	In double circle on flowered field دیرہ ضرب ۱۹ M. 25. Pl. VI. 1.

Metal No.	Mint	Date	Obverse	Reverse
AV 373 B.M.	رکاب Rikāb	1191 5	As 361. ۱۱۹۱ **W.** 168. **S.** ·75.	In double circle ضرب ب رکا ٥ M. 2. Pl. V. 15.
374 I.M.	کابل Kābul *Dāru-s-saltanat.*	1186 1	Couplet in three lines. **W.** 168. **S.** ·85.	In double circle as 343. ۱۱۸۶
375 B.M.	,,	1189 3	As 352 but no و between ماه and خور. ۱۱۸۹ **W.** 168. **S.** ·9.	In double circle السلطنة میمنت جلوس مانوس کابل ب ۳ ضر دار سنه Pl. VI. 2.
376	,,	1190 4	As 375. ۱۱۹۰ **W.** 168. **S.** 1.	As 343. ۴
377 B.M.	,,	1192 6	,, ۱۱۹۲	As 376. ٦
378	,,	1194 8	,, ۱۱۹۴ **W.** 165. **S.** ·9. Broad piece.	,, ۸
379	,,	— 11	,,	,, ۱۱
380 B.M.	,,	12-- 13	,, **W.** 165. **S.** 1·1. Broad piece.	,, ۱۳

Metal No.	Mint	Date	Obverse	Reverse
AV				
381	كابل Kābul *Dāru-s-salṭanat*	1204 18	As 356; ۱۲۰۴ l. of second line.	In double circle كابل دار السلطنة ب ضر ۱۸
382 I.M.	„	1209 21	As 356; date ۱۲۰۹ to r. over middle line. **W.** 170. **S.** ·9.	كابل دار السلطنة ب ضر ۲۱
383	كشمير Kashmīr *Dāru-s-salṭanat*	— 12	Normal couplet in three lines. **W.** 167. **S.** ·9.	In triple circle كشمير ۱۲ دار السلطنة ميمنت جلوس مانوس ضرب Pl. VI. 4.
384	Kashmīr	1203 15	Couplet in three lines; زند in place of كند. Date ۱۲۰۳ (ringed). **W.** 184. **S.** 1·0.	As 212. ۱۵ Pl. VI. 3.
385 I.M.	ملتان Multān *Dāru-l-amān*	1203 9	Couplet arranged in four lines. ۱۲۰۳ **W.** 168. **S.** ·8.	As 46. ۹ M. 20. Pl. VI. 5.
386	„	1203 10	As 385. ۱۲۰۳ **W.** 168.	As 385. ۱۰

Metal No.	Mint	Date	Obverse	Reverse
AV 387	هرات Hirāt	1192	In double circle چهرهٔ نقش تیمور شاه سکه از خورشید و ماه تا کند بر م چرخ ارد طلا و نقره **W.** 168. **S.** ·85. Characteristic style.	In triple circle ۱۱۹۲ ت مانوس هرا میمنت ضر جلوس ب
388	"	1194	As 387, but بر in top line. **W.** 167.	Slightly different from 387. ۱۱۹۴ Pl. VI. 7.
389 B.M.	"	1195	As 387. **W.** 167.	As 387. ۱۱۹۵
390 I.M.	Hirāt *Dāru-s-salṯanat*	1200	Couplet in three lines. **W.** 168. **S.** ·75.	In double circle هرا ت ۱۲۰۰ دار السلطنة میمنت جلوس مانوس ضرب
391 B.M.	"	1203	In circle از خور و ماه شید چرخ می ارد و نقره طلا برچهرهٔ نقش تیمور شاه سکه تا کند **W.** 168. **S.** ·85.	د ر ت هـر ا ا السلطنة ب ضر ۱۲۰۳

Metal No.	Mint	Date	Obverse	Reverse
AV 392	Hirāt *Dāru-s-salṭanat*	1205 1206	As 391; date ١٢٠٥ l. last line.	As 391; date ١٢٠٦.
393 I.M.	,,	1207	As 391; ١٢٠٧ l. last line. W. 167. S. ·8.	ضر ب هـــرا ا ١٢٠٧ السلطنة ت د ر
Æ 394	اتك Atak	1186 1	As 351. ١١٨٦	As 351. احد
395 B.M.	,,	1187 2	,, ١١٨٧	,, ٢
396	,,	1188 2	,, ١١٨٨	,, ٢
397	,,	1188 ۴ *sic*	,, ١١٨٨	,, ۴
398	,,	1192 ۴ *sic*	,, ١١٩٢	,, ۴
399 I.M.	,,	1193 8	,, ١١٩٣	,, ٨
400	,,	1196 10	,, ١١٩٦	,, ١٠
401 B.M.	,,	1197 11	,, ١١٩٧	,, ١١
402 I.M.	,,	1197 12	,, ١١٩٧	,, ١٢
403	,,	1198 12	,, ١١٩٨	,, ١٢
404	,,	— 14	,,	,, ١۴

Metal No.	Mint	Date	Obverse	Reverse
AR 404 A Bah.	اتك Atak	— 16	As 351.	As 351. ١٦
405	احمد شاهی Aḥmad Shāhī *Ashrafu-l-bilād*	1187 2	As 352. ١١٨٧ **W.** 175. **S.** ·85.	In circle on dotted field احمد شا میمنت نو ٢ جلوس ماس هی سنه ب ضر اشرف البلاد Pl. VI. 8.
406	,,	1187 3	,, ١١٨٧	As 405. ٣
407	,,	—	As 353, but date off coin. **W.** 176. **S.** ·95.	In triple circle as 353.
408	,,	1189	As 352; date ١١٨٩ under third line. **W.** 176.	As 354: date off coin.
409 B.M.	,,	1191	As 353. **W.** 175.	As 352; ١١٩١ l. third line.
410 B.M.	,,	1192	As 352. ١١٩٢	As 352.
411 B.M.	,,	1193 —	As 391; ١١٩٣ l. last line. **W.** 176. **S.** ·95.	,, Pl. VI. 9.
412	,,	1193 21 *sic*	As 354. ١١٩٣	As 354. ٢١

Metal No.	Mint	Date	Obverse	Reverse
AR 413	احمد شاهی Aḥmad Shāhī *Ashrafu-l-bilād*	1194 9	Couplet in four lines; date ۱۱۹۴ l. last line. **W.** 175.	As 354. ۹
414	„	1195 —	As 408, but تا is at beginning of third line. ۱۱۹۵	„ Date off coin.
415	„	1197 12	As 354. ۱۱۹۷ **W.** 177.	As 354. ۱۲
416 B.M.	„	— 12	As 352; date off coin.	As 352. ۱۲
417 I.M.	„	1198	As 352; date off coin. **W.** 176.	As 354; date ۱۱۹۸ over سنه.
418	„	1198 1199	As 352. ۱۱۹۹ **W.** 178.	As 354; ۱۱۹۸ over سنه.
419 B.M.	„	1204 —	As 356.	As 356. ۱۲۰۴
420 B.M.	„	1205 —	„	„ ۱۲۰۵
421	„	1205 19	„ **W.** 177. **S.** ·95.	As 357. ۱۲۰۵ ۱۹
422	„	1206 20	„ **W.** 177.	„ ۱۲۰۶ ۲۰

Metal No.	Mint	Date	Obverse	Reverse
Æ 423	احمد شاهی Aḥmad Shāhī *Ashrafu-l-bilād*	1207 **21** (writ-ten **12**)	As 356. **W.** 177.	شاه حمد ا ا د ف ١٢٠٧ البلا ب ضر شر ١٢
424 B.M.	"	1207 **21** (writ-ten **12**)	"	As 357. ١٢٠٧ ١٢ Pl. VI. 10.
425 I.M.	ام البلاد *Ummu-l-bilād* (Balkh)	1195	As 361. **W.** 171. **S.** ·85.	مانوس ميمنت ١١٩٥ جلوس سنه ضرب ام البلاد
426 B.M.	"	1198	"	" (١١٩)٨ Pl. VI. 11.
427 B.M.	بهکهر Bhakhar	1186	In small foliated area تيمور شا سکه ٤ Remainder of couplet filling margin, beginning at twelve o'clock and reading outwards. **W.** 177·5. **S.** ·9.	Bounded by triple foliation on dotted field جلوس ميمنت مانوس بهکهر ب ضر ١١٨٦ Pl. VI. 12.
428	"	1186	As 427.	As 427; date differently arranged.

Metal No.	Mint	Date	Obverse	Reverse
AR **429** I.M.	بهکهر Bhakhar	1187	As 427.	مانوس میمنت جلوس ١١٨٧ بهکهر ضرب
430 B.M.	„	1187	As 361.	In triple circle بهکهر ١١ ضرب ٨٧ At top of coin outside area M. 26.
431	„	1188	As 427.	As 429. ١١٨٨
432	„	1189	„	„ ١١٨٩ M. 29. Pl. VI. 13.
433	„	1189	„	In foliated area مانوس میمنت جلوس بهکهر ١١ ٨٩ ضرب
434	„	1189	As 361, but M. 27 below word نقش.	In triple circle بهکهر ١١٨٩ ضرب
435	„	1190	Couplet in four lines; in loop of ش of نقش M. 28.	As 434. ١١٩٠
436	„	1191	As 427.	As 429. ١١٩١

Metal No.	Mint	Date	Obverse	Reverse
Æ 437	بهکهر Bhakhar	1192	As 427.	As 429. ۱۱۹۲
438	,,	1193	In triple circle, couplet in four lines. W. 177.	In elaborate circular border as 434; date ۱۱۹۳ and M. 27 above mint name.
439	,,	1195	As 438.	As 438. ۱۱۹۵
440	,,	1195	As 427.	In triple circle جلوس میمنت مانوس بهکهر ۱۱۹۵ ضرب
441	,,	1195	In small foliated area شاه تیمور Rest of couplet round it beginning at twelve o'clock and reading outwards.	In foliated area within triple circle as 429. ۱۱۹۵ Pl. VI. 14.
442	,,	1196	As 438.	As 434. ۱۱۹۶ Pl. VI. 16.
443	,,	1196	As 441.	As 441; ۱۱۹۶ l. mint name.
444	,,	1196	As 441, but superior style.	As 443.
445	,,	1196	As 441.	As 441, but date ۱۱۹۶ above ب of ضرب; in three places of field M. 30.

Metal No.	Mint	Date	Obverse	Reverse
Æ 446	بهکهر Bhakhar	1197	As 438.	As 434. ۱۱۹۷
447	„	1197	As 441.	As 445. M. 31.
448 B.M.	„	1197	„	As 445 with same marks. ۱۱۹۷
449	„	1197	As 427. **W.** 172. **S.** ·8.	In foliated area surrounded by broad margin as 429. ۱۱۹۷ Pl. VI. 15.
450	„	1198	As 438.	As 438. ۱۱۹۸
451	„	1198	As 441.	As 445. ۱۱۹۸
452	„	1198	As 441.	In triple circle مانوس میمنت جلوس ۹۸ بهکهر ۱۱ سنه ضرب M. 32 in three places.
453	„	1199	„	As 452. ۱۱۹۹
454 I.M.	„	1200	„	„ but ۱۲۰۰ to l. of mint name.
455 I.M.	„	1200	As 438.	As 438. ۱۲۰۰

Metal No.	Mint	Date	Obverse	Reverse
Æ 456	بهکهر Bhakhar	1201	As 441.	As 454. ١٢٠١
457	„	1202	„	„ ١٢٠٢
458 I.M.	„	1202	As 438.	As 438. ١٢٠٢
459 I.M.	„	1203	As 441.	As 454. ١٢٠٣
460	„	1204	„	In triple circle as 429. ١٢٠٤
461 I.M.	„	1206	„ **W.** 176. **S.** ·9.	As 429, but ١٢٠٦ under ضرب.
462	Bakhar	—	As 360, but words چهره and نقره interchanged. **W.** 176.	As 360, but date off coin.
463 B.M.	„	— 19	As 360. **W.** 177. **S.** ·85.	As 360. ١٩
464 B.M.	Bhakhar	1207	As 441. **W.** 175. **S.** ·9.	As 461. ١٢٠٧
465	„	1172 *sic*	„ **W.** 176.	As 441; date ١١٧٢ over ب of ضرب.
466	پشاور Pashāwar	1186 1	As 361. ١١٨٦ **W.** 175. **S.** ·85.	As 361. احد M. 2. Pl. VII. 1.

Metal No.	Mint	Date	Obverse	Reverse
Æ 467	پشاور Pashāwar	1187 1	As 361. ۱۱۸۷	As 361. أحد
468	"	1187 2	" ۱۱۸۷	" ۲
469	"	1188 2	" ۱۱۸۸	" ۲
470	"	1188 3	" ۱۱۸۸	" ۳
471	"	1189 4	" ۱۱۸۹	" ۴
472	"	1190 5	" ۱۱۹۰	" ۵
473	"	1194 8	" ۱۱۹۴	" ۸
474	"	1195 9	" ۱۱۹۵	" ۹
475	"	1196 10	" ۱۱۹۶	" ۱۰
476	"	1196 11	" ۱۱۹۶	" ۱۱
477	"	1197 10	" ۱۱۹۷	" ۱۰
478	"	1197 11	" ۱۱۹۷	" ۱۱
479	"	1197 12	" ۱۱۹۷	" ۱۲
480	"	1198 12	" ۱۱۹۸	" ۱۲
481 B.M.	"	1199 12	" ۱۱۹۹	" ۱۲

Metal No.	Mint	Date	Obverse	Reverse
Æ 482	پشاور Pashāwar	1199 13	As 361. ۱۱۹۹	As 361. ۱۳
483	,,	1200 13	,, ۱۲۰۰	,, ۱۳
484 I.M.	,,	1201 15	,, ۱۲۰۱	,, ۱۵
485	,,	1203 17	,, ۱۲۰۳	,, ۱۷
486	,,	— 18	As 356. **W.** 177. **S.** ·9.	In flowing style as 367. ۱۸
487 B.M.	,,	— 19	As 356.	As 369, but date under نو ۱۹
488	,,	1206 20	,, ۱۲۰۶ l. of second line. **W.** 178.	As 487. ۲۰ Pl. VII. 2.
489	,,	1207 20	As 488. ۱۲۰۷	,, ۲۰
490 B.M.	تتہ Tatta	—	Fragment of usual couplet in large characters; date off coin. **W.** 177. **S.** ·75.	مانوس میمنت سنہ جلوس ب ضر تتہ
491 I.M.	,,	120– —	As 490; date ۱۲۰– r. top line. **W.** 182.	As 490; regnal date illegible.

Metal No.	Mint	Date	Obverse	Reverse
Æ **492**	حیدراباد Ḥaidar-ābād *Khujista bunyād*	—	Couplet in three lines. **W.** 174. **S.** ·8.	In circle surrounded by broad margin بنیاد خجسته ب ضر حیدراباد Pl. VII. 3.
493 B.M.	Ḥaidar-ābād Sind	—	In foliated area تیمور شاه سکه Rest of couplet around area reading outwards. **W.** 117. **S.** ·75.	مانوس میمنت سنه جلوس سند ب اباد ضر حیدر Pl. VII. 10.
494 B.M.	دیره Dera	1186 **1**	در دران شاه ۱۱۸۶ تیمور شاه باد کـــــــ سکه مبار **W.** 177. **S.** ·8.	In triple circle احد سنه ب ضر دیره M. 13. Pl. VII. 4.
495 B.M.	"	1186 **1**	In circle سکه تیمور شاه نقش ماه تا کند بر چهره نقره از خورشید و طلا و چرخ می ارد ۱۱۸۶ **W.** 177. **S.** ·8.	In double circle as 494. M. 11. Pl. VII. 5.
496	"	— **1**	Couplet in four lines.	As 495.
497	"	1188 **2**	As 496. ۱۱۸۸	" ۲

Metal No.	Mint	Date	Obverse	Reverse
Æ 498 B.M.	دیره Dera	1188 3	As 496. ۱۱۸۸	As 495. ۳
499	,,	1189 3	As 496. ۱۱۸۹	,, ۳
500	,,	1190 4	As 371. ۱۱۹۰	,, ۴
501	,,	1191 5	,, ۱۱۹۱	,, ۵
502	,,	1192 6	,, ۱۱۹۲	,, ۶
503	,,	1193 7	,, ۱۱۹۳	,, ۷
504	,,	1194 8	,, ۱۱۹۴	,, ۸
505	,,	1195 9	,, ۱۱۹۵	,, ۹
506	,,	1196 10	,, ۱۱۹۶	,, ۱۰
507 I.M.	,,	1197 11	,, ۱۱۹۷	,, ۱۱
508	,,	1198 12	,, ۱۱۹۸	,, ۱۲
509	,,	1199 13	,, ۱۱۹۹	,, ۱۳
510	,,	1200 14	,, ۱۲۰۰	,, ۱۴
511	,,	1200 15	,, ۱۲۰۰ written ۱۲:	,, ۱۵
512	,,	1201 16	,, ۱۲۰۱	,, ۱۶

Metal No.	Mint	Date	Obverse	Reverse
Æ 513	ديره Dera	1202 17	As 371. ١٢٠٢ **W.** 175. **S.** ·8.	As 495. ١٧ In high relief.
514	"	1203 18	" ١٢٠٣ **W.** 176.	" ١٨
515	"	1204 19	" ١٢٠۴	" ١٩
516	"	1204 19	In double circle as 372. **W.** 177. **S.** ·9.	In double circle as 372.
517	"	1205 20	" ١٢٠٥	" ٢٠
518	"	1206 21	" ١٢٠٦	" ٢١
519	"	1207 21	" ١٢٠٧	" ٢١
520	"	1207	Part of couplet in large characters. **W.** 173. **S.** ·85.	In double circle ١٢٠٧ ضرب ديره No mark. Pl. VII. 6.
521 B.M.	ديرجات Derajāt	1192 8	As 371; date ١١٩٢ beneath word نقش **W.** 170. **S.** ·8.	٨ سنه ب ضر ت ديرجا

Metal No.	Mint	Date	Obverse	Reverse
Æ 522	Derahjāt	1194	As 356. **W.** 170. **S.** ·9.	In double circular margin ornamented with dots and rays سنه ت دیرہ جا ب ضر ۱۱۹۴
523 B.M.	Derajāt	1196 10	Couplet in four lines; date ۱۱۹۶ over second line. **W.** 171. **S.** ·85.	In double circle ۱۰ سنه ت دیرجا ضرب M. 33. Pl. VII. 7.
524	Derahjāt	1197	As 356.	As 522. ۱۱۹۷
525 I.M.	Derajāt	1197 11	As 371. ۱۱۹۷ **W.** 170. **S.** ·85.	In double circle with rays and dots ۱۱ سنه ت ب ضر دیرجا M. 34 to l. of top line.
526	"	1198 12	" ۱۱۹۸	As 525. ۱۲
527	Derahjāt	12	As 356.	As 522; ۱۲ l. last line.
528 I.M.	Derajāt	1199 13	As 371. ۱۱۹۹	As 525. ۱۳

Metal No.	Mint	Date	Obverse	Reverse
Æ 529	Derajāt	1199 15	As 371. ١١٩٩	As 525. ١٥ M. 35.
530	"	1200 15	" ١٢٠٠	" ١٥ M. 36.
531	"	1201 16	" ١٢٠١	" ١٦
532 B.M.	"	1202 17	" ١٢٠٢ W. 170.	" ١٧
533	"	1202 18	" ١٢٠٢	" ١٨
534	"	1203 18	" ١٢٠٣	" ١٨
535 I.M.	"	1204 18	" ١٢٠٤	" ١٨
536	Derahjāt	— 18	As 356. W. 171. S. 1.	As 522, but date ١٨.
537	"	1205 19	" Date ١٢٠٥ under middle line.	As 536. ١٩ Pl. VII. 12
538	"	1206 19	As 537. ١٢٠٦	" ١٩
539 I.M.	"	1206 19	" but date ١٢٠٦ l. last line.	" ١٩

Metal No.	Mint	Date	Obverse	Reverse
Æ **540** I.M.	Derahjāt	1206 **20**	As 537. ۱۲۰۶	As 536. ۲۰ M. 37 l. top line.
541	„	1207 **20**	As 537, but date ۱۲۰۷ above middle line.	As 540 ; no mark. ۲۰
542	„	1207 **22**	As 541. ۱۲۰۷ **W**. 170.	As 536. ۲۲ M. 38 l. middle line.
543 I.M.	„	1207	As 536.	As 522. ۱۲۰۷
544 I.M.	„	1208	„ **W**. 168.	„ ۱۲۰۸
545 B.M.	رکاب Rikāb *Mubārak*	— **11**	می آرد چرخ طلا و از خورشید و ماه نقره تا کند بر تیمور شاه - - - - - - - **W**. 176. **S**. 1.	رکا مبارک ب ضرب جلوس میمنت مانوس ۱۱ سنه Pl. VII. 11.
546	Rikāb	—	Couplet in four lines. **W**. 177. **S**. ·9. Also B.M. and I.M.	In circle surrounded by broad margin رکا ب ضرب Pl. VII. 13.

Metal No.	Mint	Date	Obverse	Reverse
Æ 547	سند Sind	1198	As 493. **W.** 170·5. **S.** ·9.	In foliated area مانوس میمنت ۹۸ ۱۱ جلوس سنه ب ضر سند Pl. VII. 9.
548	„	—	„ **W.** 121. **S.** ·8.	As 547 but no date.
549 B.M.	„	1240	„ **W.** 168. **S.** ·8.	مانوس میمنت جلوس ۱۲۴۰ ضرب سند
550 B.M.	„	1242	„ **W.** 171. **S.** ·75.	As 549; date ۱۲۴۲. Pl. VII. 8.
551 B.M.	„	1255	„ **W.** 121. **S.** ·8.	As 547. ۱۲۵۵
552 B.M.	„	1257	„ **W.** 120. **S.** ·75.	As 547; ۵۷ under س of مانوس and ۱۲ in loop of س of جلوس.
553	کابل Kābul *Dāru-s-salṭanat*	1186 1	Couplet in three lines. **W.** 177. **S.** ·85.	As 343. ۱۱۸۶ احد
554	„	1187 1	„	„ ۱۱۸۷ احد

Metal No.	Mint	Date	Obverse	Reverse
Æ 555	كابل Kābul *Dāru-s-salṭanat*	1187 2	As 553.	As 343. ۱۱۸۷ ۲
556	„	1188 2	„	„ ۱۱۸۸ ۲
557	„	1188 3	„	„ ۱۱۸۸ ۳
558	„	1189 3	„ **W.** 178.	„ ۱۱۸۹ ۳
559	„	1189 3	As 352. ۱۱۸۹ **W.** 173. **S.** ·9.	As 375. ۳
560	„	1189 3	As 352. ۱۱۸۹	As 343. ۳
561	„	1190 4	„ ۱۱۹۰	„ ۴
562	„	1191 4	„ ۱۱۹۱	„ ۴
563	„	1191 5	„ ۱۱۹۱ **W.** 176. **S.** ·95.	„ ۵
564	„	1191 5	Couplet in four lines. ۱۱۹۱	„ ۵
565	„	1192 6	As 352. ۱۱۹۲	As 343. ۶

Metal No.	Mint	Date	Obverse	Reverse
Æ 566	كابل Kābul *Dāru-s-salṭanat*	1193 7	As 352. ١١٩٣	As 343. ٧
567	,,	1194 8	,, ١١٩٤	,, ٨
568	,,	1195 9	,, ١١٩٥	,, ٩
569	,,	1197 11	,, ١١٩٧	,, ١١
570	,,	— 12	,, Date off coin.	,, ١٢
571 I.M.	,,	1200 13	,, ١٢٠٠	,, ١٣
572 B.M.	,,	1201	In large coarse lettering; couplet in four lines. **W.** 171. **S.** ·85.	As obverse كابل دار السلطنة ب ضر ١٢٠١ Under بل M. 39.
573	,,	— 15	As 352; date off coin.	As 343. ١٥
574	,,	— 16	,,	,, ١٦
575	,,	1203 17	,, ١٢٠٣ **W.** 178.	,, ١٧
576 B.M.	,,	1204 —	,, ١٢٠٤	,, Date off coin.

Metal No.	Mint	Date	Obverse	Reverse
Æ 577	كابل Kābul *Dāru-s-salṭanat*	1204 18	As 356; date ۱۲۰۴ l. middle line. **W**. 180. **S**. 1·0.	As 572. ۱۸
578	„	1204 18	As 577 but date ۱۲۰۴ above middle line.	As 577. ۱۸
579	„	1204 19	As 578. ۱۲۰۴	„ ۱۹
580	„	1205 19	As 577. ۱۲۰۵	„ ۱۹
581 B.M.	„	— 19	As 578 but broad coin; date off flan. **W**. 179. **S**. 1·35.	„ ۱۹
582 B.M.	„	1206 20	As 578; a fine broad coin. ۱۲۰۶ **W**. 178·5. **S**. 1·25.	„ ۲۰
583	„	1206 20	As 578. ۱۲۰۶ **W**. 178.	„ ۲۰
584 B.M.	„	1207 21	„ ۱۲۰۷ **W**. 176.	„ ۲۱
585	„	1207 21	As 356 but ۱۲۰۷ under word نقش. **W**. 177. **S**. ·95.	„ ۲۱

Metal No.	Mint	Date	Obverse	Reverse
Æ 586 B.M.	کشمیر Kashmīr	1187 1	In triple circle نقش سکهٔ تیمور شاه ۱۱۸۷ چهـــــــرهٔ از خورشید و ماه تا زند بر نقـــــــرهٔ چرخ می آرد طلا و **W.** 170. **S.** 1·0.	On dotted field مانوس میمنت احد سنهٔ جلوس کشمیـــــر ضرب
587 B.M.	„	— 5	As 586; date off coin.	As 586. ۵
588 Srī.	„	— 6	„ Srīnagar Museum.	„ ۶
589	„	1195 8	„ ۱۱۹۵	„ ۸
590 B.M.	„	1195 8	„ ۱۱۹۵ Counterstruck with the word صحیح.	„ ۸
591 Edin.	„	1198 6	„ ۱۱۹۸ Cp. 205.	„ ۶
592 Edin.	„	1198 7	„ ۱۱۹۸	„ ۷
593 B.M.	„	119– 9	سکهٔ تیمور شاه نقـــــش و ماه تا زند بر چهرهٔ شـــــــید نقرهٔ از خور مـ ۱۱ ۹– چرخ آرد طلا و **W.** 169. **S.** ·95. A specimen at Edinburgh has date 1196.	مانوس میمنت ۹ سنهٔ جلوس ب ضر کشمیر

Metal No.	Mint	Date	Obverse	Reverse
Æ 594	کشمیر Kashmīr	1197 10	As 384; date ١١٩٧ l. middle line.	مانوس میمنت س سنه ١٠ جلو کشمیر ضرب
595 B.M.	"	1198 10	As 594. ١١٩٨	As 594. ١٠
596	"	1198 —	" ١١٩٨	" but date uncertain.
597 B.M.	"	1198 11	As 594 but counter-struck with word صحیح. ١١٩٨	As 594. ١١
598 B.M.	"	1199 12	As 594. ١١٩٩ **W.** 168. **S.** ·9.	مانوس میمنت ١٢ سنه جلوس ب ضر کشمیر Pl. VII. 14.
599 B.M.	"	1200 12	" ١٢٠٠	As 598. ١٢
600 B.M.	"	1200 13	" ١٢٠٠ **W.** 168.	As 586. ١٣
601 B.M.	"	1201 13	" ١٢٠١ **W.** 167.	" ١٣
602	"	1201 14	" ١٢٠١ **W.** 169.	" ١۴

Metal No.	Mint	Date	Obverse	Reverse
Æ 603	کشمیر Kashmīr	1202 15	As 594. ۱۲۰۲	As 586. ۱۵ Pl. VII. 16.
604	"	1204 16	" ۱۲۰۴	" ۱٦
605 B.M.	"	1204 17	" ۱۲۰۴ W. 167.	" ۱۷
606 B.M.	"	1205 17	" ۱۲۰۵	" ۱۷
607[1] B.M.	"	1206 19	" ۱۲۰٦	" ۱۹
608 B.M.	"	1207 19	" ۱۲۰۷ W. 167.	" ۱۹
609	"	1208 20	" ۱۲۰۸ W. 168.	" ۲۰
610	ملتان Multān *Dāru-l-amān*	1194 3	Couplet in four lines. ۱۱۹۴ W. 176. S. ·85.	As 46. ۳ M. 40.
611	"	1194 3	Much as 610. Date ۱۱۹۴ under word سکہ. W. 178.	As 610. ۳
612	"	1195 4	As 611. ۱۱۹۵ W. 178.	" ۴

[1] Date 18 in Kashmīr Museum.

Metal No.	Mint	Date	Obverse	Reverse
Æ 613 B.M.	ملتان Multān *Dāru-l-amān*	— 5	As 611 ; date illegible.	As 610. ٥
614	„	1197 5	Couplet in four lines. ١١٩٧ **W.** 176.	„ ٥
615	„	1198 5	As 614. ١١٩٨	„ ٥
616	„	1198 6	„ ١١٩٨	„ ٦
617	„	1198 7	„ ١١٩٨	„ ٧
618	„	1199 7	„ ١١٩٩	„ ٧
619	„	1200 7	„ ١٢٠٠	„ ٧
620 I.M.	„	1201 7	„ ١٢٠١	, ٧
621	„	1203 9	„ ١٢٠٣	„ ٩
622	„	1203 10	„ ١٢٠٣	„ ١٠
623	„	1204 10	„ ١٢٠٤ **W.** 177.	„ ١٠
624	„	1204 18	As 356 ; date ١٢٠٤ under middle line. Fine broad coin. **W.** 180. **S.** 1·0.	In foliated area on dotted field دار الامان ب ضر ملتان ١٨ Pl. VII. 17.

Metal No.	Mint	Date	Obverse	Reverse
Æ 625	ملتان Multān *Dāru-l-amān*	1205 18	As 624 but not so well struck. ١٢٠٥ W. 178. S. ·85.	As 624. ١٨
626	„	1205 19	„ ١٢٠٥	„ ١٩
627	„	1206 19	„ ١٢٠٦	„ ١٩
628	„	1207 20	„ ١٢٠٧ W. 178. S. ·8.	„ ٢٠
629 B.M. I.M.	هرات Hirāt	1184	As 387 ; date ١١٨٤ below word نقش. Distinctive style. W. 176. S. ·9.	In triple circle on dotted field ت نوس هرا میمنت جلوس ضرب ما of مانوس is missing.
630	„	1184	As 629.	In triple circle on dotted field هر ت نوس ا میمنت جلوس ضرب ما of مانوس is missing.
631 I.M.	„	1187	As 629 but date ١١٨٧. W. 176.	As 630.
632 B.M.	„	1187	As 629. ١١٨٧ W. 176. S. ·85.	In circle ١١٨٧ ت مانوس هرا میمنت ضرب جلوس

Metal No.	Mint	Date	Obverse	Reverse
Æ 633 B.M.	Hirāt *Dāru-s-salṭanat*	1188	As 629. ١١٨٨ **W.** 176. **S.** ·85.	In circle هرات لسلطنة دار ضرب In margin an arabesque at each of the four cardinal points; elsewhere three marks or letters. Pl. VII. 15.
634	Hirāt	1188	As 629. **W.** 177.	As 632 but date ١١٨٨, and ما of مانوس missing.
635 B.M.	„	1188	Couplet in three lines.	As 634.
636 I.M.	„	1189	Couplet something like 495. **W.** 176.	In triple circle ١١٨٩ ت مانوس هرا ميمنت ضر جلوس ب
637	„	1189	Couplet in three lines.	As 636. ١١٨٩
638 B.M.	„	1189	As 610 but no date. **W.** 172.	„ ١١٨٩
639	„	1190	As 636 but date off coin.	„ ١١٩٠
640 I.M.	„	1191	As 636 but no date visible.	„ ١١٩١

Metal No.	Mint	Date	Obverse	Reverse
AR 641 I.M.	Hirāt	1192	Couplet in three lines. W. 176.	As 636. ١١٩٢
642	„	1192	Couplet in four lines. W. 176.	„ ١١٩٢
643	„	1193	As 642. ١١٩٣ W. 177. S. ·85.	„ ١١٩٣
644 I.M.	„	1194	As 387.	In quadruple circle ١١٩٤ ت نوس هرا ميمنت ضر جلوس ما ب
645	„	1195	Couplet in three lines. W. 175·5.	As 636. ١١٩٥
646	„	1194 1196	As 645; date ١١٩٦ over middle line. W. 176. Also in B.M.	„ ١١٩٤
646 A Bah.	„	1197	As 645.	„ ١١٩٧
647	„	1197	Couplet in three lines. W. 175.	In triple circle ضرب جلوس ١١٩٧ ميمنت مانوس هرات Pl. VII. 18.

Metal No.	Mint	Date	Obverse	Reverse
Æ **648**	Hirāt	1198	As 647; no date visible.	As 636. ۱۱۹۸
649	Hirāt *Dāru-s-saltanat*	1200	چرخ می ارد طـــــلا و نقره از خور و ماه بر چهره شـــــیـــــد تا نقش سکهٔ تیمور شاه کـــــنـــــد **W.** 177. **S.** ·85.	In triple circle هرا ت ۱۲۰۰ دار السلطنة میمنت جلوس مانوس ضرب
650	”	1201	چرخ می ارد طـــــلا و نقره از خور تیمور شاه شـــــیـــــد و ماه تا کند بر نقش سکهٔ چهره	ت دار السلطنة هرا ۱۲۰۱ میمنت جلوس مانوس ضرب
651	”	1202	As 650. **W.** 176.	As 650 but date at top of coin.
652	”	1203	” **W.** 177. **S.** ·85.	As 651. ۱۲۰۳ Pl. VII. 19.
653	”	1204	”	” ۱۲۰۴
654	”	1204	As 356; date ۱۲۰۴ over middle line. **W.** 178. **S.** ·95.	On dotted field د ر ت هر ا ا السلطنة ب ضر ۱۲۰۴

Metal No.	Mint	Date	Obverse	Reverse
Æ 655 B.M.	Hirāt *Dāru-s-salṭanat*	1205	As 654. ١٢٠٥	As 654. ١٢٠٥
656	„	1205	As 391. **W**. 178. **S**. 1·0.	On dotted field د ر ت هر ا ا السلطنة ب ضر ١٢٠٥ Pl. VII. 20.
657	„	1206	As 656. ١٢٠٦	As 656. ١٢٠٦
658	„	1207	„ ١٢٠٧ **W**. 178.	„ ١٢٠٧
659 B.M.	„	1207	As 656 but word تا at end of second line. **W**. 179.	On dotted field ضر ب هر ١٢٠٧ السلطنة ا ا ت د ر Pl. VIII. 1.
660	„	1208	As 656. ١٢٠٨ **W**. 178.	As 659. ١٢٠٨
661 I.M.	„	1208	„ ١٢٠٨ **W**. 178.	On dotted field د ر هر ت ا ١٢٠٨ ا السلطنة ب ضر

Metal No.	Mint	Date	Obverse	Reverse
Æ **662**	Hirāt *Dāru-s-saltanat*	1209	As 656. ١٢٠٩	As 659. ١٢٠٩
663 B.M.	,,	1209	,, ١٢٠٩ Also in I.M.	As 661 but date ١٢٠٩ in small figures over ت of هرات; over س of سلطنة M. 41.
664	,,	1210	,, ١٢١٠	As 659. ١٢٠١ [*sic*]
665	,,	1211	,, but date ١٢١١ under third line.	,, ١٢١١
666 I.M.	,,	1211	As 656. ١٢١١	,, ١٢١١
667 I.M.	,,	1211	,, **W.** 14. **S.** ·5. A small piece.	As 656. ١٢١١
668 I.M.	,,	1214 1200	,, but date ١٢٠٠ over third line.	As 659. ١٢١٤
669	,,	1216 1200	,, but date ١٢٠٠ over third line.	,, ١٢١٦
670	,,	1216	As 656; date ١٢١٦ plainly visible.	,, ١٢١٦
671	,,	1221?	As 649.	In circle surrounded by empty margin هرا ت دار السلطنة ١٠٢١ ضرب Over س of سلطنة M. 42.

Metal No.	Mint	Date	Obverse	Reverse
AR 672	Hirāt *Dāru-s-salṭanat*	?	As 650. **W.** 177. **S.** ·85.	As 650, but date blundered and is written ۱۳۲.
Æ 673	بلخ Balkh	1202	In circle تیمور ه شا فلوس **W.** 140. **S.** ·9.	In circle ۱۲۰۲ بلخ ضرب
674	"	1205	As 673. **W.** 107.	As 673. ۱۲۰۵
675 B.M.	"	1206	" **W.** 162. **S.** ·9.	" ۱۲۰۶ Pl. VIII. 2.
676	"	—	In circle تیمور شاه - - - - سکه **W.** 173. **S.** ·9. Much rubbed.	In star surrounded by circle بلخ ضرب
677 B.M.	بهکهر Bhakhar	— 8	In triple circle تیمور شا هم فلوس **W.** 247. **S.** ·95.	In triple circle بهکهر ۸ ضرب
678 B.M.	"	— 9	As 677. **W.** 192. Much rubbed.	As 677, but at top of field ۹.

Metal No.	Mint	Date	Obverse	Reverse
Æ 678 A R.B.	بکهر Bakhar	1194	On flowered field تیمور شاه فلوس **W.** 200. **S.** ·9. Collection of Sir Richard Burn.	In triple circle on flowered field بکهر ب ضر ۱۱۹۴
679 B.M.	Bhakhar	1198	As 677. **W.** 249. **S.** ·95. Dates 1192 and 1196 given in Leggett Catalogue.	In triple circle بهکهر ۱۱۹۸ ضرب Pl. VIII. 3.
680 P.T.	پشاور Pashāwar	1186 1	تیمور شاه بادشاه غاز سکه مبار ۱۱۸۶ **W.** 194. **S.** ·9. Collection of P. Thorburn.	فلوس ضرب پشاور احد
681 B.M.	,,	11-- 4	As 680 with ۱۱-- r. top line. **W.** 172.	As 680. ۴ M. 43. Pl. VIII. 4.
682 B.M.	,,	— 8	As 680. **W.** 176.	,, ۸
683 B.M.	,,	—	,, **W.** 158.	In ornamental margin as 680.
684	,,	—	,, **W.** 124.	Eight-leaved star surrounded by the legend reading inwards فلوس ضرب پشاور Pl. VIII. 8.

Metal No.	Mint	Date	Obverse	Reverse
Æ 685	پشاور Pashāwar	—	As 680. W. 121.	Seven-foil area with seven-lobed star in centre, surrounded by legend reading outwards فلوس ضرب پشاور
686	„	—	„ W. 170.	Much as 685 but legend reads inwards.
687	„	—	„ W. 115 (rubbed).	Quatrefoil with legend as 686.
688 B.M.	ديره Dera	1199	تيمور - - - - شاه در درانى ١١٩٩ - - - - - W. 175. S. ·9.	ديره ضرب جلوس مبارك
689 B.M.	„	—	در دران شـــــاه تيمور شاه باد كـــــ سكه مبار W. 187. S. ·9.	As 688.
690 B.M.	„	— –6	در درانى تيمور شاه باد شـــــاه فلوس W. 184. S. ·9.	ديره ضرب جلوس مبارك ٦ – Pl. VIII. 7.
691	كشمير Kashmīr	118–1	تيمور انى شاه در سكه فلوس Date ١١٨ – under تيمور. W. 270. S. ·85.	احد سنه كشمير ضرب

Metal No.	Mint	Date	Obverse	Reverse
Æ 692 B.M.	کشمیر Kashmīr	119- *sic* 1	As 691 but ۱۱۹-. **W.** 256. **S.** ·85.	As 691. احد
693 B.M.	"	— 9	" **W.** 293. **S.** ·9.	" ۹ Pl. VIII. 6.
694 B.M.	"	1195 —	" ۱۱۹۵ **W.** 266.	"
695 B.M.	"	1197 —	" ۱۱۹۷ **W.** 243.	"
696 B.M.	"	1200 —	In triple circle ۱۲۰۰ تیمور شاه درانی سکهٔ فلوس **W.** 291. **S.** ·85.	سنه کشمیر ضرب
697	"	1201 13	As 696. ۱۲۰۱ **W.** 287. Date 12. W.K. 2852.	۱۳ سنه کشمیر ب ضر Pl. VIII. 5.
698	"	1201 13	" ۱۲۰۱ **W.** 267.	As 697.
699 B.M.	"	1201 14	As 696. ۱۲۰۱ **W.** 245.	" ۱۴

Metal No.	Mint	Date	Obverse	Reverse
Æ 700 B.M.	کشمیر Kashmīr	1201 15	As. 696. ۱۲۰۱ **W.** 214; rubbed.	As 697. ۱۵
701	„	1202 15	„ ۱۲۰۲ **W.** 270.	„ ۱۵
702 B.M.	ملتان Multān	1181 *sic*	تیمور شاه بادشاه در درا نی فلوس ۱۱۸۱ **W.** 211. **S.** ·95.	ملتان ضرب جلوس مبارک Pl. VIII. 10.
703	„	1194 3	As 702. ۱۱۹۴ **W.** 165; rubbed. **S.** ·85.	As 702; date ۳ l. of مبارک.
704	„	1196 —	در درا نی تیمور شاه باد شـــــاه فلوس ۱۱۹۶ **W.** 180. **S.** ·85.	As 702.
705	„	1197 6	As 704. ۱۱۹۷ **W.** 180.	„ ۶
706	„	1200 7 *sic*	„ ۱۲۰۰ **W.** 195. **S.** ·9.	„ ۷
707 B.M.	„	1201 10	„ ۱۲۰۱ **W.** 175.	„ ۱۰

Metal No.	Mint	Date	Obverse	Reverse
Æ 708 B.M.	ملتان Multān	1201 —	As 704. ١٢٠١ **W.** 180.	As 702.
709 B.M.	,,	1202 10	,, ١٢٠٢ **W.** 185. Another dated 1204 in Cabinet of the late Mr. R. Sutcliffe.	,, ١٠
710 B.M.	,,	1205 19	در درا نی ١٢٠٥ تیمور شاه باد شـــــاه **W.** 185. **S.** ·85.	ملتان ضرب فلوس ١٩
711 L.D.	,,	1205 —	As 710 but date ١٢٠٥ at bottom of coin. **W.** 184. Longworth Dames Cabinet.	As 710.
712 B.M.	,,	1205 19	در درا نی تیمور بادشـــاه ١٢٠٥ شـــاه **W.** 179.	,, ١٩ Pl. VIII. 9.
713 B.M.	,,	1206 20	As 712. ١٢٠٦ **W.** 178.	,, ٢٠
714 B.M.	,,	1207 19 *sic*	,, ١٢٠٧ **W.** 185.	,, ١٩

HUMĀYŪN

(At Qandahār)

A.H. 1207. A.D. 1793.

Metal No.	Mint	Date	Obverse	Reverse
AV 715 Bah.	احمد شاهی Ahmad Shāhī *Ashrafu-l-bilād*	1207	As 716. **W.** 167. **S.** ·8.	As 716. Pl. VIII. 11.
			The couplet is on these lines:— سیم زر در جهان شد روشنتر از خورشید و ماه تاکه بر او ـ ـ ـ ـ ـ نقش نام همایون بادشاه 'Silver and gold in the world became brighter than the sun and moon So long as on it ... the pattern of the name of the emperor Humāyūn.'	
AR 716	احمد شاهی Ahmad Shāhī *Ashrafu-l-bilād*	1207	On dotted field تر از خورشید و ماه تا که ـــــــــد یو شاه بر او نقش نام هما ن باد شـــــــــن سیم زر در س رو جهان ١٢٠٧ **W.** 177. **S.** 1.	In double circle on dotted field شاهی ف د البلا حمد اا ١٢٠٧ ب ضر شر Pl. VIII. 12.

III

SHĀH ZAMĀN

A.H. 1207–1216. A.D. 1793–1801.

Metal No.	Mint	Date	Obverse	Reverse
AV 717	احمد شاهی Aḥmad Shāhī *Ashrafu-l-bilād*	1209 2	یافت بحکم خدای قـرار لت بنام شاه زمان سـکـه هر دو جهان رواج دو **W.** 168. **S.** ·9. The couplet (Z 1) is:— قرار یافت بحکم خدای هر دو جهان رواج سکه دولت بنام شاه زمان 'Obtained permanency by command of the Lord of both Worlds, Current coin of the realm through the name of Shāh Zamān.'	On dotted field as 716; date ۱۲۰۹.
718 I.M.	,,	1215 7 *sic*	As 717, with couplet Z 1. **W.** 167. **S.** ·85.	In circle شاهـ حمد ا ا د فـ البلا ۱۲۱۵ ب ضر شر ۷ In four marginal compartments, beginning at six o'clock, reading from the outside, couplet Z 2. Cp. silver coin illustrated at Pl. IX. 5.

Metal No.	Mint	Date	Obverse	Reverse
AV 718 I.M. (*cont.*)	احمد شاهی Aḥmad Shāhī *Ashrafu-l-bilād*	1215 7 *sic*	The second couplet (Z 2) is :— سکه زد بر سیم و زر بحکم الهی زمان شاه یمین و یساری 'Struck coin on silver and gold by the Divine command, Zamān Shāh, right hand and left hand (of the State).'	
719 B.M.	,,	1215 8	As 717. **W.** 168. **S.** ·75.	As 718. ١٢١٥ ٨
720 Bah.	بکهر Bakhar	— 2	Couplet Z 1.	بکهر میمنت ب ضر جلوس مانوس ٢
721	پشاور Pashāwar	— 2	Couplet Z 1. **W.** 168. **S.** ·95.	As 369. ٢
722	,,	— 3	As 721. **W.** 168. **S.** ·85.	,, ٣
723	,,	1215 8	Couplet Z 1 in circular area surrounded by marginal couplet Z 2, beginning at three o'clock and reading outward; date ١٢١٥ l. of middle line. **W.** 168. **S.** ·85.	As 369; date ٨ on edge of field at nine o'clock.
724 I.M.	دیرة Dera	1208 1	Couplet Z 1; date ١٢٠٨ over last line to l. **W.** 169. **S.** ·75.	In double circle حد سنة ١ ب ضر دیرة M. 11.

Metal No.	Mint	Date	Obverse	Reverse
AV				
725 B.M.	ديره Dera	1208 **2**	As 724. ١٢٠٨	As 724. ٢
726	,,	1210 **3**	,, ١٢١٠ **W.** 168. **S.** ·75.	,, ٣
727 B.M.	ديره‌جات Derahjāt	1211 **2** *sic*	Couplet Z 1 arranged thus خدای هر دو جهان سکه لت شاه زمان رواج دو بنام ١٢١١ بحکم قرار یافت **W.** 167. **S.** 1·0.	In circle with rays and dots ٢ سنه ت ديره جا ب ضر M. 44. Pl. VIII. 13.
728	قندهار Qandahār	1211 **5**	Couplet Z 1; ١٢١١ under first line. **W.** 161. **S.** ·9.	On dotted field مانوس میمنت ٥ ب قندهار ضر سنه جلوس Pl. IX. 1.
729 B.M.	کابل Kābul *Dāru-s-salṭanat*	1208 **1**	On dotted field couplet Z 1; date ١٢٠٨ below top line. Fine broad coin; also in I.M. **W.** 168. **S.** 1·1.	In triple circle on floral field کابل دار السلطنة ب ضر احد Pl. VIII. 14.

Metal No.	Mint	Date	Obverse	Reverse
AV 730	کابل Kābul *Dāru-s-salṭanat*	1209 2	As 729, but not so broad. ۱۲۰۹ **W.** 166. **S.** ·8.	As 729. ۲
731	,,	1209 3	As 730.	,, ۳
732 I.M.	,,	1211 4	As 729. ۱۲۱۱ **W.** 168. **S.** 1·15.	,, ۴
733 I.M.	,,	12-- 5	Couplet Z 2 arranged thus -- ۱۲ بحکم الہ سکہ زد بر سیم و زر م زمان شاہ یمین و یسار **W.** 170. **S.** 1·0.	,, ۵
734	,,	1213 6	۱۲۱۳ بحکم الہ زمان شاہ یمین و یسار م سکہ زد بر سیم و زر **W.** 168. **S.** ·85.	,, ۶
735	لاہور Lāhor *Dāru-s-salṭanat*	1211 4	Couplet Z 1; date ۱۲۱۱ above last line. **W.** 169. **S.** ·8.	In triple circle ر هو دار لا السلطنة ب ۴ ضر سنة

Metal No.	Mint	Date	Obverse	Reverse
AV 736	لاهور Lāhor *Dāru-s-salṭanat*	— 4	As 735 but date off coin. **W.** 168.	As 735. Pl. IX. 3.
737 Bah.	ملتان Multān *Dāru-l-amān*	1210 1 *sic*	Couplet Z 1; date ١٢١٠ above فت of یاقت in top line.	ملتان ضرب احد دار الامان
738 B.M.	هرات Hirāt *Dāru-s-salṭanat*	1212	Couplet Z 2 as on 847, but date ١٢١٢ to l. of top line. **W.** 168. **S.** ·75.	In triple circle on dotted field ضر ب هرا ١٢١٢ السلطنة ۱ ت د ر Pl. IX. 2.
739 Bah.	„	1214	As 738. ١٢١٤	As 738. ١٢١٤
AR 740	احمد شاهی Aḥmad Shāhī *Ashrafu-l-bilād*	1207	As 717 but date ١٢٠٧ to l. of last line, and و of دولت in middle line. **W.** 178. **S.** ·95.	As 716. Pl. IX. 4.
741 I.M.	„	1207	As 740 but no date on obverse.	As 740 but date ١٢٠٧ to l. of last line.
742 I.M.	„	1208	As 740.	As 741. ١٢٠٨
743	„	1208	„	As 716. ١٢٠٨
744	„	1209 2	„ **W.** 178. **S.** 1·0.	„ ١٢٠٩ Also ٢ to l. of last line.

Metal No.	Mint	Date	Obverse	Reverse
AR **745**	احمد شاهی Aḥmad S͟hāhī *As͟hrafu-l-bilād*	1211 4	As 740. **W.** 177. **S.** ·9.	As 716. ١٢١١ ٤ to l. of last line.
746	„	1212 —	„ **W.** 178. **S.** ·9.	„ ١٢١٢ Regnal date off the coin.
747	„	1212 5	Couplet Z 2; to r. of top line ١٢١٢. **W.** 178. **S.** ·9.	On dotted field as 716; date ٥ to l. of last line.
748	„	1212 5	As 747 but date ١٢١٢ below middle line. **W.** 178. **S.** ·95.	As 747.
749	„	1213 —	As 748. ١٢١٣	As 747 but date ١٢١٣; regnal date off coin.
750 I.M.	„	1213 5	As 747. ١٢١٣	As 716 but date ١٢١٢ *sic*; ٥ to l. of last line.
751 P.T.	„	7	In circular area couplet Z 1; around it couplet Z 2 beginning at six o'clock and reading from the outside. **W.** 346. **S.** 1·15. Double rupee; P. Thorburn.	In double circle as 716; date ٧. Illustrated in *Num. Chron.*, 1888, Pl. XIII. 9.
752	„	1214 7	As 717. **W.** 177.	As 718 but legend in field arranged as 717. ١٢١٤ ٧
753	„	1214 7	„ Also in B.M. **W.** 177. **S.** ·95.	As 752 but dates arranged thus in last line ٧ ضر ١٤ شر ١٢ Pl. IX. 5.

Metal No.	Mint	Date	Obverse	Reverse
Æ 754	احمد شاهی Aḥmad Shāhī *Ashrafu-l-bilād*	1214 8	As 717. W. 178.	As 718. ١٢١٤ ٨
755	,,	1214 8	,, W. 177.	As 718 but ١٢ over ب of ضرب and ١٤ over ب of بلاد. ٨
756 P.T.	,,	1214 8	,, **W.** 353. **S.** 1·1. Double rupee; P. Thorburn.	As 755. ١٢١٤ ٨
757	,,	1215	,,	As 718 but no regnal year. ١٢١٥
758	,,	1215 8	,, **W.** 178. **S.** ·85.	As 718 but Hijri date over ب of بلاد. ١٢١٥ ٨
759 B.M.	بهکهر Bhakhar	—	In foliated area زمان شاه Around it fragments of a couplet Z 3 which appears to be different from either of the usual two couplets Z 1 and Z 2. **W.** 177. **S.** ·85.	مانوس میمنت جلوس بهکهر ضرب
760 B.M.	Bakhar	1215?	On dotted field couplet Z 1. **W.** 177·3.	On dotted field بکهر میمنت ب ضر س س جلو ما نو Below last line what may be intended to be ١٢١٥.

Metal No.	Mint	Date	Obverse	Reverse
AR 761	بکهر Bakhar	?	As 760 but rude style. W. 178.	As 760; date, if any, cannot be read with certainty.
762 B.M.	پشاور Pashāwar	1208 1	یافت بحکم خدای ۱۲۰۸ قـــــرار دولت بنلم شاه زمان ســـــکه هر دو جهان رواج W. 178. S. ·9.	ضرب میمنت س س ور ما چلو نو پشا احد
763 I.M.	"	— 2	As 762. W. 178.	As 762. ۲
764	"	1211 3	" Date ۱۲۱۱ l. of last line. W. 178.	" ۳
765	"	1211 4	As 764. ۱۲۱۱ W. 178.	" ۴
766	"	1212 4	" ۱۲۱۲ W. 178.	" ۴
767	"	— 4	As 733. W. 178.	" ۴
768	"	1211 5	" ۱۲۱۱ W. 178.	" ۵ Pl. IX. 6.

Metal No.	Mint	Date	Obverse	Reverse
Æ 769	پشاور Pashāwar	1212 5	As 733. ١٢١٢ W. 177.	As 762. ٥
770	„	— 5	„ Date off coin.	„ ٥
771	„	1213 6	„ ١٢١٣ W. 178.	„ ٦
772	„	1213 6	„ ١٢١٣ W. 178.	„ Date ٦ l. of پشا of پشاور.
773	„	1213 6	„ ١٢١٣ W. 178. S. ·9.	„ Date ٦ l. of ور of پشاور.
774 B.M.	„	1215 8	„ ١٢١٥ W. 178.	As 773. ٨
775	„	1215 8	In circle couplet Z 1; surrounding it reading outwards and beginning at three o'clock couplet Z 2. Whole contained in double circle. Date ١٢١٥ l. of middle line of couplet Z 1. W. 178. S. ·95.	„ ٨
776	„	1215 8	As 775; good specimen. ١٢١٥ W. 176.	„ ٨

Metal No.	Mint	Date	Obverse	Reverse
Æ 777 I.M.	پشاور Pashāwar	1215 1216	As 775. ١٢١٥	As 773. Counterstruck with ١٢ رائج ١٦ in small lozenge.
778	"	1215 9	" ١٢١٥	As 773. ٩
779	"	1216 9	" ١٢١٦	" ٩
			W. 178. S. ·9.	
780 B.M.	ديره Dera	1208 1	خدای هر دو جهان سکه رواج بنام شاه زمان دولت بحکم قرار یافت Date ١٢٠٨ above ت of یافت. W. 178. S. ·85.	double circle احد سنه ب ضر ديره To l. of top line M. 13.
781	"	— 1	As 780 but date off coin.	As 780.
782 I.M.	"	1208 2	As 780. ١٢٠٨	" ٢
783	"	1210 3	" ١٢١٠	" ٣
784	"	1211 4	" ١٢١١	" ٤
			W. 178.	
785 B.M.	"	1213 5	" ١٢١٣	" ٥
			W. 177.	Pl. IX. 7.

Metal No.	Mint	Date	Obverse	Reverse
Æ 786 B.M.	ديره Dera	1214 6	As 780. ١٢١۴	As 780. ٦
787 B.M.	„	1215 7	„ ١٢١٥ W. 177.	„ ٧
788	„	1121 *sic* Possibly 1211	As 789. W. 172. S. ·75.	As 789. ١١٢١
789 B.M.	„	1215	Fragments of couplet Z 1 in different style from 780. Also in I.M. W. 173. S. ·75.	ديره ب ضر ١٢١٥ To l. of top line M. 9.
790	ديرهجات Derahjāt	1207	هر دو خدای جهان سـکـه لت شاه زمان رواج دو بنام بحـکم قرار يافت W. 170. S. ·9.	In circular ornamentation سنه ت ديره جا ب ضر ١٢٠٧
791 B.M.	„	— 1	As 790. W. 170.	As 790 but no Hijri year; to l. of top line احد.
792	„	1208	„ Date ١٢٠٨ l. of last line. W. 170.	As 790; date ١٢٠٧ *sic.*
793 I.M.	„	1208	„ Date off coin. W. 171.	As 790. ١٢٠٨

Metal No.	Mint	Date	Obverse	Reverse
Æ 794	دیرهجات Derahjāt	1209 2	As 790 but date thus ۹ بنام ۱۲۰ W. 170.	As 791. ۲ over word سنه.
795	,,	1210 2	As 794. ۱۲۱۰ W. 170.	As 794. ۲
796	,,	1210 2	As 790, but date thus بنام ۱۲۱۰ W. 170.	,, ۲
797	,,	1211 2	As 796. ۱۲۱۱ W. 170.	,, ۲
798	,,	1211 2	,, ۱۲۱۱ W. 170.	,, ۲ Also M. 45 l. of ه of دیرهجات.
799	دیرجات Derajāt[1]	1212 2	,, ۱۲۱۲ W. 170.	۲ سنه ت دیرجا ب ضر In middle line M. 46 and هو. Cp. *Num. Chron.*, 1888, Pl. XIII. 10.
800 I.M.	,,	1212 —	As 794, but ۱۲ under ج of رواج. W. 170.	As 799; date off coin.

[1] Mr. Longworth Dames has recorded Derajāt rupees dated 1212, 6 : 1213, 7 and 1215, 8.

Metal No.	Mint	Date	Obverse	Reverse
Æ 801 I.M.	ديرجات Derajāt	— 6	As 796, but date illegible. **W.** 170.	As 799. ٦
802	,,	1214 7	As 796. ١٢١٤	,, ٧
803 B.M.	,,	— 8	,, **W.** 169.	,, ٨
804	كابل Kābul *Dāru-s-saltanat*	1207 1	يافت بحكم خداى قرار دولت بنام شاه زمان سكه هر دو جهان رواج Date ١٢٠٧ under top line. **W.** 177. **S.** ·95.	كابل دار السلطنة ب ضر احد
805	,,	1208 1	As 804. ١٢٠٨ **W.** 178.	As 804. احد
806	,,	1208 2	,, ١٢٠٨ **W.** 178.	As 804, but ٢ سنه
807	,,	1209 2	,, ١٢٠٩ **W.** 177.	As 806. ٢
808	,,	1209 3	,, ١٢٠٩ **W.** 178.	,, ٣

Metal No.	Mint	Date	Obverse	Reverse
Æ 809	کابل Kābul *Dāru-s-salṭanat*	— 3	As 804. Top line off coin.	As 806. ٣
810	„	1210 4	„ ١٢١٠ **W.** 180.	„ ۴
811	„	1211 4	„ ١٢١١ **W.** 177. **S.** 1.	„ ۴
812 B.M.	„	1212 *sic* 4	In triple circle as 733. Very broad thin coin. Ringed. **W.** 180. **S.** 1·4.	In triple circle as 806. ۴
813 B.M.	„	— 5	As 804. Date off coin.	As 806. ٥
814	„	1211 5	As 733. ١٢١١ **W.** 178. **S.** ·95.	As 806. ٥
815 B.M.	„	121– —	As 734. Half rupee. **W.** 84. **S.** ·7.	„ Date rubbed.
816 B.M.	„	—	As 734; date off coin. Quarter rupee. **W.** 44. **S.** ·55.	As 806; date illegible.

Metal No.	Mint	Date	Obverse	Reverse
Æ 817	كابل Kābul *Dāru-s-salṭanat*	1212 5	On dotted field in elaborate circular border couplet Z 1, arranged as on 717. Around it, reading outwards and beginning at four o'clock, couplet Z 2; under the word سكه the date ۱۲۱۲. Double rupee. **W**. 354·5. **S**. 1·05.	On dotted field within elaborate border, as 806. ٥ Specimen illustrated is in Fitzwilliam Museum, Cambridge. Pl. IX. 14.
818 B.M.	,,	1212 6	As 817. ۱۲۱۲ Double rupee. **W**. 356.	As 817. ٦
819 B.M.	,,	1213 6	As 817, but date ۱۲۱۳ above word سكه. Double rupee. **W**. 359·5.	,, ٦
820	,,	1212 or 1213 6	As 734. ۱۲۱۲ (or ۳) **W**. 178.	As 806. ٦
821	,,	1213 7	,, ۱۲۱۳ **W**. 179.	,, ٧
822 B.M.	,,	1215 7	As 804. ۱۲۱٥ **W**. 178.	,, ٧
823	,,	1215 8	,, ۱۲۱٥ **W**. 177.	,, ٨

Metal No.	Mint	Date	Obverse	Reverse
Æ 824 B.M.	کابل Kābul *Dāru-s-salṭanat*	1258	On dotted field بحکم خدای قرار یافت بنام شاه زمان لت هر دو جهان رواج سکهٔ دو Date ۱۲۵۸ above middle line. **W.** 146. **S.** ·9. A posthumous coin struck by Zamān's full brother Shāh Shujā' in his third reign.	On dotted field ضرب دار کابل السلطنة Date ۱۲۵۸ written downwards ۱۲۵۸ کابل Cp. Pl. XIV. 16.
825 B.M.	کشمیر Kashmīr	1208 2	In triple circle on flowered field یافت بحکم خدای ۱۲۰۸ قــــــــرار دولت بنام شاه زمان ســـــــکه هر دو جهان رواج **W.** 170. **S.** ·9.	On flowered field in multifoil area surrounded by circle of dots مانوس میمنت ۲ سنه جلوس کشمیر ضرب Pl. IX. 8.
826 B.M.	"	1209 2	As 825. ۱۲۰۹ **W.** 167.	As 825. ۲
827	"	1209 3	" ۱۲۰۹ **W.** 165.	" ۳
828 B.M.	"	1210 3	" ۱۲۱۰ **W.** 168.	" ۳

Metal No.	Mint	Date	Obverse	Reverse
Æ 829 B.M.	كشمير Kashmīr	1211 4	As 825. ١٢١١ **W.** 168.	As 825. ۴
830 B.M.	,,	1211 5	,, ١٢١١ **W.** 166.	,, ٥
831 B.M.	,,	1212 5	,, ١٢١٢ **W.** 167.	,, ٥
831 A Sri.	Kashmīr *Khitta*	1211 5	,, ١٢١١ Kashmir Museum, Sri-nagar. **W.** 167.	كشمير ٥ سنه خطه ب ضر
832 B.M.	,,	1212 5	,, ١٢١٢ **W.** 167. **S.** ·9.	As 831 A. ٥ Pl. IX. 9. (rev.)
833 B.M.	,,	1213 6	,, ١٢١٣ ١٢ under top line, ١٣ over middle line.	,, ٦
834 B.M.	,,	1213 6	As 833. ١٢١٣ **W.** 172.	In central circular area ٦ ب ضر كشمير خطه Margin bounded by double circle.

Metal No.	Mint	Date	Obverse	Reverse
Æ 835 B.M.	كشمير Kashmīr *Khiṭṭa*	1213 7	As 833. ١٢١٣ W. 172.	As 834. ٧ Pl. IX. 9 (obv.) and Pl. IX. 10.
836 R.S.	"	1214 7	" ١٢١٤ For R.S. *see* 209.	" ٧
837 L.D.	Kashmīr	1214 7	" ١٢١٤ W. 173. S. ·9.	In central foliated area ٧ سنه كشمير ضرب Margin bounded by double circle.
838 B.M.	"	12-- 8	" ١٢-- Date 1215 on a specimen in the Kashmir Museum. W. 172.	As 837. ٨ Pl. IX. 11.
839	لاهور Lāhor *Dāru-s-salṭanat*	1211 4	As 825, but date ١٢١١ to l. of last line. W. 178. S. ·9.	As 735. ۴
840 B.M.	"	1213 6	On flowered field couplet Z 2 as on 734. A fine broad coin; good metal. W. 178. S. ·1.	On flowered field دار هـــور ١ لا لسلطنة ب ٦ ضر سنه Pl. IX. 12.

Metal No.	Mint	Date	Obverse	Reverse
Æ 841 B.M.	ملتان Multān *Dāru-l-amān*	1207 1	خدای هر دو جهان رواج یافت ۱۲۰۷ بحکم بنام شاه زمان لت طراز سکه دو **W.** 178. **S.** ·8.	In foliated lozenge surrounded by circle of dots ملتان ضرب دار الامان احد At top M. 40. Pl. IX. 13.
842	„	1207 1	As 841, but last line off coin. **W.** 178.	As 841.
843	„	1208 1	As 842. ۱۲۰۸ **W.** 178.	„ احد
844	„	1209 1 *sic*	„ ۱۲۰۹	„ احد
845	„	1210 1 *sic*	„ but date ۱۲۱۰ over ت of یافت. **W.** 178.	„ احد
846	„	1215 8	As 842. ۱۲۱۵	As 841, but no mark. ۸
847 I.M.	هرات Hirāt *Dāru-s-salṭanat*	1212	As 734, but ر of زر begins first line; ۱۲۱۲ under بحکم. **W.** 178. **S.** ·85. Half rupee. *Num. Zeit.*, Vienna, 1904, p. 101.	As 738. ۱۲۱۲
48 .M.	„	1212	As 734. **W.** 177. **S.** ·85.	„ ۱۲۱۲

Metal No.	Mint	Date	Obverse	Reverse
AR 849 I.M.	هرات Hirāt *Dāru-s-salṭanat*	1212	زر بحکم الهی زمان شاه یمین و یسار ١٢ ی سکه زد بر سیم و ١٢ W. 177.	„ ١٢١٢
850	„	1213	As 849. ١٢١٣ W. 177·5.	„ ١٢١٣
851	„	1213	As 849, but date ١٢١٣ over middle line. W. 177·5.	„ but date written ١٣١٢.
852 I.M.	„	1213	As 849, but ١٢ above word یمین and ١٣ below it. W. 177·5.	As 851. ١٣١٢
853	„	1214	As 849, but ١٢ below letter ا and ١۴ above س of یساری W. 177·5.	As 738. ١٢١۴
854 I.M.	„	1214	As 851. ١٢١۴ W. 176·5.	„ ١٢١۴
855	„	1215	„ ١٢١٥ W. 177.	„ ١٢١٥
856 B.M.	„	1215	„ ١٢١٥ W. 175.	As 654, but date ١٢١٥ above س of سلطنة.

Metal No.	Mint	Date	Obverse	Reverse
Æ 857 B.M.	بهکر Bhakkar	—	In dotted circle زمان شاه فلوس **W.** 227. **S.** ·95.	In central dotted circle surrounded by margin بهکر ضرب
858	دیره Dera	1209 **2**	در درا نی ۱۲۰۹ زمان شاه Also in B.M. M. 47. **W.** 153. **S.** ·85.	دیره ضرب فلوس ۲ Pl. IX. 15.
859 B.M.	کشمیر Kashmīr	1208 —	In triple circle ۱۲۰۸ زمان شاه درا نی سکه فلوس **W.** 267. **S.** ·9.	In triple circle — سنه کشمیر ب ضر
860	,,	1210 **3**	زمان شاه سکه فلوس ۱۲۱۰ Two B.M. specimens weigh 158 and 166 grains. **W.** 191. **S.** ·8.	As 859. ۳
861	,,	—	As 860, but date off coin. **W.** 143.	As 859, but date off coin.
862 B.M.	,,	1212 —	زمان شاه ۱۲۱۲ سکه فلوس **W.** 148. **S.** ·8.	— سنه کشمیر ب ضر Upright sword.

Metal No.	Mint	Date	Obverse	Reverse
Æ 863	کشمیر Kashmīr	1212 5	In eight-rayed star ۱۲ ة ۱۲ ز ن ما شا **W.** 110. **S.** ·85.	In dotted circle ٥ کشمیر ضرب
864	„	— 5	As 863 but rude style. **W.** 135.	As 863. ٥
865 B.M.	„	1212 5	As 863. **W.** 161. **S.** ·8.	„ ٥ Pl. IX. 16.
866 B.M.	„	1212 5	As 863 but date ۱۲۱۲ to r. **W.** 167. **S.** ·7.	„ ٥
867	„	1212 5	In circle ۱۲۱۲ شــــاه زمان **W.** 167. **S.** ·8.	As 863. ٥
868	„	1212 6	As 867. ۱۲۱۲ **W.** 164.	„ ٦ Pl. X. 1.
869	„	1213 6	As 867. ۱۲۱۳ **W.** 167. **S.** ·9.	As 863. ٦
870 B.M.	„	1214 7	In double circle ۱۲۱۴ هـ زمان شا **W.** 212. **S.** ·95.	In circle ٧ ضرب کشمیر

Metal No.	Mint	Date	Obverse	Reverse
Æ 871 B.M.	کشمیر Kashmīr	1214 7	As 870. ۱۲۱۴ **W.** 167. **S.** ·9.	As 870. ۷
872	„	1214 8	„ ۱۲۱۴ **W.** 168. **S.** ·9.	„ ۸
873 B.M.	„	1215 8	As 870. ۱۲۱۵ **W.** 170. **S.** ·9.	„ ۸ Pl. X. 2.
874	„	1215 —	„ ۱۲۱۵ **W.** 123.	„ Date off coin.
875	ملتان Multān	1208 1	در درا نی ۱۲۰۸ زمان شاه باد شاه **W.** 178. **S.** ·85.	ملتان ضرب فلوس احد
876 B.M.	„	1209 2	As 875 but ۱۲۰۹ under last line. **W.** 185. **S.** ·9.	As 875. ۲
876 A R.B.	„	1210 4	As 875. Cabinet of Sir Richard Burn. **W.** 181.	„ ۴
877 B.M.	„	1211 —	As 875 but date ۱۲۱۱ under زمان. **W.** 187.	„ Date illegible.

Metal No.	Mint	Date	Obverse	Reverse
Æ 878 B.M.	ملتان Multān	1211 4	As 875. ١٢١١ W. 178.	„ ۴
879 B.M.	„	1212 5	„ ١٢١٢ W. 185.	„ ٥
880	„	1215 8	„ ١٢١٥ W. 183. S. ·85.	„ ٨ M. 8. Pl. X. 3.

IV

SHUJĀ'U-L-MULK SHĀH

First reign A.H. 1216. A.D. 1801.

Maḥmūd Shāh defeated Shāh Zamān in the summer of A.D. 1801 and succeeded him at Kābul. Shāh Shujā', the full brother of Zamān, proclaimed himself at Pashāwar (p. xxvii) and advanced against the capital but was defeated in September 1801. No coins can at present be assigned with certainty to this brief reign at Pashāwar.

V

MAḤMŪD SHĀH

(At Hirāt)[1]

A.H. 1216–1245. A.D. 1801–1829.

Metal No.	Mint	Date	Obverse	Reverse
Æ 881	هرات Hirāt *Dāru-s-saltanat*	1216	In elaborate circular border بر زر زد بتوفيق اله سکه محمود شاه ن ستا خسرو گیتی **W.** 177. **S.** ·8.	In double circle ضر ب هر ا ا ۱۲۱۶ السلطنة ت د ر Pl. X. 16.
			The couplet is:— سکه بر زر زد بتوفیق اله خسرو گیتی ستان محمود شاه 'Struck coin on gold with the aid of God The world-conquering Cyrus, Maḥmūd Shāh.'	
882	"	1217	As 881.	As 881. ۱۲۱۷
883	"	1217 2	As 881 but date ۲ to l. of last line and ۱۲۱۷ written perpendicularly inwards l. of middle line.	" ۱۲۱۷
884	"	1218	As 881 but date ۱۲۱۸ under word محمود.	" ۱۲۱۸

[1] There is a gold coin in the British Museum with the Hirāt reverse of A.H. 1216, but the obverse bears the couplet of Taimūr Shāh.

Metal No.	Mint	Date	Obverse	Reverse
AR 885 I.M.	هرات Hirāt *Dāru-s-salṭanat*	1218 2	As 884. **W.** 177.	As 881, but addition of ٢ over ر of د.
886	„	1218	„ ١٢١٨ **W.** 177·3. **S.** ·8.	د ر ت هر ١١ ١٢١٨ السلطنة ب ضر
887 I.M.	„	1219	الله خسرو گیتی ستا محمود شاه ن ١٢١٩ سکه بر زر زد بتوفیق **W.** 178.	As 886. ١٢١٩ ٢ to l. of ضرب?
888 I.M.	„	1219	In elaborate circular border بتوفیق الله ه شـا و گیتی ستان محمود ١٢ ١٩ خسر سکه بر زر زد The position of the ه of شاه varies on some of the following specimens. **W.** 177. **S.** ·8.	As 886. ١٢١٩
889	„	1219	As 888. ١٢١٩ **W.** 175.	As 881. ١٢١٩

Metal No.	Mint	Date	Obverse	Reverse
Æ 890 B.M.	هرات Hirāt *Dāru-s-salṭanat*	1219	As 888, but date ۱۲۱۹ under word محمود.	As 881. ۱۲۱۹
891 I.M.	„	1219	As 888, but no date.	As 886. ۱۲۱۹
892	„	1220	As 888. ۱۲۲۰	„ ۱۲۲۰
893 I.M.	„	1220	As 888, but date ۱۲۲۰ under محمود.	„ ۱۲۲۰
894 I.M.	„	1220	As 891. **W.** 177.	„ ۱۲۲۰
895 I.M.	„	1220	„	As 881. ۱۲۲۰
896	„	1221	As 888, but date ۱۲۲۱ under r. of top line.	As 886. ۱۲۲۱
897 B.M.	„	1221	As 891.	„ ۱۲۲۱
898	„	1222	„ **W.** 177.	„ ۱۲۲۲
899	„	1223	„	„ ۱۲۲۳
900 I.M.	„	1223 5?	As 891, but date (?) ۵ under middle of second line.	„ ۱۲۲۳
901	„	1224	As 891. **W.** 176.	In triple circle ضر دار ب ۱۲ ۲۴ السلطنة ت هر ا

Metal No.	Mint	Date	Obverse	Reverse
Æ **902** I.M.	هرات Hirāt *Dāru-s-saltanat*	1224 5?	As 900. **W.** 177.	As 901. ١٢٢٤
903 I.M.	„	1225 5?	„	„ ١٢٢٥
904	„	1225	As 891.	„ ١٢٢٥
905 I.M.	„	1225	„	As 886. ١٢٢٥
906 I.M.	„	1226	„	As 881. ١٢٢٦
907 B.M.	„	1226	„	As 886. ١٢٢٦
908 I.M.	„	1227	As 888. ١٢٢٧	As 881. ١٢٢٧
909 B.M.	„	1227	As 891.	„ ١٢٢٧
910	„	1228	As 888. ١٢٢٨ **W.** 175.	„ ١٢٢٨
911 B.M.	„	1228	As 891.	„ ١٢٢٨
912	„	1229	„ **W.** 175.	„ ١٢٢٩
913 I.M.	„	1230	بتوفيق الله ستا وگيتی ن محمود شاه خسر سکه بر زر زد **W.** 177.	As 886. ١٢٣٠

Metal No.	Mint	Date	Obverse	Reverse
Æ 914 B.M.	هرات Hirāt *Dāru-s-salṭanat*	1230	As 913. W. 177.	As 886, but date ۱۲۳۰ over هر of هرات.
915 I.M.	"	1231	"	As 886. ۱۲۳۱
916 I.M.	"	1232	" W. 175.	" ۱۲۳۲
917 I.M.	"	1233	"	" ۱۲۳۳
918 I.M.	"	1234	"	" ۱۲۳۴
919 I.M.	"	1235	" W. 176. Also half rupee—P. Thorburn.	" ۱۲۳۵
920 I.M.	"	1236	" W. 180.	" ۱۲۳۶
921 I.M.	"	1237	"	" ۱۲۳۷
922 I.M.	"	1238	" W. 171.	" ۱۲۳۸
923[1] I.M.	"	1242	" W. 172.	" ۱۲۴۲
924 I.M.	"	1242	" Half rupee. W. 84. S. ·65.	" ۱۲۴۲

[1] Mr. P. Thorburn has a quarter rupee of A.H. 1241.

Metal No.	Mint	Date	Obverse	Reverse
AR 925 I.M.	هرات Hirāt *Dāru-s-salṭanat*	1242	As 913. Quarter rupee. **W.** 43. **S.** ·45.	As 886. ۱۲۴۲
926 I.M.	”	1243	” Half rupee. **W.** 79. **S.** ·73.	In circle ت هــــرا ۱۲۴۳ الســلطنة دار ضرب Pl. XI. 1.
927 I.M.	”	1243	” Half rupee.	As 926, but words يا هو interpolated above ت of هرات.
928	”	1254	As 888. **W.** 173. **S.** ·75.	As 901. ۱۲۵۴ The date may be intended for 1245, the year of Maḥmūd's death.

MAḤMŪD SHĀH

First reign A.H. 1216–1218. A.D. 1801–1803.

Metal No.	Mint	Date	Obverse	Reverse
AV 929 B.M.	احمد شاهی Aḥmad Shāhī *Ashrafu-l-bilād*	1218 3	In double circle بتوفيق الله شــــــاه و گيتی ستان محمود خســــــر سكه بر زر زد The couplet is the same as that on coin 881. **W.** 168. **S.** ·8.	In double circle شاهی د حمد ا ا ف ۱۲۱۸ البلا ب ضر شر ۳ In niche at top of coin يا محمود. Pl. X. 4

Metal No.	Mint	Date	Obverse	Reverse
AV 930 I.J.M.	احمد شاهی Aḥmad Shāhī *Ashrafu-l-bilād*	1218 3	As 929. In weight this coin is equivalent to the Persian *ashrafī*. For I.J.M. see p. vi. **W.** 54. **S.** 1·0.	As 929.
931 B.M.	بهاولپور Bahā-walpūr	1217 1	In dotted circle on flowered field زد بر زر بتوفيق الله سـکـه محمود شاه ۱۲۱۷ خسرو گيتی ستان Double mohur; an unmilled specimen of an issue normally milled. **W.** 341. **S.** 1·1.	In dotted circle on flowered field مانوس ميمنت ۱ سنه جلوس ضرب بهاولپور M. 48. Pl. X. 7.
932 B.M.	„	1217 1	As 931, but inferior in style and obliquely milled; ال instead of الله. ۱۲۱۷ Double mohur. **W.** 342. **S.** 1·1.	As 931.
933 Bab.	„	1217 2	As 932. ۱۲۱۷ Double mohur.	„ ۲
934 Bab.	„	1218 2	„ ۱۲۱۸ Double mohur.	„ ۲
935 Bab.	„	1218 2	„ ۱۲۱۸ **W.** 170. **S.** ·85.	„ ۲

Metal No.	Mint	Date	Obverse	Reverse
Æ 936 B.M.	احمد شاهی Aḥmad Shāhī *Ashrafu-l-bilād*	1216	اله خسرو گیتی / شاه ستان محمود ۱۲۱۶ سکه / زد بر زر بتوفیق **W.** 177. **S.** ·8.	As 716, but date ۱۲۱۶ l. last line. Pl. X. 5.
937 B.M.	„	1216	As 888. No date visible. **W.** 177.	As 936. ۱۲۱۶
938 I.M.	„	1217	As 937.	As 936, but date ۱۲۱۷ below r. of middle line.
939	„	1217 2	„ **W.** 178. **S.** ·85.	As 929. ۱۲۱۷ ۲
940	„	1218 3	„	„ ۱۲۱۸ ۳ Pl. X. 6.
941	„	1218 3	„ **W.** 176.	As 929, but یا عزیز instead of یا محمود. ۱۲۱۸ ۳
942	بهاولپور Bahāwalpūr *Dāru-s-surūr*	1217	Legend as 932; no milling. Date ۱۲۱۷ to l. of middle line. **W.** 177. **S.** ·8.	In double circle دار السرور ضرب بهاولپور M. 49. Pl. X. 8.
943	Bahāwalpūr	1217 1	As 932; oblique milling and date ۱۲۱۷. Double rupee. **W.** 356. **S.** 1·1.	As 931. ۱

Metal No.	Mint	Date	Obverse	Reverse
AR 944 I.M.	بهاولپور Bahā-walpūr	1217 1	As 943, but گیتے instead of گیتی. Double rupee; oblique milling.	As 931. ١
945 I.M.	„	1217 1	As 932; oblique milling. ١٢١٧ W. 177. S. ·1.	„ ١
946 B.M.	„	1217 1	As 944. W. 177.	„ ١
947 B.M.	„	1217 2	As 932. ١٢١٧ W. 178.	„ ٢
948	„	1218 2	As 932; oblique milling. W. 178. S. ·1.	„ ٢
949	بکهر Bakhar	—	زد بتوفیق الله سکه بر زر محمود شاه خسرو گیتی ستان W. 177.	بکهر میمنت ضرب س ما س جلو نو Pl. XII. 15.
950 B.M.	پشاور Pashāwar	1216 1	Legend as 929, but زد بر زر and خسرو; date ١٢١٦ to l. of last line. W. 177. S. ·9.	In circular border ضرب میمنت س س ور احد ما جلو نو پشا Pl: X. 9.

Metal No.	Mint	Date	Obverse	Reverse
Æ 951 B.M.	پشاور Pashāwar	1217 2	الہ محمود شاہ خســـــــرو بتوفیق گیتی ستان ســـــــکہ زد بر زر ۱۲۱۷ **W.** 178.	In circle پشاور ۲ سنہ ضرب Pl. X. 11.
952 B.M.	,,	1218 3	As 951. ۱۲۱۸ **W.** 177.	As 951. ۳
953	دیرہ Dera	1216 1	زد بر زر ســـــکہ بتوفیق الہ گیتی خســـــــرو ستان محمود شاہ ۱۲۱۶ **W.** 177. **S.** ·8.	In double circle احد سنہ ب ضر دیرہ To l. of top line M. 13. Pl. X. 10.
954 B.M.	,,	— 2	As 953. **W.** 178.	As 953. ۲
955	دیرہجات Derahjāt	1216 1	As 949; date ۱۲ under first line and ۱۶ over second line. **W.** 170. **S.** ·8.	In circle احد سنہ ت دیرہ جا ب ضر Pl. X. 12.
956	,,	1217 2	As 955, but date ۱۲۱۷ beneath second line. **W.** 170. Also 1218, 2 (*L. D.*).	As 955. ۲

Metal No.	Mint	Date	Obverse	Reverse
Æ **957**	کابل Kābul *Dāru-s-saltanat*	1216 1	On flowered field بتوفیق اله شـــــاه گیتی ستان محمود خســـــرو سکه زد بر زر ۱۲۱۶ **W.** 177. **S.** ·9.	In border on flowered field کابل دار السلطنة ب احد ضر سنه
958 B.M.	,,	1217 1	As 957. ۱۲۱۷ **W.** 176.	As 957. احد
959	,,	1217 2	As 957. ۱۲۱۷ **W.** 177.	As 957. ۲
960 B.M.	,,	1218 2	اله شاه محـــــمود بتوفیق گیتی ستان خســـــرو سکه زد بر زر ۱۲۱۸ **W.** 178.	As 957. ۲
961 I.M.	,,	1218 —	As 960. ۱۲۱۸ **W.** 177.	In circle ضرب دار کابل ا لسلطنة Date off the coin (probably at top).
962 B.M.	کشمیر Kashmīr	12-- 1	بتوفیق اله شـــــاه خسرو گیتی ستان محمود ۱۲-- ســـــــــکه بر زر زد **W.** 169. **S.** ·9.	In foliated central area, margin bounded by double circle احد سنه کشمیر ضرب

Metal No.	Mint	Date	Obverse	Reverse
Æ 963	كشمير Kashmīr	1217 **2**	As 962. ١٢١٧ **W.** 170.	As 962. ٢
964 B.M.	„	1217 **2**	In triple circle ١٧ محمود شاه ١٢ **W.** 39. **S.** ·6.	In foliated diamond ٢ كشمير ضرب Pl. X. 13.
965 B.M.	„	1218 3	As 962. ١٢١٨ **W.** 170.	As 962. ٣ B.M.
966 B.M.	Kashmīr *Khiṭṭa*	1218 3	„ ١٢١٨ **W.** 172. **S.** ·9.	In triple circle ٣ ستة كشمير خطه ضرب Pl. X. 14.
967	ملتان Multān *Dāru-l-amān*	1216 1	As 932, but date ١٢١٦. **W.** 178. **S.** ·85.	ملتان ضرب احد دار الأمان In ن of امان M. 8. Pl. X. 15.
968 I.J.M.	„	1218 1 *sic*	As 932, but ١٢١٨. For I.J.M. see p. vi.	As 967.

Metal No.	Mint	Date	Obverse	Reverse
Æ 969 B.M.	کشمیر Kashmīr	1216 1	In triple circle ۱۲۱۶ عازی محمود شاه **W.** 157. **S.** 1·0.	In triple circle احد سنه کشمیر ب ضر
970 B.M.	Kashmīr	— 2	Fragmentary as 969. **W.** 61. **S.** ·6.	In double circle ۲ سنه کشمیر ضرب
971 B.M.	„	1217 —	• ۱۲ شاه ۱۷ محمود **W.** 67. **S.** ·6.	سنه کشمیر ضرب
972 B.M.	„	1217 2	شاه محمود ۱۷ **W.** 59. **S.** ·6.	۲ سنه کشمیر ضرب Pl. XIII. 8.

SHUJĀ'U-L-MULK SHĀH

Second reign A.H. 1218–1224. A.D. 1803–1809.

Metal No.	Mint	Date	Obverse	Reverse
AV 973 B.M.	احمد شاهی Ahmad Shāhī *Ashrafu-l-bilād*	1220	In double circle چون مهر و ماه شــــاه دین پرور شجاع الملك شـــاه سکه زد بر سیم و زر **W.** 167. **S.** ·75.	In double circle with four mihrabs projecting into margin enclosed by outer dotted circle, like 929; date ١٢٢.. Pl. XI. 3.
974 B.M.	”	1222	In double circle and on dotted field as 973. Thin broad coin equivalent to the Persian *ashrafī*. Cp. 930. **W.** 47. **S.** 1·1.	In square with projecting mihrabs, all contained in outer double circle, as 973. ١٢٢٢

The couplet is:—

سکه زد بر سیم و زر چون مهر و ماه
شاه دین پرور شجاع الملك شاه

'Struck coin on silver and gold like the sun and moon,
The king, the fosterer of the Faith, Shujā'u-l-mulk Shāh.'

Metal No.	Mint	Date	Obverse	Reverse
975 B.M.	بهاولپور Bahā-walpūr	1218 1	In dotted circle on flowered field زد برسیم و زرچون مهر وماه سکه شجاع الملك شاه شـــاه دین پرور ١٢١٨ Double mohur; obliquely milled. **W.** 341. **S.** 1·0.	As on obverse مانوس میمنت احد سنه جلوس ضرب بهاولپور To r. of middle line M. 48. Pl. XI. 2.

Metal No.	Mint	Date	Obverse	Reverse
AV 976	بهاولپور Bahā-walpūr	12-- 1	As 975, but ہ of شاہ to l. of last line; ۱۲ to r. of middle line. Obliquely milled. W. 170. S. ·95.	As 975.
977	,,	12-- 1	As 976, but different die. W. 169.	,,
978 Bab.	ديره Dera	1218 1	Couplet much as n 975.	احد سنه ب ضر ديره To l. of top line M. 11.
979	رکاب Rikāb[1] *Mubārak*	1219	Couplet as on 973. W. 168. S. ·7.	In circle within margin contained by outer dotted circle, the margin occupied by eight mihrabs. ۱۲۱۹ ب مبارك رکا ضرب Pl. XI. 4.
980 B.M.	كابل Kābul *Dāru-s-salṭanat*	1223 —	As 1028. ۱۲۲۳ W. 169. S. ·85.	ضرب كابل دار السلطنة Pl. XI. 5.

[1] There is a close resemblance between coins Pl. XI. 4 and Pl. XI. 11; this Rikāb issue appears to have been struck in the Qandahār region.

Metal No.	Mint	Date	Obverse	Reverse
AV 981	ملتان Multān *Dāru-l-amān*	1218 1	Much as 975; date ۱۲۱۸. W. 171. S. ·8.	ملتان ضرب دار الامان احد In loop of ن of امان M. 8. Pl. XI. 6.
982 L.D.	„	1224 8	As 981. ۱۲۲۴ W. 171. S. ·7.	As 981. ۸
AR 983 B.M.	احمد شاهی Aḥmad Shāhī *Ashrafu-l-bilād*	1218	In double circle as 973. W. 177. S. ·9. This coin in style corresponds precisely with 940. It is a broad well-struck piece.	In double circle within margin bounded by dotted circle, as 973. ۱۲۱۸ Pl. XI. 8.
984	„	1218	As 983. W. 176.	As 983.
985 B.M.	„	1218	As 983. A beautiful quarter rupee. W. 44. S. ·55.	„ ۱۲۱۸ Pl. XI. 11.
986	„	— 2	As 983. W. 176. S. ·75.	„ Date ۲ l. last line.
987	„	1219	„ W. 177. S. ·8.	„ ۱۲۱۹

Metal No.	Mint	Date	Obverse	Reverse
Æ **988**	احمد شاهی Aḥmad Shāhī *Ashrafu-l-bilād*	1220	As 983. **W.** 177.	As 983. ۱۲۲۰
989 I.M.	„	1220	„ **W.** 177.	As 983, but legend enclosed in a square with mihrabs projecting from each side. ۱۲۲۰
990	„	1221	„ **W.** 176.	As 983, but foliated border inside circle. ۱۲۲۱
991	„	1222	In double circle الملك شاه ه مهر و ماه شجاع چون دین پرور شـــــــــــا سکه زد بر سیم و زر **W.** 177.	In foliation within dotted circle شاهی د حمد الـبـلا ۱۲۲ اا ۲ ف شر
992	„	1223	As 991. **W.** 177.	As 983. ۱۲۲۳
993	„	1224	„ **W.** 175. **S.** ·7.	„ ۱۲۲۴
994 B.M.	„	1224	„ **W.** 178. **S.** ·8.	In foliated lozenge شاهی البلاد أشر احمد ۱۲۲۴ ف ضرب Pl. XI. 9.

Metal No.	Mint	Date	Obverse	Reverse
Æ 995 B.M.	بکهر Bakhar	1218	زد چون مهر و ماه سـکه شجاع الملك شاه شـاه برسیم و زر دین پرور W. 178. S. ·9.	بکهر میمنت ب ضر س س جلو ۱۲۱۸ مانو Pl. XI. 10.
996	„	1219?	As 995, but inferior in style. W. 177.	As 995, but date ١١٩١ *sic* below س of مانوس.
997	„	—	As 996. W. 178.	As 996; date, if any, off coin.
998	بهاولپور Bahā-walpūr	1218 1	In dotted circle on flowered field زد برسیم از فضل خاص کردگار سـکه شاه شجاع نامدار خسـرو گیتی ستان ۱۲۱۸ Obliquely milled. Double rupee. W. 356. S. 1·1.	As on obverse. مانوس میمنت احد جلوس سنه ضرب بهاولپور To r. of middle line M. 48. Pl. XI. 7.

The couplet is:—

سکه زد برسیم از فضل خاص کردگار
خسرو گیتی ستان شاه شجاع نامدار

'Struck coin on silver through the special grace of the Creator,
The world-grasping Cyrus, the illustrious Shāh Shujā'.'

Metal No.	Mint	Date	Obverse	Reverse
Ꜳ 999 B.M.	بهاولپور Bahā-walpūr	1218 1	As 998. ۱۲۱۸ Obliquely milled. **W.** 177. **S.** ·95.	As 998. احد
1000	„	1218 2	„ ۱۲۱۸ Obliquely milled. **W.** 177. **S.** ·95.	„ ٢
1001 I.M.	„	1218 1	As 975. ۱۱۲۸ *sic* Obliquely milled. **W.** 178. **S.** ·95.	As 975. احد
1002 B.M.	„	1219 1	As 975; ۱۲ to r. of middle line and ۱۹ to r. of last line. Obliquely milled. **W.** 178. **S.** ·95.	„ احد
1003 B.M.	„	— 1	As 975, but M. 57 in loop of ن of دين. Not milled. **W.** 173. **S.** ·85.	„ احد
1004 I.M.	„	1222	As 1003; not milled. ۱۲ to r. of middle line. **W.** 174. **S.** ·85.	As 975, but ۱۲ to l. of last line and ۲۲ above سنه. Pl. XI. 12.
1005	„	1222	As 975, but ۱۲ to r. of last line and ۲۲ to r. of middle line. Not milled. **W.** 174. **S.** ·9.	As 975, but ۱۲۲۲ above سنه.

Metal No.	Mint	Date	Obverse	Reverse
Æ 1006 I.M.	بهاولپور Bahā- walpūr	1222	As 975; ١٢ to r. of middle line and ٢ to r. of last line. Not milled. **W.** 175. **S.** 1·0.	As 975, but ١٢٢٢ above سنه and no mark.
1007 I.M.	„	1212 *sic*	As 1003; not milled. **W.** 174. **S.** ·95.	As 975, but ١٢١٢ *sic* above سنه.
1008 B.M.	پشاور Pashāwar	1218 1	Couplet arranged as on 973; date ١٢١٨ to l. of middle line. **W.** 178. **S.** ·9.	In double circle نو ر س س و هيمنت جلو ما پشا ب احد ضر سنه Pl. XI. 15.
1009 B.M.	„	1218 1	As 1008. ١٢١٨ **W.** 178. **S.** ·9.	In double circle پشاور احد سنه ضرب Pl. XI. 16.
1010	„	— 1	As 1008, but date off coin. **W.** 178.	As 1009. احد
1011	„	1219 2	As 1008. ١٢١٩ **W.** 177. **S.** ·9.	As 1008. ٢

Metal No.	Mint	Date	Obverse	Reverse
Æ 1012	پشاور Pashāwar	1220 3	As 1008. ۱۲۲۰ **W.** 177. **S.** ·85.	In double circle س ور جلو پشا ب ۳ ضر سنه
1013 B.M.	,,	1221 4	,, ۱۲۲۱ **W.** 177. **S.** ·8.	As 1012. ۴
1014 B.M.	,,	— 6	As 1008; date off coin. **W.** 178. **S.** ·85.	,, ۶
1015 B.M.	دیره Dera	— 1	Parts of مهر و ماه couplet. **W.** 178. **S.** ·8.	In double circle احد سنه ب ضر دیره M. 11 to l. of top line. Pl. XII. 1.
1016	,,	— 4	As 1015. **W.** 178. **S.** ·85.	As 1015. ۴
1017	,,	— 5	,, **W.** 178. **S.** ·8.	,, ۵
1018	دیره جات Derahjāt	1218 1	دین پرور شـــاه شا ه شجا ۸ ع الملک ۱۲۱ زد سکه بر سیم و زر چون مهر و ماه **W.** 170. **S.** ·8.	احد سنه ت دیره جا ب ضر

Metal No.	Mint	Date	Obverse	Reverse
Æ 1019	دیرہجات Derahjāt	1218 2	As 1018. ۱۲۱۸ W. 170.	As 1018. ۲
1020 I.M.	„	1219 2	„ but ۱۹ in loop of ع. ۱۲۱۹ W. 169.	„ ۲
1021 I.M.	„	1220 2	„ but ۱۲۲۰ in small figures under middle line. W. 167.	„ ۲
1022	„	1220 3	As 1021. ۱۲۲۰ W. 169.	„ ۳
1023 B.M.	„	1221 4	„ ۱۲۲۱ W. 168. S. ·85.	„ ۴ Pl. XII. 3.
1024	„	1221 5	„ ۱۲۲۱ W. 169.	„ ٥
1025	„	12-- 5	„ ۱۲-- W. 169.	„ ٥
1026	„	— 6	„ Date off coin. W. 168.	„ ٦

Metal No.	Mint	Date	Obverse	Reverse
Æ 1027 B.M.	كابل Kābul *Dāru-s-saltanat*	— 1	On flowered field دين پرور شـــــاه ماه شجاع الملك شاه مهر و و زر چون ســــــم سكه زد بر Date off coin **W.** 178. **S.** ·8.	On flowered field ضرب كابل دار السلطنة سنه احد
1028 B.M.	,,	1219 2	As 1027, but to l. of چون the date سنه ۱۲۱۹. **W.** 178. **S.** ·8.	As 1027. ۲
1029 B.M.	كشمير Kashmīr *Khitta*	1218 1	In triple circle on dotted field شاه بحر و بر الملك حق بر سيم و زر شه شجاع ۱۲۱۸ فضـــــل سكه زد از **W.** 171. **S.** ·9.	As on obverse احد سنه كشمير خطه ضرب

The couplet is:—

سکه زد از فضل حق بر سیم و زر
شه شجاع الملك شاه بحر و بر

'Struck coin by the grace of the Truth on silver and gold,
The king of sea and land, Shah Shujā'u-l-mulk.'

Metal No.	Mint	Date	Obverse	Reverse
1030	,,	1219 2	As 1029, but date ۱۲۱۹ over middle line. **W.** 171.	As 1029. ۲ Pl. XII. 2.
1031 B.M.	,,	12-- 2	As 1029, but ۱۲ in loop of ل of فضل; rest of date off coin. **W.** 169.	,, ۲

Metal No.	Mint	Date	Obverse	Reverse
Æ 1032 B.M.	کشمیر Kashmīr *Khitta*	1220 3	As 1030. ۱۲۲۰ W. 170.	As 1029. ۳
1033	"	1221 4	As 1029, but ۱۲۲۱ to l. of last line. W. 170.	" ۴
1034	"	1222 5	As 1033. ۱۲۲۲ W. 170.	" ۵
1035 L.D.	"	1223 —	" ۱۲۲۳	"
1036	ملتان Multān *Dāru-l-amān*	1218 1	As 981. ۱۲۱۸ W. 178. S. ·8.	As 981. احد
1037	"	1219 —	" ۱۲۱۹ W. 177. S. ·8.	" Date off coin.
Æ 1038	بهکهر Bhakhar	—	In double circle شجاع الملك شـــــــاه فلوس Countermarked with word شجاع in small square. W. 214. S. ·95.	In circular border ۱۲-- بهکهر ضرب

Metal No.	Mint	Date	Obverse	Reverse
Æ 1039 B.M.	کشمیر Kashmīr	1218	الملك غازی ۱۸ شاه شجاع **W.** 113. **S.** ·7.	. . . . . سنه کشمیر . . . . .
1040 B.M.	„	1220 3	شاه الملك ۱۲۲۰ شجاع **W.** 114. **S.** ·65.	In double circle ۳ کشمیر ضرب
1041 B.M.	„	1220 3	As 1040, but broader and thinner. ۱۲۲۰ **W.** 95. **S.** ·8.	As 1040. ۳
1042 B.M.	„	—	الملك شاه فلوس شجاع This reading is tentative. **W.** 140. **S.** ·75.	. . . . . سنه  کشمیر ضرب
1043 B.M.	„	1220	In circle ۲۰ الملك شاه شجاع **W.** 124. **S.** ·75.	In triple circle, crossed swords. 
1044	„	1221 4	۱۲۲۱ ۴ الملك ع شجـــا شـــا **W.** 122. **S.** ·8. The date is sometimes written ۱۲۶۱.	۴ سنه 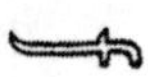 Pl. XII. 6.

Metal No.	Mint	Date	Obverse	Reverse
Æ 1045 B.M.	ملتان Multān	1224 5	در درا نی شجاع الملك شاه ۱۲۲۴ بادشاه W. 188. S. ·8.	ملتان ضرب فلوس ٥ Pl. XII. 7.
1046 B.M.			Copper coin hammered out so that original inscriptions are illegible. On one side overstruck in small square الملك شجاع W. 193.	Pl. XII. 5.
1047 B.M.			Copper coin, possibly of Jahāngīr, counterstruck on one side with الملك شجاع and illegible date in small square; on other side رائج in small circle. W. 221. S. ·9.	

SHUJĀ'U-L-MULK SHĀH

(At Pashāwar and Kashmīr)

A.H. 1227–1228. A.D. 1812–1813.

Metal No.	Mint	Date	Obverse	Reverse
Æ 1048 B.M.	پشاور Pashāwar	1227 1	On dotted field in circle within broad margin contained by dotted circle ۱۲۲۷ السلطان شجاع الملك شاه W. 177. S. ·9.	Within elaborate circular border س ور جلو پشا ب احد ضر سنة Pl. XI. 13.

Metal No.	Mint	Date	Obverse	Reverse
Æ 1049 B.M.	پشاور Pashāwar	1227 1	In dotted circle شاه ۱۲۲۷ شجاع الملك W. 14·5 (rubbed). S. ·45. See p. xxvii.	In dotted circle پشاور ب ضر احد Pl. XII. 4.
Æ 1050 B.M.	کشمیر Kashmīr	1228 1	۱۲۲۸ سنه فلوس W. 139. S. ·8.	احد سنه کشمیر ضرب
1051 B.M.	„	1228 1	۱۲۲۸ سنه فلوس W. 116. S. ·65. The attribution of these copper coins to Shāh Shujā' is tentative, pp. xxvii–xxviii.	احد The mint name is absent, but the coin can be attributed with certainty to Kashmīr. This piece is described and illustrated on pp. 242, 243 of W. H. Valentine's *Copper Coins of India*, Part 2.

SHUJĀ'U-L-MULK SHĀH

(At Pashāwar)

Probably in A.H. 1233. A.D. 1818.

Metal No.	Mint	Date	Obverse	Reverse
Æ 1052 B.M.	پشاور Pashāwar	— 1	In double circle on flowered field بر سیم و زر سکه شاه شجاع نامور شد . . . . . . W. 164. S. ·9.	In ornate octagon on flowered field ضرب س ور جلو پشا احد سنه Pl. XI. 14.

This is a unique coin with a new couplet. In the absence of a Hijri date, attribution is difficult; the piece in weight and reverse design corresponds with Shāh Maḥmūd's Pashāwar rupees of years 1230 to 1233. I believe the coin was struck when Shāh Shujā' entered Pashāwar in A.D. 1818—see page xxviii.

QAIṢAR SHĀH

(At Qandahār)

A.H. 1218. A.D. 1803.

Metal No.	Mint	Date	Obverse	Reverse
AV 1053 B.M.	احمد شاهی Aḥmad Shāhī *Ashrafu-l-bilād*	1218	In double circle on flowered field جهان الد بحـــكم رائج بنام قیصر شاه گشت سیم و زر در **W.** 168. **S.** ·75. The couplet is:— سیم و زر در جهان بحکم الہ گشت رائج بنام قیصر شاه 'Silver and gold in the world by God's command Became current in the name of Qaiṣar Shāh.'	In square with mihrabs, the whole contained in a double circle شا هـ د حمد ا ا ف ۱۸ ۱۲ البـلا ب ضر شر Pl. XII. 8.
AR 1054	„	1218	As 1053. **W.** 178. **S.** ·9.	As 1053. ۱۲۱۸ Pl. XII. 9.

QAIṢAR SHĀH

(At Kābul and Kashmīr)

A.H. 1222–1223. A.D. 1807–1808.

Metal No.	Mint	Date	Obverse	Reverse
1055 B.M.	کابل Kābul *Dāru-s-salṭanat*	1222 1	. . . . . . ـــــــد . . . سلطان قیصر . . . . ———— . . سکه . . . ۱۲۲۲ **W.** 180. **S.** ·9. Further material is required to elucidate the new couplet on this unique coin.	In double eight-sided foliation ضرب کابل ۱ دار لسلطنة احد سنه Pl. XII. 10.

Metal No.	Mint	Date	Obverse	Reverse
Æ 1056 B.M.	کشمیر Kashmīr *Khitta*	1222 1	On flowered field الله بفضل رائج بنام قیصر شاه ۱۲۲۲ گشت سکه زد در جهان **W.** 171. **S.** ·9.	In triple circle احد سنه کشمیر خطه ضرب Pl. XII. 11.

The couplet is :—

سکه زد در جهان بفضل الله
گشت رائج بنام قیصر شاه

'Coin struck in the world by the grace of God
Became current in the name of Qaiṣar Shāh.'

Metal No.	Mint	Date	Obverse	Reverse
1057 B.M.	,,	1223 2	As 1056. ۱۲۲۳ **W.** 171. **S.** ·9.	As 1056. ۲

MAḤMŪD SHĀH[1]

Second reign A.H. 1224–1233. A.D. 1809–1818.

Metal No.	Mint	Date	Obverse	Reverse
AV 1058[2] B.M.	احمد شاهی Aḥmad Shāhī *Ashrafu-l-bilād*	1224 ?	In double circle on dotted ground, couplet of first reign much as on 929. Probably Persian denomination. **W.** 37·5. **S.** 1·1.	On dotted ground in square with mihrabs as 1053. The coin is rubbed and the dates are uncertain.
1059 B.M.	بهاولپور Bahā-walpūr	1225 1	As 931, but different style; ۲۵ beneath middle line. **W.** 171. **S.** ·85.	As 931, but سنه احد. M. 48.

[1] Maḥmūd was driven out of Kābul by the Bārakzais in A.D. 1818, A.H. 1233. He ruled on sufferance at Hirāt till his death in 1245.

[2] This coin is noteworthy for its light weight. I attribute the piece to Maḥmūd's second reign because of its style. The framework of the reverse legend is that of Qaiṣar Shāh's Aḥmad Shāhī money, so the coin was probably struck after 1218.

Metal No.	Mint	Date	Obverse	Reverse
AV 1060[1] L.D.	کابل Kābul *Dāru-s-saltanat*	1224 2	Couplet as below. **W.** 169. **S.** ·9. The couplet is:— سکه دولت بزر و سیم فزود حسن دیگر سلطان محمود 'Made abundant coin of the realm on gold and silver The second Hasan, Sultān Mahmūd.'	٢ سنة ضرب دار السلطنة کابل
1061 B.M.	"	122– 8	In triple circle on flowered field, couplet as 1060. Date to r. under top line.	In *tughrā*, surrounded by triple border, as 1060. ٨ Pl. XII. 14.
AR 1062	احمدپور Ahmad-pūr	1217 *sic* 48	Couplet arranged as on 931; l. middle line ١٢١٧. **W.** 128. **S.** ·8.	مانوس میمنت ۴۸ سنة جلوس ب ضر احمدپور To r. of middle line M. 48.
1063 B.M.	"	12–– 48	As 1062, but ١٢ above middle line. **W.** 127.	As 1062.
1064	"	— 49	As 1062, but no Hijri date visible. **W.** 129.	" ۴۹

[1] I repeat the description, with modifications, from Coin 80 of Longworth Dames's monograph. I suggest that what was read by Mr. Dames and Mr. Rodgers as خسرو دیگر is حسن دیگر *vide* Appendix. Coin 13 of Mr. Dames's own Plate shows distinctly that the title is not خسرو دیگر. On all coins known to me the forms فزود and بزر are used, not افزود and بر زر as read by Mr. Dames.

Metal No.	Mint	Date	Obverse	Reverse
AR 1065 I.M.	احمدپور Aḥmad-pūr	12--	As 1063. **W**. 127.	As 1062 ; ١٢ to l. of ب. Pl. XII. 13.
1066	احمد شاهی Aḥmad Shāhī *Ashrafu-l-bilād*	1222	بتوفيق اله شــــــاه و گیتی ستان محمود خســـــــــــر سکه بر زر زد **W**. 177. **S**. ·8.	In foliated area شاه د حمد ا ا البلا ١٢٢٢ ف شر
1067	„	1224	As 1066. **W**. 176. **S**. ·8.	In foliated diamond شاه اشر البلاد حمد ا ١٢٢٤ ف ضرب
1068 B.M.	„	1224	As 1066. **W**. 178. **S**. ·7.	On dotted field احمد شاه ا ا د شر ف لبلا ١٢٢٤ ضرب In central cartouche یا محمود Pl. XII. 17.
1069 I.M.	Aḥmad Shāhī	—	Maḥmūd's first couplet arranged as on 931. **W**. 175. **S**. ·9.	In double circle surrounded by broad margin contained in dotted circle, on floral field هی احمد شا ب ضر

Metal No.	Mint	Date	Obverse	Reverse
Æ 1070	احمد شاهی Aḥmad Shāhī	1225	As 1066. **W.** 176.	On dotted field شاه د حمد ف ا ا ۱۲۲۵ البلا ب ضر شر
1071	„	1226	As 931. **W.** 175. **S.** ·7.	On dotted field شاه د ف البلا حمد ا ا ۱۲۲۶ ب ضر شر
1072	„	1226	„ **W.** 177.	Like 1067, but date ۱۲۲۶ over ب of ضرب.
1073 B.M.	Aḥmad Shāhī *Ashrafu-l-bilād*	1226	As 1064. **W.** 177. **S.** ·7.	As 1072. ۱۲۲۶
1074 I.M.	Aḥmad Shāhī	1229	On dotted field couplet of 1060. **W.** 159. **S.** ·85.	On dotted field in *ṯughrā* ۱۲۲۹ احمد شاه ب ضر

Metal No.	Mint	Date	Obverse	Reverse
Æ 1075 I.M.	احمد شاهی Aḥmad Shāhī	1230	As 1074. W. 160.	In tughrà ۱۲۳۰ احمد شاهی ضرب
1076 B.M.	„	1231	„ W. 159. S. ·85.	As 1075. ۱۲۳۱ Pl. XII. 1
1077 B.M.	„	1233	„ W. 158. S. ·85.	Contained as 1069. احمد شاهی ضرب ۱۲۳۳
1078 I.M.	بکهر Bakhar[1]	1241 ?	Couplet of 949 in four lines; above it ۴۱۱۲ سنة W. 177. S. 1·2.	As 949.
1079 B.M.	„	—	As 1078, but date off top of coin.	„
1080 I.M.	Bhakhar	1245	Within central foliated area شاه محمود The rest of the couplet, that of 881 with سیم instead of زر, is arranged round the area. The die is usually too large for the flan. W. 176. S. ·85.	مانوس میمنت ۴۵ جلوس ب ضر بهکهر

[1] I attribute these broad pieces to Maḥmūd's second reign because of the barbarous style and the difference in arrangement from 949.

Metal No.	Mint	Date	Obverse	Reverse
Æ 1081 I.M.	بهکهر Bhakhar	1255	As 1080. M. 50 above word شاه. **W.** 153. **S.** ·9.	As 1080 but M. 50 in loop of س of جلوس. Good specimens have the ١٢ of the date ١٢٥٥ to the left of the ب of بهکهر.
1082 B.M.	”	1255	As 1081. **W.** 152.	As 1081, but M. 51. ١٢٥٥
1083	”	1256	As 1081, but M. 52. **W.** 152. **S.** ·9.	As 1081, but M. 52 and ١٢٥٦.
1084	”	1256	As 1081, but above شاه bird (pigeon?) to r. alighting from flight. **W.** 153.	As 1081, but M. 53. ١٢٥٦
1085 B.M.	”	1258	As 1084, but pigeon to l. **W.** 152. **S.** ·85.	As 1081, but peafowl to r. with cobra in its beak, and ١٢٥٨. Pl. XII. 16 (obverse only).
1086	”	1258	As 1084, but a crouching hare. The head, ears, and fore-legs of the hare are in the area; the body and hind-legs in the margin. **W.** 152.	As 1085. ١٢٥٨ Pl. XII. 18.
1087	”	1259	As 1086. **W.** 153. **S.** ·85.	As 1085, but lion counter rampant guardant and ١٢٥٩. Pl. XIII. 2.
1088 I.M.	”	1261	” **W.** 152. **S.** ·8.	As 1087. ١٢٦١
1089 B.M.	”	1265	As 1083. **W.** 153. **S.** ·9.	As 1083. ١٢٦٥

Metal No.	Mint	Date	Obverse	Reverse
Æ 1090 I.M.	بهکهر Bhakhar	1267	As 1080. W. 153. S. ·8.	مانوس میمنت ۶۷ . . . جلوس ب ضر بهکهر M. 50 to r. of جلوس.
1091 I.M.	بهاولپور Bahā-walpūr	1224 1	As 931; ۱۲ to l. of last line and ۲۴ to l. of middle line. W. 174. S. ·85.	مانوس میمنت احد سنه جلوس ضرب بهاولپور To r. of middle line M. 48. Over ج of جلوس M. 54.
1092 I.M.	"	1239 1 *sic*	As 931; ۳۹ over محمود. W. 172. S. ·9.	As 1091, but without M. 54; mint name written بهاولپور.
1093 I.M.	"	1240	As 1092, but ۴۰ above محمود and ۱۲ below it. Obliquely milled. W. 170. S. ·95.	As 1092, but ۴۰ over سنه.
1094 I.M.	"	1241	As 1093, but ۱۲ and ۴۱. Obliquely milled. W. 172. S. 1·0.	As 1092. ۴۱
1095 I.M.	"	1242	As 1093, but ۱۲ and ۴۲. Obliquely milled. W. 172. S. 1·0.	As 1092; ۴۲ above سنه and ۱۲ below جلوس.
1096 B.M.	"	1244	As 1093, but ۱۲ and ۴۴. Obliquely milled. W. 170. S. ·95.	As 1092. ۴۴

Metal No.	Mint	Date	Obverse	Reverse
Æ 1097 I.M.	بهاولپور Bahā-walpūr	1244 1245	As 1093, but ١٢ and ٣٥. Obliquely milled. **W.** 171.	As 1092, but ١٢٤٤ above middle line.
1098 I.M.	,,	1249	As 1093, but ١٢٤٩ above middle line. Obliquely milled. **W.** 170. **S.** ·9.	As 1095, but ١٢ and ٤٩.
1099	,,	1249	As 1098. ١٢٤٩ Obliquely milled. **W.** 170. **S.** ·95.	As 1092, but additional mark M. 55 and date ١٢٤٩ in loop of س of جلوس.
1100	,,	1249 1250	,, ١٢٤٩ Obliquely milled. **W.** 171. **S.** 1·05.	As 1092, but ١٢٥٠ beneath word سنه.
1101 I.M.	,,	1250 1249	As 1098, but ١٢٥٠. Obliquely milled. **W.** 171. **S.** 1·0.	As 1100, but ١٢٤٩.
1102	,,	1250	As 1098. ١٢٥٠ **W.** 171.	As 1099, but ١٢٥٠ below word سنه.
1103 I.M.	,,	1250	,, **W.** 171.	As 1100, but ٥٠ below word سنه.
1104 B.M.	پشاور Pashāwar	1226 2	فزود سکه دو لت سلطان محمود ١٢٢٦ سیم حسن دیگر بزر و **W.** 173. **S.** ·85.	On flowered field in double square with arabesques in margins س ور جلو پشا ب ٢ ضرب سنه

Metal No.	Mint	Date	Obverse	Reverse
Æ 1105	پشاور Pashāwar	1227 3	As 1104. ۱۲۲۷ **W.** 176. **S.** ·9.	As 1104. ۳
1106 B.M.	,,	1228 4	,, ۱۲۲۸ **W.** 177.	,, ۴
1107 B.M.	,,	123– 6	,, **W.** 158 (rubbed).	On flowered field in octagonal border ضرب س ور جلو پشا ٦ سنة
1108[1] B.M.	,,	1230 7	,, **W.** 160. **S.** 1·0.	As 1107. ۷ Pl. XIII. 3.
1109 B.M.	,,	1231 7	,, ۱۲۳۱ **W.** 164. **S.** 1·0.	,, ۷
1110 B.M.	,,	1231 8	,, ۱۲۳۱ **W.** 163. **S.** ·95.	,, ۸

[1] A fine specimen of this coin in the Fitzwilliam Museum, Cambridge, weighs 165 grains.

Metal No.	Mint	Date	Obverse	Reverse
Æ 1111	بشاور Pashāwar	1232 8	In foliated diamond on flowered field محمود سلطان ١٢٣٢ Within four marginal compartments:— Low right سكه دولت Low left حسن ديگر High right فزود High left بزر و سيم **W.** 164. **S.** 1·0.	As 1107. ٨ Pl. XIII. 1.
1112	,,	1232 9	As 1111. ١٢٣٢ **W.** 165.	,, ٩
1113	,,	1233 9	,, ١٢٣٣ **W.** 165.	,, ٩
1114 B.M.	,,	1233 10	,, ١٢٣٣ **W.** 164. **S.** ·85.	,, ١٠
1115	ديرهجات Derahjāt	1224 1	بتوفيق اله شـــاه ستا ١٢٢٤ گيتى ن محمود خســـرو سكه بر زر زد **W.** 168. **S.** ·75.	احد سنه ت ديره جا ب ضر
1116 B.M.	,,	1226 3	As 1115. ١٢٢٦ **W.** 170.	As 1115. ٣

Metal No.	Mint	Date	Obverse	Reverse
Æ 1117	دیرہجات Derahjāt	1227 3	As 1115. ۱۲۲۷ **W.** 166.	As 1115. ۳
1118 I.M.	"	1227 —	As 1115, but ۱۲۲۷ in small figures in loop of ن of ستان. **W.** 165. **S.** ·8.	As 1115, but regnal date off coin.
1119 I.M.	"	1234 —	As 1115, but ۱۲ above و of محمود ; ۳ and ۴ in the loops of ن and ی of ستان and گیتی respectively. **W.** 164. **S.** ·8.	As 1115, but regnal date off coin.
1120 I.M.	"	1236 —	As 1115, but ۲۳۶ in loop of ی of گیتی. **W.** 170.	As 1119.
1121 I.M.	"	1237 —	As 1115. ۱۲۳۷ **W.** 166. **S.** ·85.	"
1122 I.M.	"	1240 —	" ۱۲۴۰ **W.** 167.	"
1123 B.M.	"	1241 —	" ۱۲۴۱ **W.** 166.	"
1124 I.M.	"	1242 4 *sic*	" ۱۲۴۲ **W.** 168.	As 1115. ۴

Metal No.	Mint	Date	Obverse	Reverse
AR 1125 B.M.	دیرہ‌جات Derahjāt	1244 —	As 1115, but ۴۴ in loop of ن of ستان. **W.** 167. **S.** ·75.	As 1119.
1126 I.M.	”	1244 —	As 1115, but ۱۲ in ن of ستان and ۴ over ۴ in ی of گیتی. **W.** 166.	”
1127 I.M.	”	1245	As 1125. ۱۲۴۵ **W.** 167. **S.** ·7.	As 1115. ۴۵
1128 L.D.	”	1246 —	” ۱۲۴۶ **W.** 166.	”
1129 I.M.	”	1247 —	As 1115. ۱۲۴۷ M. 48 in loop of ی of گیتی. **W.** 167. **S.** ·7.	As 1119.
1130	”	1248 —	As 1129. ۱۲۴۸ **W.** 166.	”
1131 I.M.	”	1250 —	As 1115. ۱۲۵۰ M. 48 and M. 50. **W.** 167. **S.** ·7.	”
1132	”	1251 —	As 1131. ۱۲۵۱ **W.** 166. **S.** ·75.	”

Metal No.	Mint	Date	Obverse	Reverse
Æ 1133	ديرهجات Derahjāt	12-- 1	As 1115, but ١٢ below و of محمود and M. 54 above it; word شاه at end of middle line. **W.** 168. **S.** ·8.	As 1115. احد
1134	,,	— 2	Legend arranged as on 931 and similar style; date (illegible) below word محمود. **W.** 170. **S.** ·8.	,, ٢ M. 56 to r. of ٢.
1135 B.M.	کابل Kābul *Dāru-s-saltanat*	1225 2	سکه دولت ب ١٢٢٥ سلطان محمود . . . . **W.** 178. **S.** ·7.	کابل دار السلطنة ب ٢ ضر سنه
1136 B.M.	,,	1228 5	On dotted field لت سلطا سکه دو ن محـــمود ١٢٢٨ دیگر سیم فزود حسن بزر و **W.** 176. **S.** ·95.	In double circle within wide margin کابل السلطنة دار ٥ ضرب
1137 B.M.	,,	1228 5	As 1136. ١٢٢٨	As 1136. ٥ but surcharged with رائج in small incuse.
1138 B.M.	,,	— 8	As 1135, but date off coin. **W.** 165. **S.** ·85.	Much as 1061. ٨

Metal No.	Mint	Date	Obverse	Reverse
Æ 1139 I.M.	کابل Kābul *Dāru-s-salṭanat*	۱۲-- —	حسن دیگر بزر و سیم فزود ۱۲-- لت سلطا محمود سکهٔ دو ن **W.** 165. **S.** ·85.	Much as 1061. Pl. XIII. 4.
1140 B.M.	کشمیر Kashmīr *Khitta*	122– 6	On flowered field بتوفیق اله شاه ۱۲ گیتی ستان محمود ۲– خسرو سکهٔ زد بر زر **W.** 165. **S.** ·85.	On flowered field ۶ سنهٔ کشمیر خطهٔ ضرب
1141 B.M.	„	1225 7	As 1140. ۱۲۲۵ **W.** 171.	As 1140. ۷
1141 A Edin.	„	1228 6	„ ۱۲۲۸ For Edin., see 205.	„ ۶
1141 B Edin.	„	1229 —	„ ۱۲۲۹	„ Regnal date off coin.
1142 B.M.	„	1230 8	„ ۱۲۳۰ **W.** 170.	„ ۸
1143 B.M.	„	1230 10	„ ۱۲۳۰ **W.** 172.	„ ۱۰

Metal No.	Mint	Date	Obverse	Reverse
AR 1144 B.M.	کشمیر Kashmīr *Khitta*	1232 10	As 1140, but entire date ١٢٣٢ over ستان. **W.** 171.	As 1140, but mint name written کشمیر and different style. ١٠
1145 B.M.	,,	1233 10	As 1144. ١٢٣٣ **W.** 170.	As 1144. ١٠ Pl. XIII. 5.
1146	,,	1233 11	,, ١٢٣٣ **W.** 169. **S.** ·85.	As 1140. ١١
Æ 1147	پشاور Pashāwar	123–	١٢٣– محمود . . . . ——— بادشاه . . . **W.** 176. **S.** ·8. A B.M. specimen has the date ١٢٣– clearly enough.	فلوس ضرب پشاور Pl. X. 17.
1148 B.M.	کشمیر Kashmīr	— 1	 Date illegible. **W.** 72 (rubbed). **S.** ·8.	In foliated lozenge احد کشمیر ب ضر
1149 B.M.	,,	— 1	As 1148. **W.** 111.	As 1148.
1150 B.M.	,,	— 1	As 1148. **W.** 121.	In foliated lozenge احد کشمیر ضرب

Metal No.	Mint	Date	Obverse	Reverse
Æ 1151 B.M.	کشمیر Kashmīr	1230 6	As 1148; date ۳۰ under ح of محمود. W. 145. S. ·8.	٦ کشمیر ضرب
1152	,,		As 1148. W. 150.	Not legible.
1153 B.M.		12--	۱۲-- شاه محمود Date may be 1229 or 1239. W. 121. S. ·7.	کشمیر ضرب
1154	,,	12--	As 1153. W. 115.	As 1153.
1155 B.M.	ملتان Multān	1227 1	در درانی ۱۲۲۷ محمود شاه بادشاه W. 180. S. ·9.	ملتان ضرب فلوس احد
1156	,,	1227 2	As 1155. W. 188. S. ·8.	As 1155. ۲
1157 B.M.	,,	1228 —	,, ۱۲۲۸ W. 187.	,, Regnal date illegible.
1158 B.M.	,,	1228 3	,, ۱۲۲۸ W. 188. Square.	,, ۳

Metal No.	Mint	Date	Obverse	Reverse
Æ 1159 B.M.	ملتان Multān	1228 5	As 1155. ۱۲۲۸ **W.** 180 (rubbed).	As 1155. ٥
1160	„	1230 7	As 1155; different style. M. 55. ۱۲۳۰ **W.** 197. **S.** ·8.	„ ٧
1161 B.M.	„	1230	In dotted circle as 1155. ۱۲۳۰ **W.** 179. **S.** ·9.	As 1155, but date ۱۲۳۰ under word ملتان. Pl. XIII. 6.
1162	„	1230	As 1161; rubbed.	As 1161.
1163	„	1230 / 1231	As 1155. ۱۲۳۰ **W.** 181.	As 1161, but ۱۲۳۱.
1164 B.M.	„	1231 7	As 1155. M. 55 over word شاه. ۱۲۳۱ **W.** 191. **S.** ·8. Date 1232 in Cabinet of Sir Richard Burn.	As 1155. ٧
1165 B.M.	„	1231 —	As 1155; no date. **W.** 180.	ملتان ب ۱۲۳۱ ضرفلوس Regnal date off coin.
1166 B.M.	„	1235	As 1164. M. 55. ۱۲۳٥ **W.** 180 (square). **S.** ·85.	As 1155. Regnal date off coin. Pl. XIII. 7.

Metal No.	Mint	Date	Obverse	Reverse
Æ 1167 B.M.	ملتان Multān	1253	As 1164; same or similar mark. ١٢٥٣ **W.** 152.	As 1166.
1168 B.M.	„	1254	As 1167. ١٢٥٤ **W.** 141.	„
1169	„	1257	„ ١٢٥٧ **W.** 150.	„
1170	„	1263	„ ١٢٦٣ **W.** 152.	„
1171 B.M.	„	1264	„ ١٢٦٤ **W.** 151. **S.** ·9.	„
1172	„	—	„ Dates illegible; inferior style.	„
1173	„	—	As 1164; early type but dates illegible. **W.** 190.	„

SHĀH NŪRU-D-DĪN[1]

A.H. 1223–1228. A.D. 1808–1813.

Metal No.	Mint	Date	Obverse	Reverse
AV 1174	کشمیر Kashmīr *Khitta*	1225 2	In central square on flowered field ٣ سنه کشمیر خطه ضرب To r. یا شاه Above نور الدین To l. یا مخدوم Below جهان Double mohur. **W.** 335·2. **S.** ·95.	In triple circle spread over entire field ١٢٢٥ ب کلا طالبها جیفه و الدنیا 'The world is carrion and the seekers thereafter are dogs.' Pl. XIII. 10.
1175	"	1225 3	شاه نور الدین یا یا مخدوم جهان ب ٣ کشمیر سنه ضر خطه **W.** 335. **S.** ·95. The legend is the same as that on 1174, but is differently arranged. یا شاه نور الدین یا مخدوم جهان 'O Shāh Nūru-d-dīn, O Lord of the World.'	As 1174. ١٢٢٥ Pl. XIII. 11.

[1] The patron saint of rural Kashmīr. The coins are discussed on pp. xxix–xxx. The invocation on the gold pieces shows that Shāh Nūru-d-dīn is an object of veneration, a saint. The word عارف on the silver coins means one who has arrived at the knowledge of God, the highest grade to which a mystic can attain; قطب العارفین is a Ṣūfī expression sometimes used as an epithet for Plato. The word سلک can mean 'the path' in the sense of a rule of life; there is a play on words here as in other coin couplets, their only literary merit.

Metal No.	Mint	Date	Obverse	Reverse
Æ 1176 B.M.	کشمیر Kashmīr *Khitta*	1223 1	In triple circle on flowered field سکه شد روشن ز شـــــــــاه نور الدین رائج از مخدوم قطب العارفین ۱۲۲۳ **W.** 224. **S.** 1·1.	On flowered field in elaborate circular border احد سنه کشمیر خطه ضرب Pl. XIII. 12.

The couplet is:—

سکه شد روشن ز شاه نور الدین
رائج از مخدوم قطب العارفین

'Coin became bright through Shāh Nūru-d-dīn,
Current by the Lord of the Pole of Wise Men.'

Metal No.	Mint	Date	Obverse	Reverse
1177	,,	1223 1	As 1176. ۱۲۲۳ **W.** 171. **S.** ·9.	As 1176. احد
1178 B.M.	,,	1224 1	,, ۱۲۲۴ **W.** 170.	,, احد
1179 B.M.	,,	1224 2	,, ۱۲۲۴ **W.** 165.	,, ۲
1180 B.M.	,,	1225 2	,, ۱۲۲۵ **W.** 170.	,, ۲
1181 B.M.	,,	1225 3	,, ۱۲۲۵ **W.** 170.	,, ۳

Metal No.	Mint	Date	Obverse	Reverse
AR 1181 A Sri	کشمیر Kashmīr *Khitta*	1226 4	As 1176. ۱۲۲۶ Kashmir Museum, Srinagar. **W.** 168.	As 1176. ۴
1182 B.M.	"	1227 5	" ۱۲۲۷ **W.** 171.	" ٥ Pl. XIII. 13.
1182 A Sri	"	1228 5	" ۱۲۲۸ **W.** 170.	" ٥
Æ 1183	"	1225 3	In double circle نور الدین یا شـــــا ۱۲ ۲٥ یا مخدوم ۃ **W.** 116. **S.** ·65.	In double circle ۳ سنہ کشمیر خطہ ضرب Pl. XIII. 9 (B.M.).

SULṬĀN ʿALĪ

(Proclaimed by Dost Muḥammad Bārakzai at Kābul)

A.H. 1233. A.D. 1818.

No coins are known. Sulṭān ʿAlī was a son of Taimūr Shāh and half-brother of Aiyūb Shāh. He was murdered at Kābul. *Masson's Narrative* (*op. cit.*), vol. iii, pp. 51–4.

AIYŪB SHĀH[1]

A.H. 1233–1245. A.D. 1818–1829.

Metal No.	Mint	Date	Obverse	Reverse
AV 1184 B.M.	پشاور Pashāwar	— 6	خورشید و ماه شـــــاه از شعاع سکه ایوب شـــــد جهان روشن‌تر از **W.** 164. **S.** ·85. The couplet is :— شد جهان‌روشن‌تر از خورشید و ماه از شعاع سکه ایوب شاه 'Became more world-illuminating than the sun and moon, Through the rays of the stamp of Aiyūb Shāh.'	In ornate octagon on dotted field ضرب س ور جلو پشا ٦ سنه
1185	„	— 7	As 1184. **W.** 162. **S.** ·85.	As 1184. ٧
Æ 1186 B.M.	احمد شاهی Aḥmad Shāhī *Ashrafu-l-bilād*	—	On flowered field in multifoil area, the Kalima. Around it in marginal compartments ضرب اشرف البلاد احمد شاهی **W.** 154 (rubbed). **S.** 1·0.	Couplet on flowered field. Pl. XIII. 16.
1187 B.M.	پشاور Pashāwar	1233 1	In small triple diamond شاه ب ایو ١٢٣٣ Rest of couplet arranged in four marginal compartments starting at six o'clock and reading outwards.	As 1184. احد Pl. XIII. 17.

[1] Aiyūb Shāh was a son of Taimūr Shāh and half brother of Sulṭān 'Alī. He was proclaimed at Pashāwar by Muḥammad 'Aẓīm Khān Bārakzai and retired to the Panjab after the death of his protector. This took place subsequent to the Sikh victory at Nowshera in A.H. 1238. Coins continued to be struck at Pashāwar in the name of Aiyūb till A.H. 1245. I cannot read the word در in the coin legend—*C.J.R.*, 1894, p. 179.

Metal No.	Mint	Date	Obverse	Reverse
Æ 1188 B.M.	پشاور Pashāwar	1233 1	ماه از شعاع خورشـــيد و سكهٔ ايوب شاه ۱۲۳۳ شــــــــــــــد جهان روشن‌تراز W. 163. S. ·9.	As 1184. احد Pl. XIII. 18.
1189 L.D. Edin.	"	1234 2	As 1184, but date ۱۲۳۴ above ب of ايوب W. 162. For Edin., see 205.	" ۲
1189 A B.M.	"	1235 2	As 1189. ۱۲۳۵ W. 160.	" ۲
1190	"	1235 3	" ۱۲۳۵ W. 163.	" ۳
1191 B.M.	"	1237 4	" ۱۲۳۷ W. 164.	" ۴
1192 B.M.	"	1238 6	" ۱۲۳۸ W. 163.	" ۶
1193 I.M.	"	1239 7	" ۱۲۳۹ W. 162.	" ۷
1194	"	1240 7	" ۱۲۴۰ W. 161.	" ۷ Pl. XIII. 15.

Metal No.	Mint	Date	Obverse	Reverse
Æ 1194 A L.D.	پشاور Pashāwar	1240 8	As 1189. ١٢٤٠	As 1184. ٨
1195 B.M.	"	1245 ? 11	" but small mark like M. 32 above word سکه, and possible date ١٢٤٥. W. 162.	" ١١
1196	"	— 11	As 1195; date, if any, off the coin. W. 163.	" ١١
1197	"	— 12	In foliated diamond شاه ایوب سکه شعاع از Rest of couplet in four compartments, reading outwards, beginning from lower right. W. 162. S. ·9.	" ١٢ Pl. XIII. 14.
1198 B.M.	کابل Kābul *Dāru-s-salṭanat*	1237 3	On flowered field جهان روشن‌تر شد ١٢٣٧ سکه ایوب شاه شید و از خور ماه از شعاع W. 164. S. ·85.	In double square with projecting mihrabs, surrounded by triple circle. ضرب دار کابل السلطنة ٣ ١٢٣— سنه Pl. XIV. 1.

Metal No.	Mint	Date	Obverse	Reverse
Æ 1199	کشمیر Kashmīr *Khitta*	1234 1	In triple circle on dotted field کردگار عظیم سیم سکه بر زر و شاه ایوب ئید زد بتا ۱۲۳۴ **W.** 170. **S.** ·9. The couplet is :— سکه شاه ایوب بر زر و سیم زد بتائید کردگار عظیم 'Aiyūb Shāh struck coin on gold and silver By the aid of the great Creator.'	As on obverse احد سنه کشمیر خطه ضرب Pl. XIV. 3.
1200 B.M.	Kashmīr	1234 2	As 1199. ۱۲۳۴ **W.** 170. **S.** ·9.	In triple circle on dotted field مانوس میمنت ۲ سنه جلوس کشمیر ضرب Pl. XIV. 2 (obv.).
1201 B.M.	ملتان Multān	1239	In rectangular frame the Kalima; underneath it ۱۲۳۹. Below ضرب Above ملتان Reading Multān probable but not certain. **W.** 155. **S.** ·9.	Couplet on flowered field, much as 1186.

Metal No.	Mint	Date	Obverse	Reverse
Æ 1202	پشاور Pashāwar	1236 4	شاه غازی ۱۲۳۶ ایوب شاه باد ك سکه مبار W. 188. S. ·95.	In elaborate circular border ۴ پشاور فلوس Pl. XIV. 4.
1203 B.M.	,,	1237	As 1202. ۱۲۳۷ W. 185. S. ·95.	Area within elaborate circular border divided into four equal segments; the corresponding four parts of the legend read outwards. فلوس ضرب پشاور ۱۲۳۷
1204 B.M.		1238 6	As 1202. ۱۲۳۸ W. 161. S. ·85.	In circular border فلوس۶ and M. 57.
1205		—	As 1202, but date illegible. W. 175. S. ·85.	Seven-lobed figure.
1206		124–	As 1202. ۱۲۴– W. 162. S. ·8.	Animal standing to r.; legend illegible.

KĀMRĀN SHĀH

(At Hirāt)

A.H. 1245–1258 A.D. 1829–1842[1]

Metal No.	Mint	Date	Obverse	Reverse
Æ 1207 I.M.	هرات Hirāt *Dāru-s-saltanat*	1252	In double circle on dotted field از مهر--- طلا سکه کامران شاه بحت ... بر نقرهٔ از ماه W. 159. S. ·85. The couplet has been reconstructed on these lines:— [می ارد] از مهر طلا و نقرهٔ از ماه [بخت --- بر] سکه کامران شاه 'Fortune brings gold from the sun and silver from the moon, . . . on the coin of Kāmrān Shāh.'[2]	As obverse ضرب دار السلطنة هرات Date ۱۲۵۲. Pl. XIV. 6.
1208 I.M.	"	125–	As 1207. Half rupee. W. 79. S. ·75.	As 1207. Pl. XIV. 7.
1209 B.M.	Hirāt	1248	In double circle on flowered field شاه کامران ۱۲۴۸ W. 41. S. ·6.	In circle on flowered field ت ضر هرا ب ۱۲۴۸ Pl. XIV. 5.

[1] From the death of his father Maḥmūd Shāh till his assassination early in 1842.

[2] See p. 103 of E. von Zambaur's article 'Contributions à la Numismatique Orientale', *Numismatische Zeitschrift*, Vienna, 1904. The words inside the brackets are uncertain. There is another partial version of the legend on p. 388 of C. M. Fraehn's *Opusculorum Postumorum, Pars Prima*, Petropoli, 1855.

Metal No.	Mint	Date	Obverse	Reverse
Ꜳ 1210 B.M.	هرات Hirāt	۱۲--	On dotted field as 1209. **W.** 42. **S.** ·55.	On dotted field as 1209; last two figures of date illegible.

SHUJĀ'U-L-MULK SHĀH

Third reign A.H. 1255–1258 A.D. 1839–1842

Metal No.	Mint	Date	Obverse	Reverse
AV 1211 B.M.	کابل Kābul *Dāru-s-salṭanat*	1255	In triple circle on flowered field سلطان شجاع شاه الملك ۱۲۵۵ **W.** 167. **S.** ·9.	In double square with a mihrab projecting from the middle of each side ۱۲ ۵ ضرب دار ه کابل السلطنة ۱۲۵۵ Pl. XIV. 10.
1212 I.M.	„	1255	As 1211, but not so broad and execution not so good. ۱۲۵۵ **W.** 167.	As 1211. ۱۲۵۵
1213 B.M.	„	1258	As 1211, but less ornate; date off coin. **W.** 165. **S.** ·75.	As 1211, but less ornate; date ۱۲۵۸ situated thus ۱۲۵۸ کابـل
Ꜳ 1214 B.M.	احمد شاهی Aḥmad Shāhī	1255	Part of couplet as on 1220; die larger than the flan. **W.** 141. **S.** ·85.	In lobed circle surrounded by broad margin ه احمد شا ب ضر ۱۲۵۵ Pl. XIV. 13.

Metal No.	Mint	Date	Obverse	Reverse
Æ 1215 B.M.	احمد شاهی Aḥmad Shāhī	—	As 1214; die much too large for flan. A quarter rupee. W. 36. S. ·5.	As 1214; date off coin. Pl. XIV. 8.
1216	”	1255	As 1214. W. 140. S. ·85.	As 1214.
1217 S.D.	”	1256	Scott-Dodgson Sale Catalogue. J. Schulman, Amsterdam, May 5, 1908. Coin 330.	
1218 B.M.	کابل Kābul *Dāru-s-salṭanat*	1255	As 1211; fine broad coin. ١٢٥٥ W. 177. S. 1·15.	As 1211, but date at top of coin only. Pl. XIV. 12.
1219 B.M.	”	1255	As 1211. W. 145. S. ·85.	As 1211.
1220	”	1255	حامی دین نبی الملك سلطان شجاع شاه شـــــــيد و تر از خور ماه برسيم و وشن سکه زد زر ر W. 142. S. ·9.	As 1211, but with additional word سنه below, and above سنه the date ١٢٥٥. Pl. XIV. 11.

I have read the couplet, hitherto unelucidated, from four specimens—one in the British Museum, one which belonged to the late Mr. W. Coldstream, I.C.S. (retired), a third in the Fitzwilliam Museum, Cambridge, and a fourth in the Panjab Museum, Lahore. The Cambridge specimen shows the date.

The couplet is:—

سکه زد بر سیم و زر روشنتر از خورشید و ماه
سلطان حامی دین نبی شجاع الملك شاه

'Struck coin on silver and gold brighter than the sun and moon,
The Sulṭān, defender of the Faith of the Prophet, Shujā'u-l-mulk Shāh.'

Metal No.	Mint	Date	Obverse	Reverse
Æ **1221** B.M.	كابل Kābul *Dāru-s-salṯanat*	1256	As 1211. ١٢٥٦ **W.** 146. **S.** ·95.	As 1211; date ١٢٥٦ to upper left of field.
1222 B.M.	,,	1256	,, **W.** 143. **S.** ·85.	As 1211, but date thus ١٢٥٦ كابل
1223 B.M.	,,	1259	As 1211. Posthumous. **W.** 146. **S.** ·8.	As 1222, but ١٢٥٩ above ب of ضرب.
1224[1]	,,	1259	در دران شاه سلطان شجاع الملك Also B.M. and W.K. Posthumous. **W.** 143. **S.** ·9.	As 1222, but no date below. ١٢٥٩ Pl. XIV. 14.

FATH JANG

A.H. 1258 A.D. 1842

Metal No.	Mint	Date	Obverse	Reverse
Æ **1225** B.M.	احمد شاهی Ahmad Shāhī *Ashrafu-l-bilād*	1258	On flowered field غازی فتح جنگ بادشاه - - - - - - - **W.** 141. **S.** ·85.	In double circle شاهی د حمد ف ا ا ١٢٥ ٨ البلا ب ضر شر Pl. XIV. 15.

[1] I do not know of any coin of this reign dated 1257. A rupee of 1258 struck in the name of Shāh Zamān is described on p. 118.

Metal No.	Mint	Date	Obverse	Reverse
Æ 1226 B.M.	كابل Kābul *Dāru-s-saltanat*	1258	On flowered field ١٢٥٨ ح بادشاه غاز جنگ سلطان فتح **W.** 144. **S.** ·9.	On flowered field ضرب دار كابل السلطنة ١٢٥٨ Pl. XIV. 17.
1227	„	—	As 1226, but date off coin. **W.** 144. **S.** ·8.	As 1226, but no date at bottom of coin.
1228 B.M.	„	1258	On flowered field در دران شاه جنگ سلطان فتح **W.** 145. **S.** ·8.	On dotted field دار كابل السلطنة ١٢٥٨ ضرب
1229 B.M.	„	1258	On flowered field جهان فتح جنگ ---- كا معد و ---- ى ن ن --- This couplet cannot be read without the aid of more specimens. **W.** 145. **S.** ·85.	On dotted field as 1226; date ١٢٥٨ thus ١٢٥٨ كابل Pl. XIV. 16.

SHAHPŪR SHĀH

A.H. 1258. A.D. 1842.

Metal No.	Mint	Date	Obverse	Reverse
Æ 1229A B.M.	کابل Kābul *Dāru-s-salṭanat*	1258	... الطاف اله[1] شـــــاه ۱۲۵۸ شه پور ... لم ستان ... ســرو ... زد **W.** 145. **S.** ·85.	As 1226. ۱۲۵۸

(See illustration, p. 189.)

UNASSIGNED[2]

Metal No.	Mint	Date	Obverse	Reverse
Æ 1230 Vienna	قندهار Qandahār	—	In square the Kalima. To r. عثمان Below علی - - - - - **S.** ·85.	چو - - - - - ن سکه محمود جهانگیر - - - - شاه قندهار - - - - Pl. XIV. 9.
Æ 1231	دیر میان Dair-i-Miyān?	—	در درا نی [محمو]د شاه - - - - - - - - **W.** 181. **S.** ·8.	In circle دیر میان ضرب

[1] The couplet is:— [*Sikka*] *zad* [- - *-az*] *alṭāf i Ilah; Khusrū i 'ālam sitān Shahpūr Shāh.* This unique rupee was in my Cabinet. It was issued at Kābul in the name of Shahpūr, younger brother of Fatḥ Jang, during the British occupation in A.D. 1842. After the departure of the British, Shahpūr was speedily ejected by Akbar Khān, son of Dost Muḥammad Bārakzai. See Ferrier's *History of the Afghans*, p. 384, and G. P. Tate's *Kingdom of Afghanistan*, p. 148.

[2] I was inclined to attribute the silver coin to Jahāngīr, son of Kāmrān and grandson of Maḥmūd Shāh but find at the British Museum that it has been placed amongst the issues of the Ghilzai conqueror Shāh Maḥmūd; he ruled Persia from A.H. 1135 to 1137. The copper piece is in good style, and the mint is clear enough. I do not know of any place called Dair i Miyān, or half-way house. Dair means a Dervish settlement, a tavern, and occurs in Persian place names. There is also Dīr where lived the chief of the Panjkora Yūsufzais.

AUTONOMOUS COINS

Metal No.	Mint	Date	Obverse	Reverse
Æ 1 B.M.	احمد شاهی Ahmad Shāhī	1198	Sword and scabbard. W. H. V., p. 172, 21. [W.H.Valentine's *Modern Copper Coins of Muhammadan States.* Spink. London, 1911.] **W**. 130.	ضرب فلوس احمد شاهی ۱۱۹۸
2 B.M.	"	1218	Like 1. **W**. 160.	Legend as on 1. ۱۲۱۸
3	"	1225	Broken sword. *C.J.R.*, Part IV, 1895, p. 106. **W**. 119.	" ۱۲۲۵
4 B.M.	"	1255	Sword on flowered field. W. H. V., p. 176, 46. **W**. 95.	" ۱۲۵۵
5 B.M.	"	1256	Sword between palm branches. W. H. V., p. 176, 47. **W**. 95.	" ۱۲۵۶
6	Derajāt?	1217	In double circle بادشاه ۱۲۱۷ *C.J.R.*, Part IV, 1895, p. 105. **W**. 146.	In a circle رائج

Metal No.	Mint	Date	Obverse	Reverse
Æ 7 W.K.	دیرۂ فتح Dera Fatḥ	1204	Lion or cat. ۱۲۰۴ W. K. 2877.	رائج فتح
8	کابل Kābul	1201	Trefoil. *C.J.R.*, Part IV, 1895, p. 102. **W.** 101.	فلوس کابل ۱۲۰۱
9 B.M.	Kābul *Dāru-s-salṭanat*	1233	Twining flowers. **W.** 130.	دار السلطنة کابل ۱۲۳۳
10 B.M.	Kābul	1256	Scroll work. **W.** 96.	۱۲۵۶ کابل ----
11 Fraehn	هرات Hirāt	1226	Palm tree between two swords. W. H. V., p. 182, 5.	ضرب فلوس هرات ۱۲۲۶
12 B.M.	"	1227	Sun face. W. H. V., p. 182, 10.	As 11. ۱۲۲۷

Coin of Shahpūr Shāh (see p. 187.)

APPENDIX

P. xvii. *For* Yūsafzai, *read* Yūsufzai.

P. xxiv. The classic account of the invasion of A.D. 1756–7 is that contributed by W. Irvine to the *Indian Antiquary*, 1907. The terrible sack of Muttra is described on p. 62.

P. xxv, Footnote 2. For a discussion of the original authorities see Oskar Mann's Quellenstudien zur Geschichte des Aḥmed Šâh Durrânî. *Zeitschrift der deutschen morgenländischen Gesellschaft.* Leipzig, 1898.

P. xxviii. The word suggested as سکہ on Coin 1051 is probably سنہ.

P. xxxii. The Panjab States of Patiāla, Jind, Nabha, and Maler Kotla obtained the right to coin from Aḥmad Shāh. All issues were modelled on the piece of Aḥmad's fourth year, and there has been no change in the die beyond the addition of the mark of the ruling chief (*Indian Antiquary*, 1928, p. 151).

P. xxxiii. The titulars Fatḥ Jang and Shahpūr Shāh are the last of the Sadozais.

P. xxxiv. *For* rupiya, *read* rūpiya.

P. xl. Coin 1103 of A.H. 1250 is the last Durrānī rupee struck at Bahāwalpūr; the milled piece dated 1251 described on p. xl is the initial State issue. In the same year was struck an unmilled rupee with a different reverse legend, the *julūs maimanat mānūs* formula and mint Aḥmadpūr. This unmilled type is the first of a long series of light weight rupees struck at either Aḥmadpūr or Bahāwalpūr; I found all dates from 1252 to 1265 inclusive. The mint Khānpūr appears later, e g. on a rupee of year 1280.

P. liii. He (Aḥmad Shāh) remarked, 'The rupee of Farrukhābād is better looking and better made than that from any other place in India'. *Indian Antiquary*, 1907, p. 50.

P. liii. Zamān. Aḥmad Shāhī. G. 3. S. 19.

P. lxi. The epithet *Dāru-s-salṭanat* associated with Kashmīr is found three centuries earlier on gold coins of the Sultans of Kashmīr (*Num. Chron.*, 1933).

P. lxii. The closing sentence of the last paragraph is not accurate. The Afghan governor issued money in the name of the local saint (p. xxix); at the same time partisans of Kābul struck rupees of the second reign of Maḥmūd Shāh with blundered regnal dates. These dates, if anything, run straight on from the second reign of Shujā'.

P. lxiv. Mr. C. J. Rodgers published a Lahore rupee of *Sambat* 1822. *On the Coins of the Sikhs, J.A.S.B.*, 1881.

P. 157. The Shāh's title on Coins Pl. XIII. 1 and 3 and other pieces is written حسس دیگر; the name Ḥasan should be حسن. On the face of it one would expect one of the four letters ح followed by س or ش; no word of this kind suits either context or metre. The word حین 'time', or the name حُنَین do not seem likely. I cannot suggest anything better than 'the second Ḥasan'. Maḥmūd Shāh's strength lay on the Persian side of Afghanistan.

COMPARATIVE TABLE OF THE YEARS OF THE HIJRI AND CHRISTIAN ERAS

A.H.	A.D.	A.H.	A.D.	A.H.	A.D.
1140	1727, Aug. 19	1181	1767, May 30	1222	1807, Mar. 11.
1141	1728, ,, 7	1182	1768, ,, 18	1223	1808, Feb. 28
1142	1729, July 27	1183	1769, ,, 7	1224	1809, ,, 16
1143	1730, ,, 17	1184	1770, April 27	1225	1810, ,, 6
1144	1731, ,, 6	1185	1771, ,, 16	1226	1811, Jan. 26
1145	1732, June 24	1186	1772, ,, 4	1227	1812, ,, 16
1146	1733, ,, 14	1187	1773, Mar. 25	1228	1813, ,, 4
1147	1734, ,, 3	1188	1774, ,, 14	1229	1813, Dec. 24
1148	1735, May 24	1189	1775, ,, 4	1230	1814, ,, 14
1149	1736, ,, 12	1190	1776, Feb. 21	1231	1815, ,, 3
1150	1737, ,, 1	1191	1777, ,, 9	1232	1816, Nov. 21
1151	1738, April 21	1192	1778, Jan. 30	1233	1817, ,, 11
1152	1739, ,, 10	1193	1779, ,, 19	1234	1818, Oct. 31
1153	1740, Mar. 29	1194	1780, ,, 8	1235	1819, ,, 20
1154	1741, ,, 19	1195	1780, Dec. 28	1236	1820, ,, 9
1155	1742, ,, 8	1196	1781, ,, 17	1237	1821, Sept. 28
1156	1743, Feb. 25	1197	1782, ,, 7	1238	1822, ,, 18
1157	1744, ,, 15	1198	1783, Nov. 26	1239	1823, ,, 7
1158	1745, ,, 3	1199	1784, ,, 14	1240	1824, Aug. 26
1159	1746, Jan. 24	1200	1785, ,, 4	1241	1825, ,, 16
1160	1747, ,, 13	1201	1786, Oct. 24	1242	1826, ,, 5
1161	1748, ,, 2	1202	1787, ,, 13	1243	1827, July 25
1162	1748, Dec. 22	1203	1788, ,, 2	1244	1828, ,, 14
1163	1749, ,, 11	1204	1789, Sept. 21	1245	1829, ,, 3
1164	1750, Nov. 30	1205	1790, ,, 10	1246	1830, June 22
1165	1751, ,, 20	1206	1791, Aug. 31	1247	1831, ,, 12
1166	1752, ,, 8	1207	1792, ,, 19	1248	1832, May 31
1167	1753, Oct. 29	1208	1793, ,, 9	1249	1833, ,, 21
1168	1754, ,, 18	1209	1794, July 29	1250	1834, ,, 10
1169	1755, ,, 7	1210	1795, ,, 18	1251	1835, April 29
1170	1756, Sept 26	1211	1796, ,, 7	1252	1836, ,, 18
1171	1757, ,, 15	1212	1797, June 26	1253	1837, ,, 7
1172	1758, ,, 4	1213	1798, ,, 15	1254	1838, Mar. 27
1173	1759, Aug. 25	1214	1799, ,, 5	1255	1839, ,, 17
1174	1760, ,, 13	1215	1800, May 25	1256	1840, ,, 5
1175	1761, ,, 2	1216	1801, ,, 14	1257	1841, Feb. 23
1176	1762, July 23	1217	1802, ,, 4	1258	1842, ,, 12
1177	1763, ,, 12	1218	1803, April 23	1259	1843, ,, 1
1178	1764, ,, 1	1219	1804, ,, 12	1260	1844, Jan. 22
1179	1765, June 20	1220	1805, ,, 1	1261	1845, ,, 10
1180	1766, ,, 9	1221	1806, Mar. 21	1262	1845, Dec. 30

NOTE.—This table is taken from the British Museum Catalogue 'Sultāns of Dehlī', for which it was compiled by Mr. Stanley Lane-Poole from sources there quoted.

TABLE OF THE RELATIVE WEIGHTS OF ENGLISH GRAINS AND FRENCH GRAMMES

Grains.	Grammes.	Grains.	Grammes.	Grains.	Grammes.	Grains.	Grammes.
1	·064	41	2·656	81	5·248	121	7·840
2	·129	42	2·720	82	5·312	122	7·905
3	·194	43	2·785	83	5·378	123	7·970
4	·259	44	2·850	84	5·442	124	8·035
5	·324	45	2·915	85	5·508	125	8·100
6	·388	46	2·980	86	5·572	126	8·164
7	·453	47	3·045	87	5·637	127	8·229
8	·518	48	3·110	88	5·702	128	8·294
9	·583	49	3·175	89	5·767	129	8·359
10	·648	50	3·240	90	5·832	130	8·424
11	·712	51	3·304	91	5·896	131	8·488
12	·777	52	3·368	92	5·961	132	8·553
13	·842	53	3·434	93	6·026	133	8·618
14	·907	54	3·498	94	6·091	134	8·682
15	·972	55	3·564	95	6·156	135	8·747
16	1·036	56	3·628	96	6·220	136	8·812
17	1·101	57	3·693	97	6·285	137	8·877
18	1·166	58	3·758	98	6·350	138	8·942
19	1·231	59	3·823	99	6·415	139	9·007
20	1·296	60	3·888	100	6·480	140	9·072
21	1·360	61	3·952	101	6·544	141	9·136
22	1·425	62	4·017	102	6·609	142	9·200
23	1·490	63	4·082	103	6·674	143	9·265
24	1·555	64	4·146	104	6·739	144	9·330
25	1·620	65	4·211	105	6·804	145	9·395
26	1·684	66	4·276	106	6·868	146	9·460
27	1·749	67	4·341	107	6·933	147	9·525
28	1·814	68	4·406	108	6·998	148	9·590
29	1·879	69	4·471	109	7·063	149	9·655
30	1·944	70	4·536	110	7·128	150	9·720
31	2·008	71	4·600	111	7·192	151	9·784
32	2·073	72	4·665	112	7·257	152	9·848
33	2·138	73	4·729	113	7·322	153	9·914
34	2·202	74	4·794	114	7·387	154	9·978
35	2·267	75	4·859	115	7·452	155	10·044
36	2·332	76	4·924	116	7·516	156	10·108
37	2·397	77	4·989	117	7·581	157	10·173
38	2·462	78	5·054	118	7·646	158	10·238
39	2·527	79	5·119	119	7·711	159	10·303
40	2·592	80	5·184	120	7·776	160	10·368

TABLE OF THE RELATIVE WEIGHTS OF ENGLISH GRAINS AND FRENCH GRAMMES

Grains.	Grammes.	Grains.	Grammes.	Grains.	Grammes.	Grains.	Grammes.
161	10·432	201	13·024	241	15·616	290	18·79
162	10·497	202	13·089	242	15·680	300	19·44
163	10·562	203	13·154	243	15·745	310	20·08
164	10·626	204	13·219	244	15·810	320	20·73
165	10·691	205	13·284	245	15·875	330	21·38
166	10·756	206	13·348	246	15·940	340	22·02
167	10·821	207	13·413	247	16·005	350	22·67
168	10·886	208	13·478	248	16·070	360	23·32
169	10·951	209	13·543	249	16·135	370	23·97
170	11·016	210	13·608	250	16·200	380	24·62
171	11·080	211	13·672	251	16·264	390	25·27
172	11·145	212	13·737	252	16·328	400	25·92
173	11·209	213	13·802	253	16·394	410	26·56
174	11·274	214	13·867	254	16·458	420	27·20
175	11·339	215	13·932	255	16·524	430	27·85
176	11·404	216	13·996	256	16·588	440	28·50
177	11·469	217	14·061	257	16·653	450	29·15
178	11·534	218	14·126	258	16·718	460	29·80
179	11·599	219	14·191	259	16·783	470	30·45
180	11·664	220	14·256	260	16·848	480	31·10
181	11·728	221	14·320	261	16·912	490	31·75
182	11·792	222	14·385	262	16·977	500	32·40
183	11·858	223	14·450	263	17·042	510	33·04
184	11·922	224	14·515	264	17·106	520	33·68
185	11·988	225	14·580	265	17·171	530	34·34
186	12·052	226	14·644	266	17·236	540	34·98
187	12·117	227	14·709	267	17·301	550	35·64
188	12·182	228	14·774	268	17·366	560	36·28
189	12·247	229	14·839	269	17·431	570	36·93
190	12·312	230	14·904	270	17·496	580	37·58
191	12·376	231	14·968	271	17·560	590	38·23
192	12·441	232	15·033	272	17·625	600	38·88
193	12·506	233	15·098	273	17·689	700	45·36
194	12·571	234	15·162	274	17·754	800	51·84
195	12·636	235	15·227	275	17·819	900	58·32
196	12·700	236	15·292	276	17·884	1000	64·80
197	12·765	237	15·357	277	17·949	2000	129·60
198	12·830	238	15·422	278	18·014	3000	194·40
199	12·895	239	15·487	279	18·079	4000	259·20
200	12·960	240	15·552	280	18·144	5000	324·00

NOTE.—This Table is taken from the British Museum Catalogue of the Coins of the Greek and Scythic Kings of Bactria and India.

RELATIVE TABLE OF INCHES AND MILLIMETRES

Inches.	Millimetres.	Inches.	Millimetres.	Inches.	Millimetres.
·25	6·35	·70	17·78	1·15	29·21
·30	7·62	·75	19·05	1·20	30·48
·35	8·89	·80	20·32	1·25	31·75
·40	10·16	·85	21·59	1·30	33·02
·45	11·43	·90	22·86	1·35	34·29
·50	12·70	·95	24·13	1·40	35·56
·55	13·97	1·00	25·40	1·45	36·83
·60	15·24	1·05	26·67	1·50	38·10
·65	16·51	1·10	27·94	1·55	39·37

Marks on Durrānī Coins

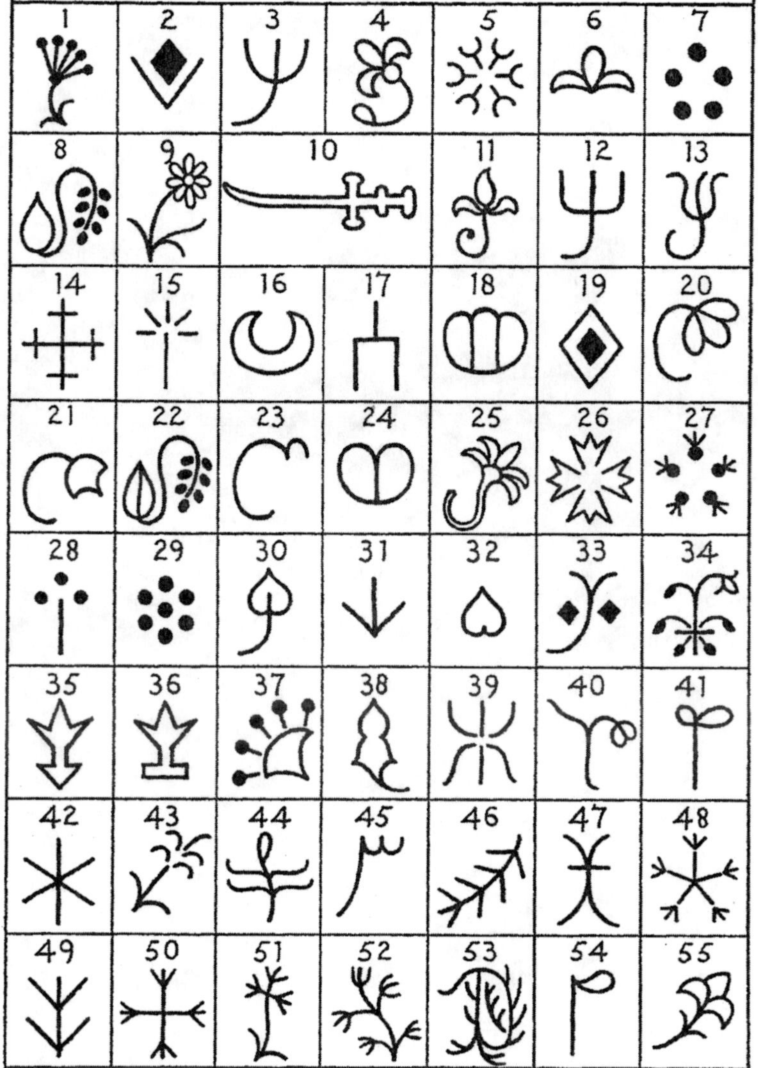

Marks on Coins of Nādir Shāh

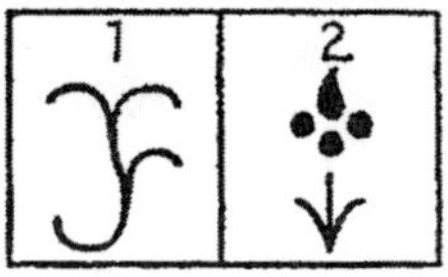

PLATE I

NĀDIR

NĀDIR—AHMAD

PLATE III

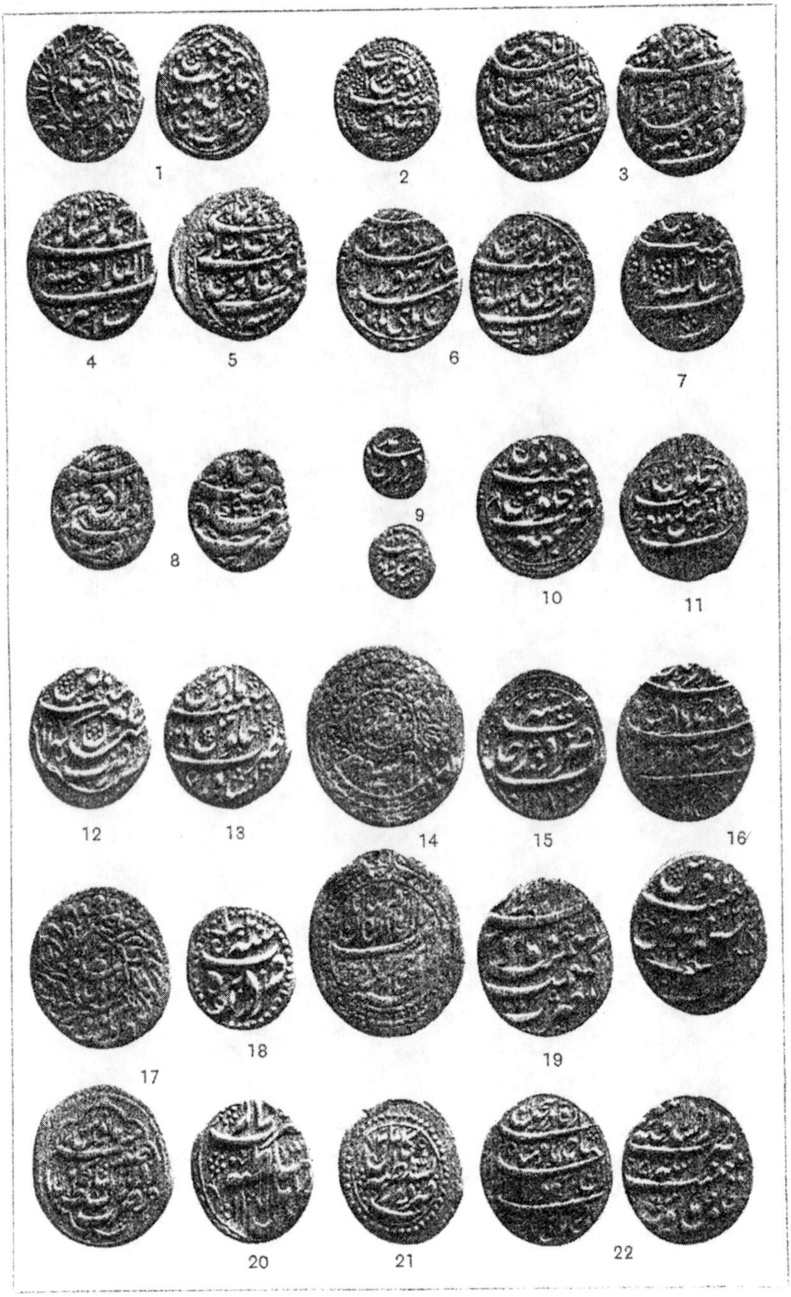

AHMAD

PLATE IV

AHMAD—TAIMŪR AS NIZĀM

PLATE V

TAIMŪR AS NIZĀM—SULAIMĀN—TAIMŪR

TAIMŪR

PLATE VII

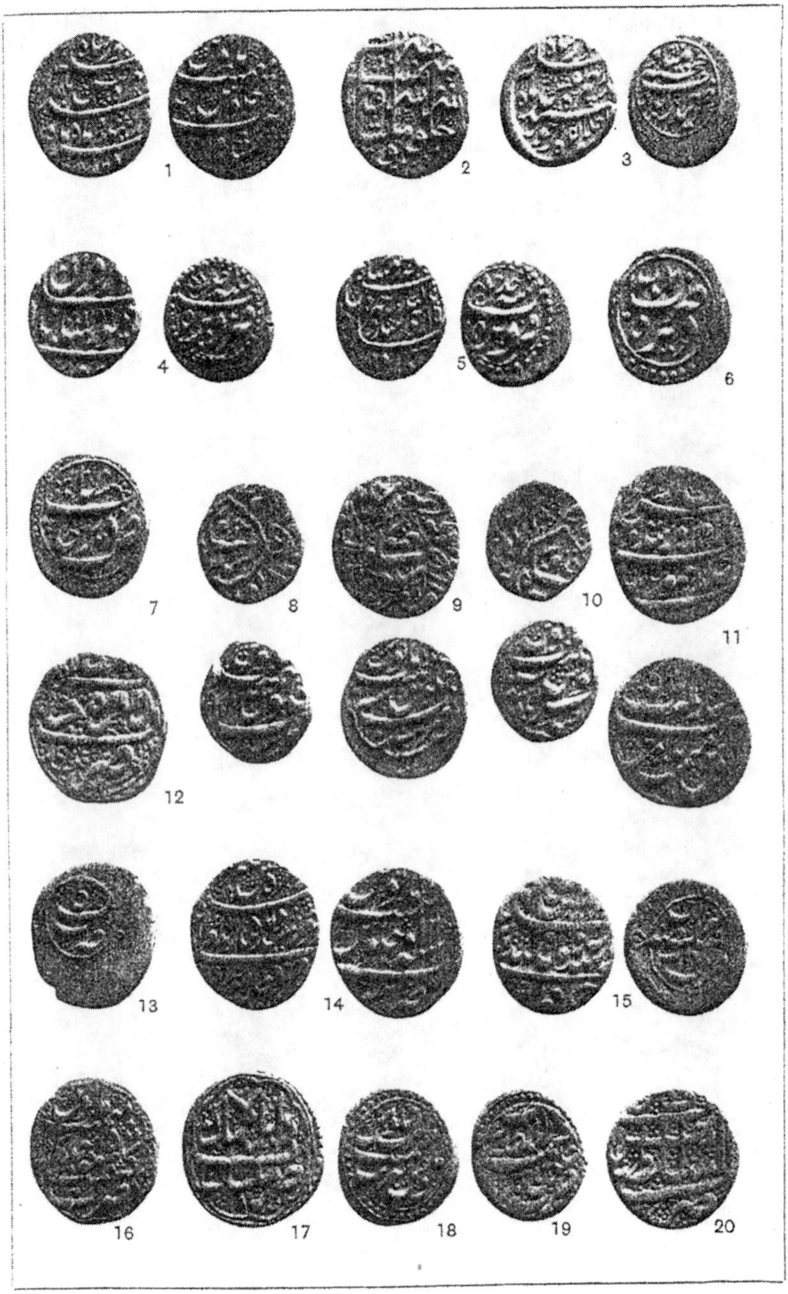

TAIMŪR

PLATE VIII

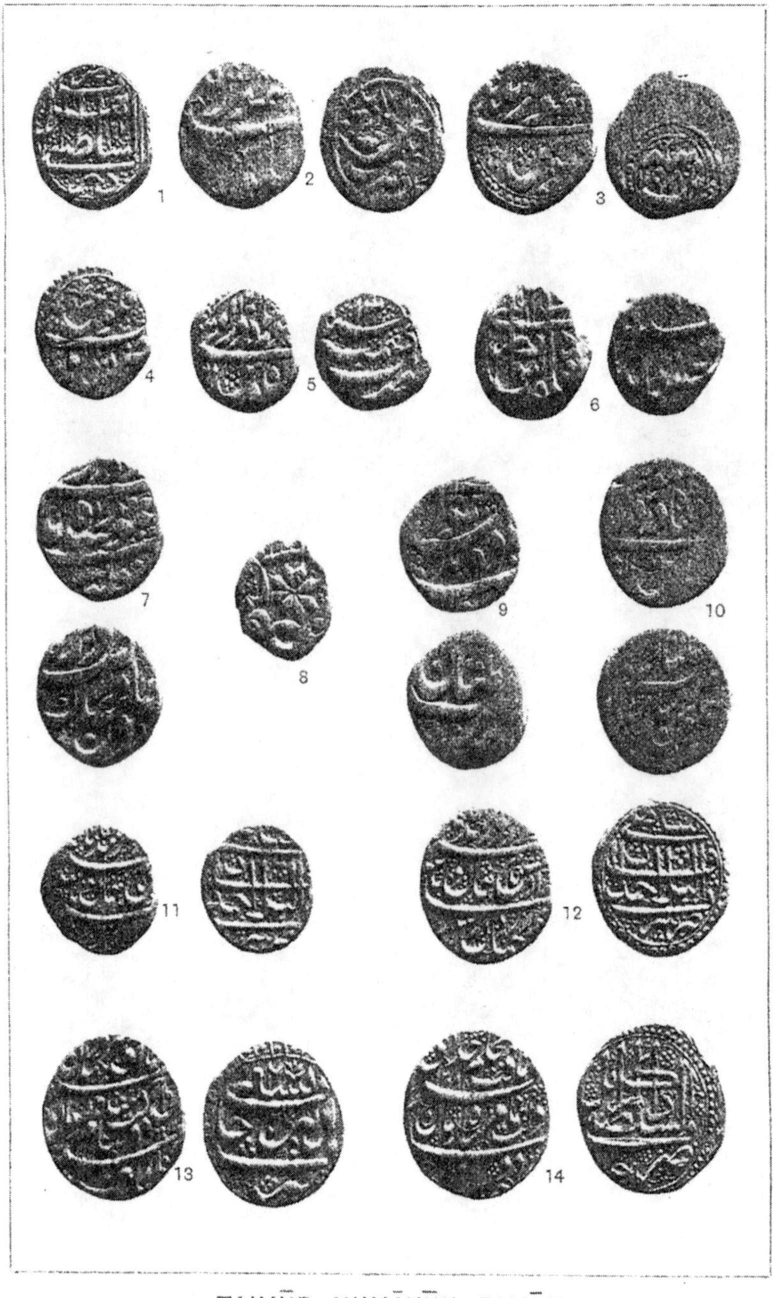

TAIMŪR--HUMĀYŪN--ZAMĀN

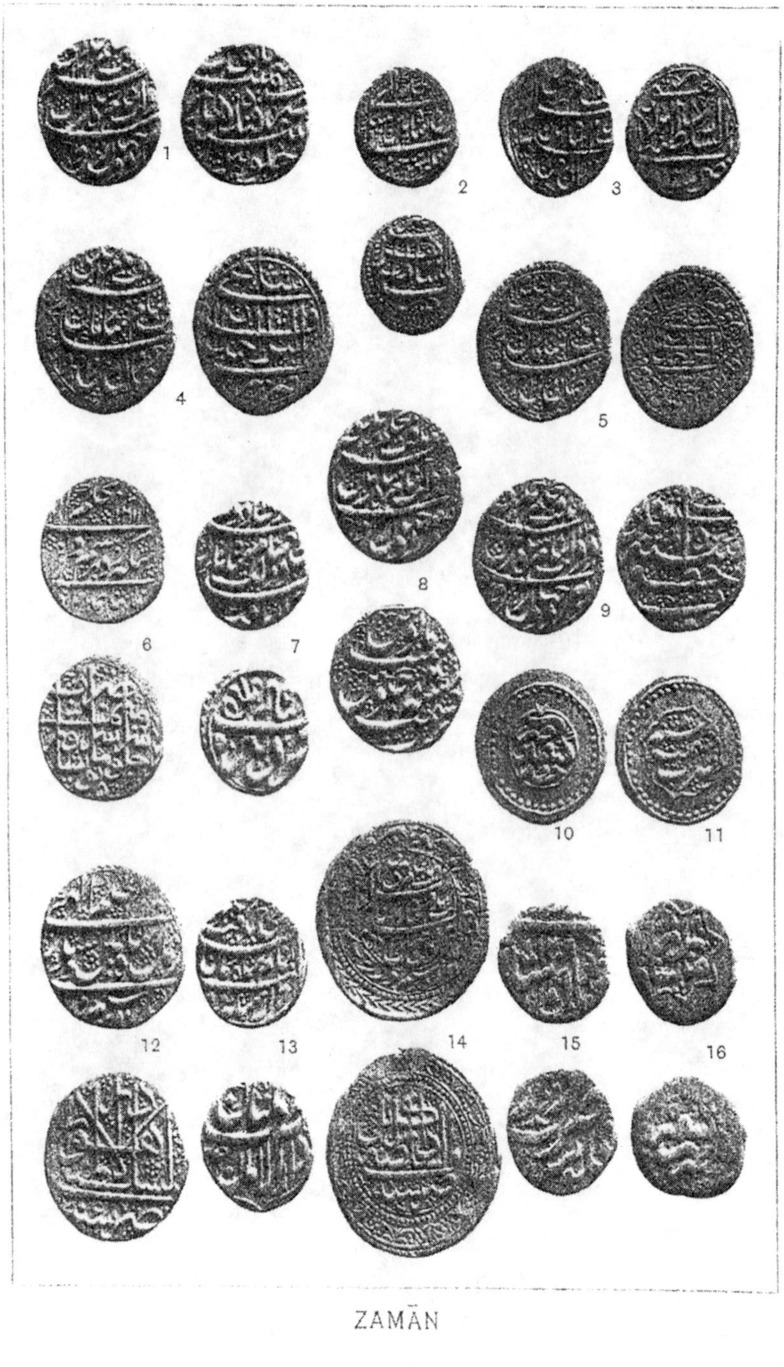

ZAMĀN

PLATE X

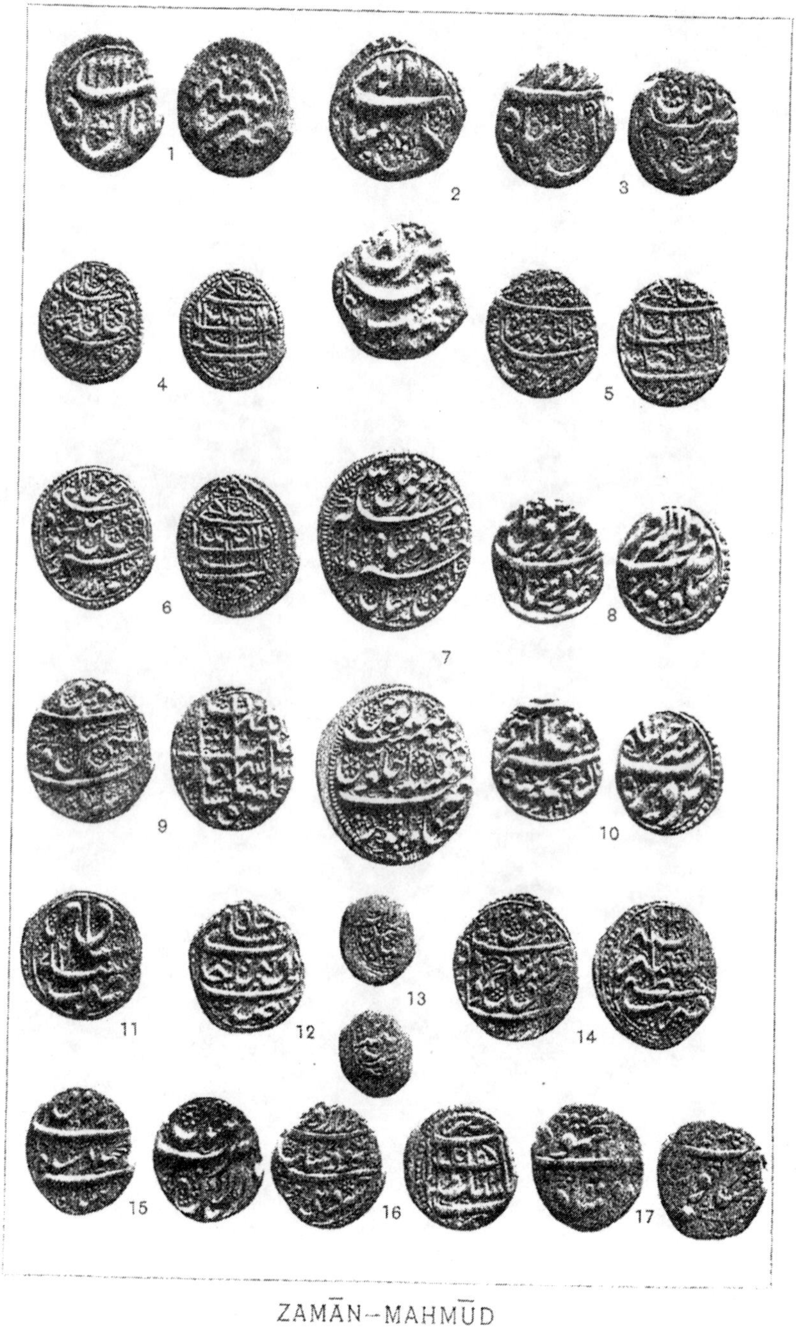

ZAMĀN–MAHMŪD

PLATE XI

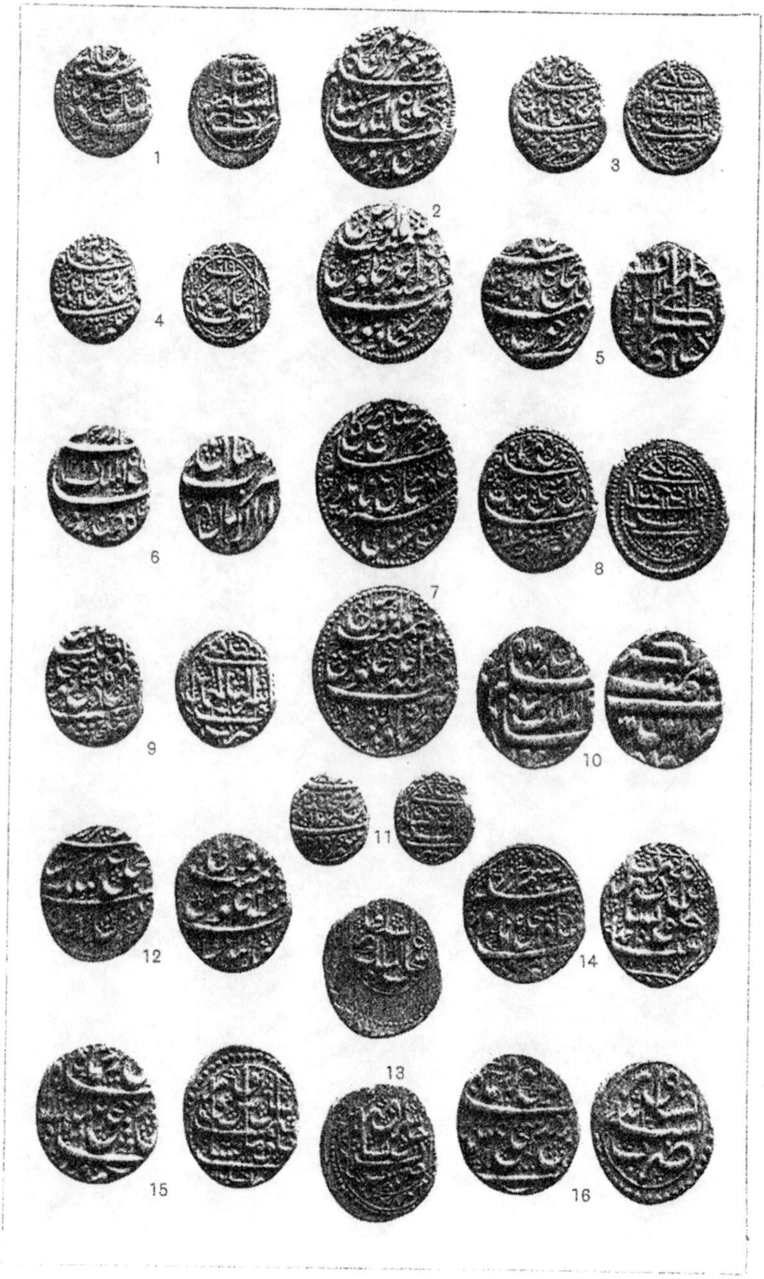

MAHMŪD–SHUJĀʿ

PLATE XII

S̲H̲UJĀ‘—QAISAR—MAHMŪD

PLATE XIII

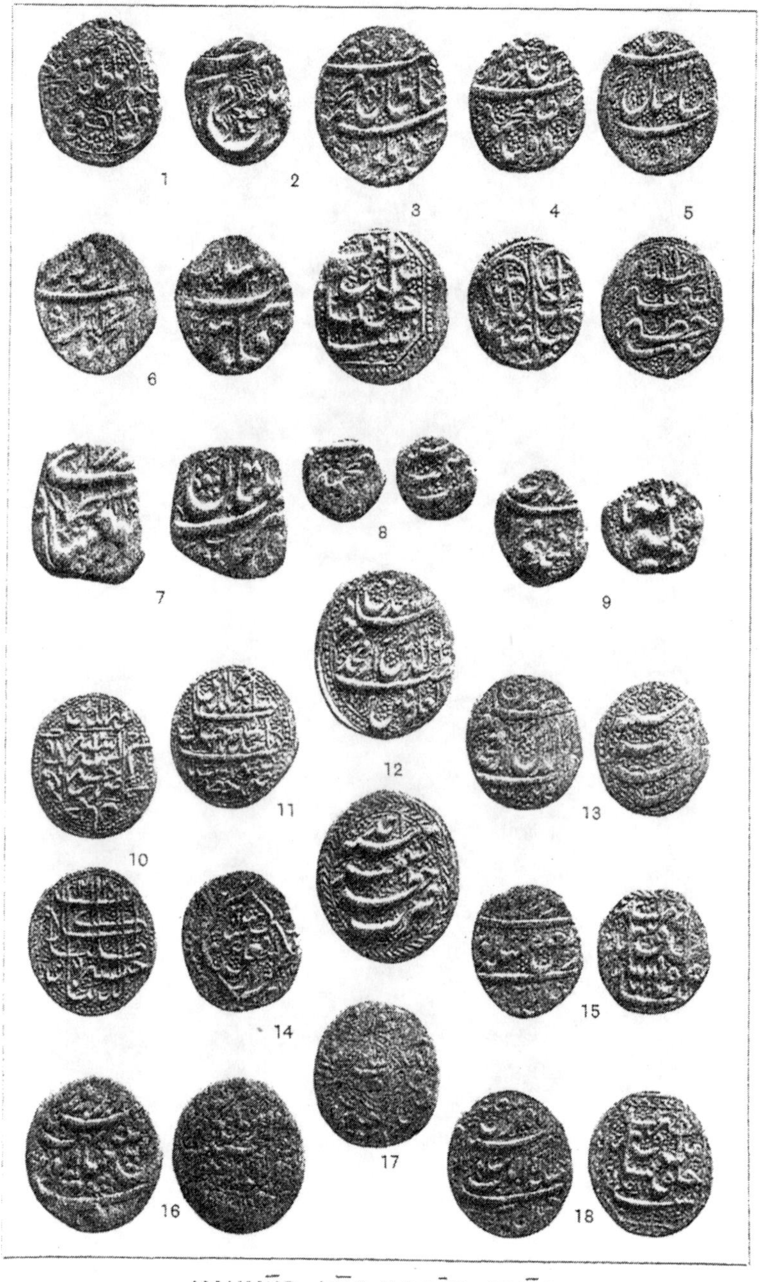

MAHMŪD–NŪR UD-DĪN–AIYŪB

PLATE XIV

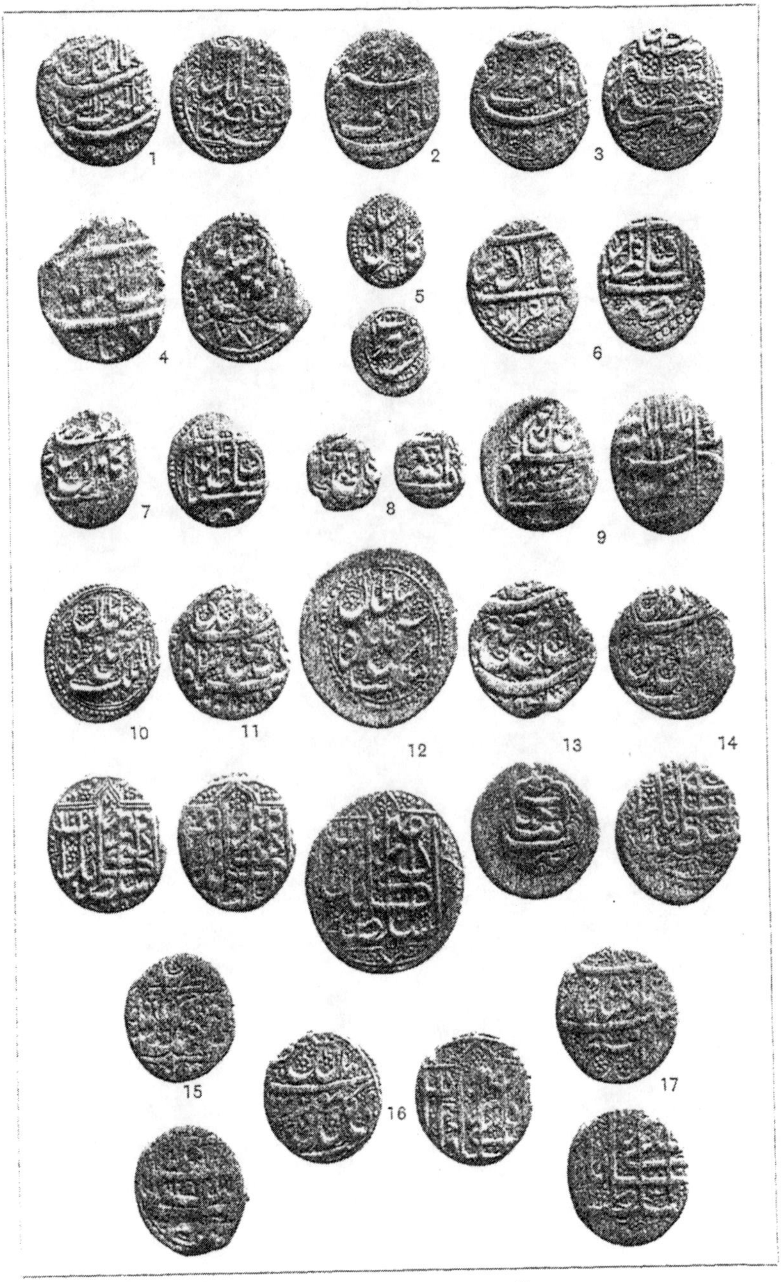

AIYŪB—KĀMRĀN—JAHĀNGĪR—SHUJĀ'—FATH JANG

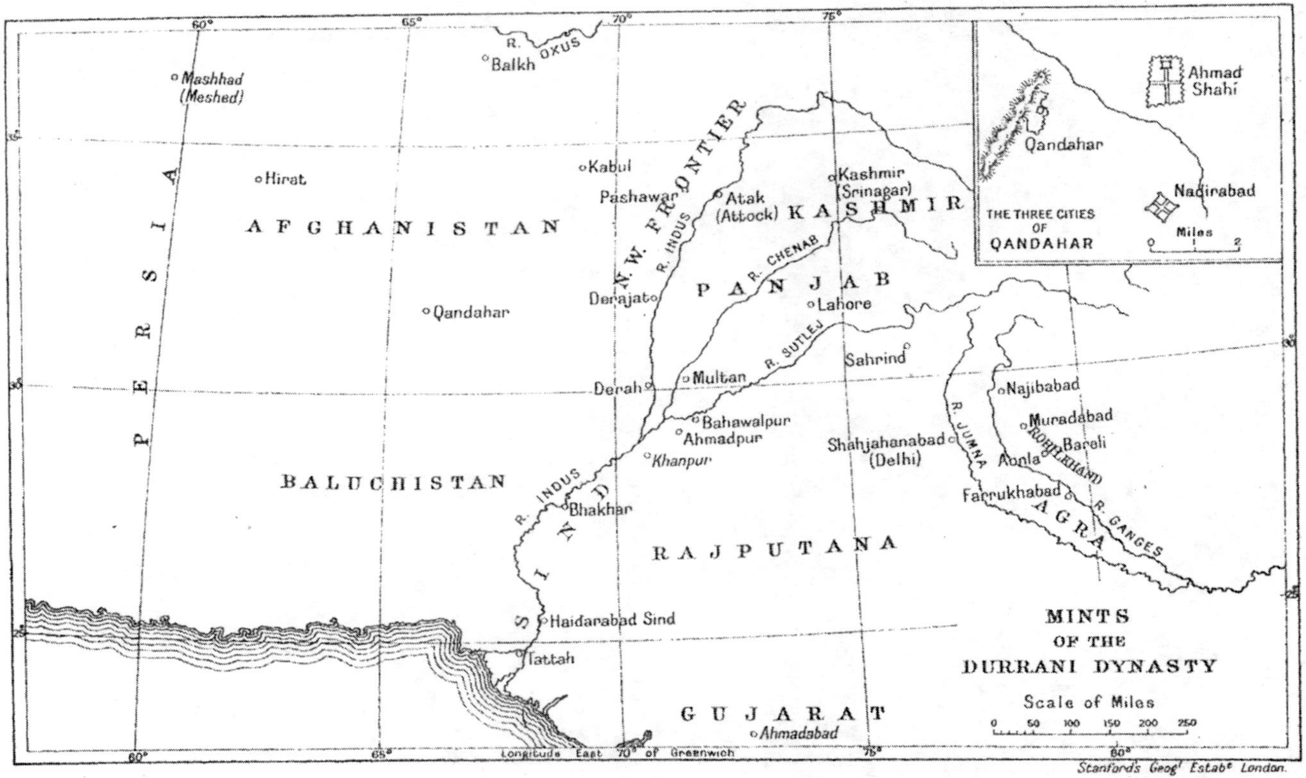
MINTS OF THE DURRANI DYNASTY
Scale of Miles
0 50 100 150 200 250
PERSIA
Mashhad (Meshed)
Hirat
AFGHANISTAN
Balkh
R. OXUS
Kabul
Pashawar
Qandahar
BALUCHISTAN
N.W. FRONTIER
R. INDUS
Atak (Attock)
KASHMIR
Kashmir (Srinagar)
R. CHENAB
PANJAB
Lahore
Derajat
R. SUTLEJ
Sahrind
Multan
Derah
Bahawalpur
Ahmadpur
Khanpur
Shahjahanabad (Delhi)
SIND
Bhakhar
RAJPUTANA
Haidarabad Sind
Tattah
GUJARAT
Ahmadabad
R. JUMNA
Najibabad
Muradabad
ROHILKHAND
Bareli
Aonla
Farrukhabad
AGRA
R. GANGES
THE THREE CITIES OF QANDAHAR
Qandahar
Ahmad Shahi
Nadirabad
Miles
0 1 2
Longitude East 70° of Greenwich
60° 65° 70° 75° 80°
Stanford's Geog' Estab' London.